GRAPHIS DESIGN 93

The International Annual of Design and Illustration

Das internationale Jahrbuch über Design und Illustration

Le Répertoire International du Design et de l'Illustration

Edited by · Herausgegeben von · Edité par:

B. Martin Pedersen

Publisher and Creative Director: B. Martin Pedersen

Editors: Heinke Jenssen, Annette Crandall

Art Directors: B. Martin Pedersen, Adrian Pulfer

Designers: Mary Jane Callister, Eric Gillett, Adrian Pulfer

Graphis Press Corp. Zürich (Switzerland)

GRAPHIS PUBLICATIONS

GRAPHIS, THE INTERNATIONAL MAGAZINE OF DESIGN AND COMMUNICATION
GRAPHIS DESIGN, THE INTERNATIONAL ANNUAL OF DESIGN AND ILLUSTRATION
GRAPHIS PHOTO, THE INTERNATIONAL ANNUAL OF PHOTOGRAPHY
GRAPHIS POSTER, THE INTERNATIONAL ANNUAL OF POSTER ART
GRAPHIS PACKAGING, AN INTERNATIONAL SURVEY OF PACKAGING DESIGN
GRAPHIS LETTERHEAD, AN INTERNATIONAL SURVEY OF LETTERHEAD DESIGN
GRAPHIS DIAGRAM, THE GRAPHIC VISUALIZATION OF ABSTRACT, TECHNICAL AND
       STATISTICAL FACTS AND FUNCTIONS
GRAPHIS LOGO, AN INTERNATIONAL SURVEY OF LOGOS
GRAPHIS PUBLICATION, AN INTERNATIONAL SURVEY OF THE BEST
       IN MAGAZINE DESIGN
GRAPHIS ANNUAL REPORTS, AN INTERNATIONAL COMPILATION OF THE BEST-DESIGNED
       ANNUAL REPORTS
GRAPHIS CORPORATE IDENTITY, AN INTERNATIONAL COMPILATION OF THE BEST IN
       CORPORATE-IDENTITY DESIGN
ART FOR SURVIVAL: THE ILLUSTRATOR AND THE ENVIRONMENT, A DOCUMENT OF ART
       IN THE SERVICE OF MAN.
THE GRAPHIC DESIGNER'S GREEN BOOK, ENVIRONMENTAL RESOURCES FOR THE DESIGN AND PRINT INDUSTRIES

GRAPHIS PUBLIKATIONEN

GRAPHIS, DIE INTERNATIONALE ZWEIMONATSZEITSCHRIFT DER VISUELLEN KOMMUNIKATION
GRAPHIS DESIGN, DAS INTERNATIONALE JAHRBUCH ÜBER DESIGN UND ILLUSTRATION
GRAPHIS PHOTO, DAS INTERNATIONALE JAHRBUCH DER PHOTOGRAPHIE
GRAPHIS POSTER, DAS INTERNATIONALE JAHRBUCH DER PLAKATKUNST
GRAPHIS PACKAGING, EIN INTERNATIONALER ÜBERBLICK ÜBER DIE PACKUNGSGESTALTUNG
GRAPHIS LETTERHEAD, EIN INTERNATIONALER ÜBERBLICK ÜBER BRIEFPAPIERGESTALTUNG
GRAPHIS DIAGRAM, DIE GRAPHISCHE DARSTELLUNG ABSTRAKTER TECHNISCHER UND
       STATISTISCHER DATEN UND FAKTEN
GRAPHIS LOGO, EINE INTERNATIONALE AUSWAHL VON FIRMEN-LOGOS
GRAPHIS MAGAZINDESIGN, EINE INTERNATIONALE ZUSAMMENSTELLUNG DES BESTEN
       ZEITSCHRIFTEN-DESIGNS
GRAPHIS ANNUAL REPORTS, EIN INTERNATIONALER ÜBERBLICK ÜBER DIE GESTALTUNG
       VON JAHRESBERICHTEN
GRAPHIS CORPORATE IDENTITY, EINE INTERNATIONALE AUSWAHL DES BESTEN
       CORPORATE IDENTITY DESIGNS
ART FOR SURVIVAL: THE ILLUSTRATOR AND THE ENVIRONMENT, EIN DOKUMENT
       ÜBER DIE KUNST IM DIENSTE DES MENSCHEN
THE GRAPHIC DESIGNER'S GREEN BOOK, UMWELTKONZEPTE DER DESIGN- UND DRUCKINDUSTRIE

PUBLICATIONS GRAPHIS

GRAPHIS, LA REVUE BIMESTRIELLE INTERNATIONALE DE LA COMMUNICATION VISUELLE
GRAPHIS DESIGN, LE RÉPERTOIRE INTERNATIONAL DE LA COMMUNICATION VISUELLE
GRAPHIS PHOTO, LE RÉPERTOIRE INTERNATIONAL DE LA PHOTOGRAPHIE
GRAPHIS POSTER, LE RÉPERTOIRE INTERNATIONAL DE L'AFFICHE
GRAPHIS PACKAGING, LE RÉPERTOIRE INTERNATIONAL DE LA CRÉATION D'EMBALLAGES
GRAPHIS LETTERHEAD, LE RÉPERTOIRE INTERNATIONAL DU DESIGN DE PAPIER À LETTRES
GRAPHIS DIAGRAM, LE RÉPERTOIRE GRAPHIQUE DE FAITS ET DONNÉES ABSTRAITS,
       TECHNIQUES ET STATISTIQUES
GRAPHIS LOGO, LE RÉPERTOIRE INTERNATIONAL DU LOGO
GRAPHIS PUBLICATION, LE RÉPERTOIRE INTERNATIONAL DU DESIGN DE PÉRIODIQUES
GRAPHIS ANNUAL REPORTS, PANORAMA INTERNATIONAL DU MEILLEUR DESIGN DE RAPPORTS
       ANNUELS D'ENTREPRISES
GRAPHIS CORPORATE IDENTITY, PANORAMA INTERNATIONAL DU MEILLEUR DESIGN D'IDENTITÉ CORPORATE
ART FOR SURVIVAL: THE ILLUSTRATOR AND THE ENVIRONMENT, L'ART AU SERVICE DE LA SURVIE
THE GRAPHIC DESIGNER'S GREEN BOOK, L'ÉCOLOGIE APPLIQUÉE AU DESIGN ET À L'INDUSTRIE GRAPHIQUE

PUBLICATION NO. 211 (ISBN 3-85709-193.2)
© COPYRIGHT UNDER UNIVERSAL COPYRIGHT CONVENTION
COPYRIGHT © 1992 BY GRAPHIS PRESS CORP., DUFOURSTRASSE 107, 8008 ZÜRICH, SWITZERLAND
JACKET AND BOOK DESIGN COPYRIGHT © 1992 BY PEDERSEN DESIGN
141 LEXINGTON AVENUE, NEW YORK, N.Y. 10016 USA
FRENCH CAPTIONS BY NICOLE VIAUD

PRINTED IN JAPAN BY TOPPAN PRINTING CO., LTD.

CONTENTS · INHALT · SOMMAIRE

REMARKS

WE EXTEND OUR HEARTFELT THANKS TO CONTRIBUTORS THROUGHOUT THE WORLD WHO HAVE MADE IT POSSIBLE TO PUBLISH A WIDE AND INTERNATIONAL SPECTRUM OF THE BEST WORK IN THIS FIELD.

ENTRY INSTRUCTIONS MAY BE REQUESTED AT: GRAPHIS PRESS CORP., DUFOURSTRASSE 107, 8008 ZÜRICH, SWITZERLAND

ANMERKUNGEN

UNSER DANK GILT DEN EINSENDERN AUS ALLER WELT, DIE ES UNS DURCH IHRE BEITRÄGE ERMÖGLICHT HABEN, EIN BREITES, INTERNATIONALES SPEKTRUM DER BESTEN ARBEITEN ZU VERÖFFENTLICHEN.

TEILNAHMEBEDINGUNGEN: GRAPHIS VERLAG AG, DUFOURSTRASSE 107, 8008 ZÜRICH, SCHWEIZ

ANNOTATIONS

TOUTE NOTRE RECONNAISSANCE VA AUX DESIGNERS DU MONDE ENTIER DONT LES ENVOIS NOUS ONT PERMIS DE CONSTITUER UN VASTE PANORAMA INTERNATIONAL DES MEILLEURES CRÉATIONS.

MODALITÉS D'ENVOI DE TRAVAUX: EDITIONS GRAPHIS, DUFOURSTRASSE 107, 8008 ZÜRICH, SUISSE

HANS VAN BLOMMESTEIN

My view of my job as art director of Avenue, *Holland's most beautiful magazine, can be illustrated by the difference between the Dutch verb "vormgeven" (to shape) and the English "to design." Designing a form sounds static and absolute. After all, once the form is determined, everything that has to be fitted into it is subjugated to that form. "Vormgeven" is a much more evocative, more dynamic, word. "Vormgeven" is the bestowing of form on contents that are continually changing and subject to new interpretations. □ For the designer there is no getting around it: The contents are the backbone of any magazine. And when you fill the roles of both art director and picture editor, as I do, you are doubly aware of this. "Vormgeven," form-giving, is what the word says: There is a message, contained in text and image, and it has to be given a form—ideally a form that makes the message clear and accessible, and, if at all possible, one that is also seductive, surprising and spectacular. But esthetics take second place: What use are visual acrobatics if the reader misses the essence? Worse yet: Will the reader bother to buy the magazine if he can't see the contents of the forest for the esthetics of the trees? □ Everyone who works for a magazine, whether in editorial or in design, must realize that he is involved in conveying information. It can be serious information, pure*

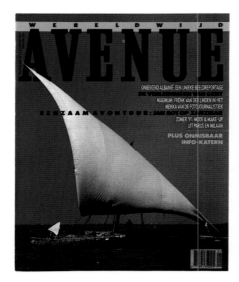 

(LEFT) COVER FROM *AVENUE* MAGAZINE, FEBRUARY 1991. ART DIRECTOR: HANS VAN BLOMMESTEIN. DESIGNER: MARISE CLASON. PHOTOGRAPHER: TAEKE HENSTRA. (RIGHT) DESIGNER: TINY LAARAKKER. ILLUSTRATOR: RONALD BLOMMESTIJN. ■

entertainment or anything in-between. □ As important as design is, photographing an exciting and expressive visual or writing an animated, informative text is no less important. If done well, the design can become a third medium for information, along with the text and the images. Through the typography and the integration of the pictures into the whole, the form itself can, at a single glance, convey information to the reader. That is the power of good "vormgeven." □ A situation such as this can be attained only if the representatives of the three disciplines—the writer, the photographer or illustrator and the designer—work together. Not too long ago, text reigned supreme, in Holland as in most countries of the world. Designers were little more than column-pasters. *Avenue* was one of the first magazines in Holland in which high-quality fashion and travel photography began to play an important role, sometimes even at the expense of the text. In this revolution lay the roots of our success. □ Now, in 1992, we have moved a step forward. The integration of form, image and text is nearly accomplished, and the rep-

resentatives of the three disciplines have learned to speak the same language: the language of communication. Everyone is asking himself the same question in his own field: Is this the best way to get my message across to the reader? An editor may not be a designer, but he is still a reader, and he will know whether a given page attracts or repels him. A designer may not write headlines, but he knows quite well whether a given headline would intrigue him as a reader. □ Making such cooperation work is one of the biggest challenges for every magazine professional. It is also one of the greatest pleasures. But there are other challenges. At a magazine you are responsible, for example, for both the design of individual productions and the coherence of the issue as a whole. One moment you're poring over the square centimeter, the next you're being asked for a bird's-eye view. And there's a third level: the continuity, the evolution. A new issue every month, year in, year out. □ Functioning successfully on all three levels, searching for a perfect balance: These are the intellectual stimuli that led me to choose this form of art direction. ■

HANS VAN BLOMMESTEIN (B. 1946) WAS TRAINED AS A GRAPHIC DESIGNER AT THE RIETVELD ACADEMY IN AMSTERDAM AND IS NOW ART DIRECTOR OF *AVENUE*. HE DESIGNS THE WORLD PRESS PHOTO YEARBOOKS, IS ON THE BOARD OF THE FOTO FESTIVAL NAARDEN, AND IS A MEMBER OF MANY JURIES FOR DESIGN AND PHOTOGRAPHY. ■

BESTSELLER-AUTEUR

ISABEL ALLENDE

"Ik heb nooit méér tarot-aanbidders
gezien dan in Californië,
en mensen die zich bezighouden
met satanische sex
en organic chicken bondage en
God mag weten wat nog meer."

Waar gebeurd: de man wilde wel eens weten hoe hij eruit zou zien als zijn benen even »

punto e
BASTA!

Meine Arbeit als Art Director bei *Avenue*, Hollands schönster Zeitschrift, lässt sich gut durch den Unterschied zwischen dem holländischen Verb «vormgeven» (formen) und dem englischen «to design» erklären. Eine Form zu «designen» klingt statisch, absolut. Wenn eine Form einmal festgelegt ist, muss sich ihr alles, was in diese Form passen soll, unterwerfen. «Vormgeven» ist evokativ, dynamischer. «Vormgeven» bedeutet, Inhalten, die sich fortwährend verändern und neuen Interpretationen ausgesetzt sind, eine Form zu verleihen. □ Der Designer kommt nicht darum herum: Der Inhalt ist das Rückgrat jeder Zeitschrift. Wenn man wie ich gleichzeitig Art Director und Bildredakteur ist, ist man sich dessen um so mehr bewusst. «Vormgeven» bedeutet wörtlich «Form geben». Es geht um eine Botschaft, die in Text und Bild enthalten ist, und dieser muss eine Form gegeben werden – und zwar im idealen Falle eine Form, die die Botschaft klar und zugänglich macht. Wenn möglich, sollte die Form ausserdem verführerisch, überraschend und spektakulär sein. Aber die Ästhetik kommt an zweiter Stelle: Was nützen visuelle Verrenkungen, wenn dem Leser das Wesentliche entgeht? Oder noch schlimmer: Wird jemand die Zeitschrift überhaupt kaufen, wenn er den Wald (Inhalt) vor lauter Bäumen (Ästhetik) nicht sehen kann? □ Jeder, der für eine Zeitschrift arbeitet, sei es redaktionell oder gestalterisch, muss sich bewusst sein, dass es um die Vermittlung von Informationen geht. Das kann ernsthafte Information sein, reine Unterhaltung oder etwas dazwischen. □ So bedeutend die Funktion von Design auch sein mag, Bild und Text sind nicht weniger wichtig. Wenn es gut ist, kann das Design – neben Bild und Text – sogar ein drittes Medium für die Information sein. Durch die Typographie und die Integration von Bildern in das Gesamtbild kann die Form selbst, auf einen einzigen Blick, dem Leser eine Botschaft vermitteln. Das ist die Stärke von gutem «vormgeving» – das man meinetwegen auch Design nennen kann. □ Eine ideale Situation kann nur entstehen, wenn die Vertreter der Disziplinen – Autor, Photograph oder Illustrator und Designer – optimal zusammenarbeiten. Vor nicht allzu langer Zeit hatte der Text absoluten Vorrang, in Holland wie überall. Designer waren kaum mehr als Reinzeichner und hatten ansonsten wenig zu sagen. *Avenue* war eine der ersten Zeitschriften in Holland, in denen erstklassige Mode- und Reisephotographie eine bedeutende Rolle zu spielen begann, manchmal (leider) auf Kosten des Textes. Auf diesem Umdenken begründet sich unser Erfolg. □ Heute, im Jahre 1992, haben wir noch einen weiteren Schritt nach vorn gemacht. Die ideale Integration von Form, Bild und Text ist so gut wie erreicht, und die Vertreter dieser drei Disziplinen haben gelernt, die gleiche Sprache zu sprechen: die Sprache der Kommunikation. Alle stellen sich in ihrem Kompetenzbereich dieselbe Frage: Ist dies die beste Art, dem Leser die Botschaft zu vermitteln? Und weil wir uns dieselbe Frage stellen, können wir die Lösungsvorschläge miteinander diskutieren. Wenn auch ein Redakteur kein Designer ist, so ist er doch Leser und kann beurteilen, ob ihn eine Seite anzieht oder abstösst. Ein Designer ist kein Texter für Headlines, aber er weiss sehr wohl, ob eine bestimmte Headline ihn als Leser ansprechen würde. □ Eine Zusammenarbeit dieser Art zu erreichen ist eine der grössten Herausforderungen für jeden Zeitschriftenmacher. Und eines der grössten Vergnügen. Aber es geht noch um mehr. Bei einer Zeitschrift ist man für das Design einzelner Beiträge und gleichzeitig für die gestalterische Geschlossenheit der Gesamtausgabe verantwortlich. In einem Moment grübelt man über ein winzigesDetail nach, im nächsten Moment muss man alles aus der Vogelperspektive sehen. Und dann kommt noch ein Kriterium hinzu, das ich noch nicht erwähnt habe: Kontinuität und Weiterentwicklung. Und jeden Monat eine neue Ausgabe, Jahr ein, Jahr aus. □ Auf diesen drei Ebenen erfolgreich zu sein, eine perfekte Ausgewogenheit zu erreichen – das ist die intellektuelle Herausforderung, die mich an dieser Form der Art Direction reizt. ■

HANS VAN BLOMMESTEIN, 1946, WURDE AN DER RIETVELD-AKADEMIE IN AMSTERDAM ALS GRAPHIK-DESIGNER AUSGEBILDET UND IST JETZT ART DIRECTOR BEI *AVENUE*. NEBEN DESIGN INTERESSIERT IHN VOR ALLEM DIE PHOTOGRAPHIE. ER IST MITGLIED DES VORSTANDS DES NAARDEN-PHOTO-FESTIVALS, UND ER WAR IN VIELEN JURYS FÜR DESIGN UND PHOTOGRAPHIE. ER GESTALTET DANEBEN AUCH DIE JAHRBÜCHER FÜR WORLD-PRESS-PHOTO. ■

Directeur artistique d'*Avenue*, le plus beau magazine qui soit publié en Hollande, ma conception de ce métier peut être illustrée par la différence qu'il y a entre le verbe hollandais «vormgeven» (donner forme) et l'anglais «to design». Ce dernier terme a un caractère plus statique, en quelque sorte absolu. Après tout, une fois la forme déterminée, tout ce qui doit y être intégré lui est subordonné. «Vormgeven» est un mot nettement plus suggestif, bien plus dynamique. □ «Vormgeven», cela consiste à donner forme à des contenus qui changent continuellement et sont sujets à de nouvelles interprétations. □ Impossible au designer d'y échapper: les contenus sont l'épine dorsale de tout magazine. Et quand vous remplissez comme moi à la fois les fonctions de directeur artistique et de responsable de l'image, vous en êtes doublement conscient. □ «Vormgeven» correspond littéralement à la signification même de ce mot. Un message est contenu dans le texte et dans l'image, et il faut lui donner une forme. Une forme, dans l'idéal, c'est ce qui rend le message clair et accessible. Et si possible, une forme qui soit aussi séduisante, surprenante et spectaculaire. Mais l'esthétique vient au second rang: à quoi servent les acrobaties visuelles si le lecteur rate l'essentiel? Ou pire encore: est-ce que le lecteur va se soucier d'acheter le magazine si l'esthétique l'empêche de saisir le contenu? □ Quiconque travaille pour un magazine, qu'il soit à la rédaction ou au département artistique, doit réaliser qu'il est impliqué dans la communication d'une information. □ Et aussi fondamentale que soit la fonction du design, photographier un visuel expressif et palpitant ou écrire un texte vivant et informatif est tout aussi important. S'il est bien fait, le design – conjointement au texte et à l'image – peut même devenir un troisième moyen d'information autonome. Grâce à l'usage optimal de la typographie et l'intégration des images dans le tout, la forme elle-même peut transmettre plus ou moins implicitement l'information au lecteur. D'un simple coup d'œil. C'est le pouvoir de la bonne «vormgeving». □ On ne peut arriver à cette situation idéale que si les responsables des trois disciplines – le rédacteur, le photographe ou l'illustrateur et le designer – travaillent vraiment main dans la main. Il n'y a pas si longtemps de cela, en Hollande aussi, le texte était souverain. Les designers se limitaient pratiquement à coller des pages de colonnes. *Avenue* fut l'un des premiers magazines en Hollande dans lequel la photographie de mode et de voyages, de toute première qualité, devait jouer un rôle important, parfois même aux dépens du texte. C'est dans cette révolution que résident les raisons de notre succès. □ Aujourd'hui, en 1992, nous avons franchi une nouvelle étape. L'intégration de la forme, de l'image et du texte est pratiquement réalisée et les responsables des trois disciplines ont appris à parler le même langage: le langage de la communication. Bien qu'un éditeur ne soit pas un designer, il est toujours un lecteur, et il peut juger si une page donnée l'attire ou au contraire le repousse. Et un designer n'est peut-être pas un rédacteur de gros titres, mais il sait très bien si un titre éveillera sa curiosité de lecteur. □ Réussir une telle collaboration constitue l'un des plus grands défis que doivent relever tous ceux qui font un magazine. Et l'un de leurs plus grands plaisirs. Mais ce n'est pas tout. Dans un magazine, vous êtes responsable à la fois du design des productions individuelles et de la cohérence du numéro tout entier. Et j'ai omis le troisième niveau: la continuité, l'évolution. Produire un nouveau numéro chaque mois. □ Réussir à fonctionner à chacun de ces trois niveaux, en quête de l'équilibre parfait: ce sont là les motivations qui m'ont conduit à choisir cette forme de direction artistique parmi les trois autres. ■

HANS VAN BLOMMESTEIN (1946) A FAIT SES ÉTUDES DE DESIGNER GRAPHIQUE À L'ACADÉMIE RIETVELD D'AMSTERDAM. IL EST ACTUELLEMENT DIRECTEUR ARTISTIQUE DU MAGAZINE *AVENUE* ET IL EST AUSSI MEMBRE DU COMITÉ DU FESTIVAL DE LA PHOTOGRAPHIE DE NAARDEN; IL EST CHARGÉ DE LA CONCEPTION DES ANNUAIRES WORLD PRESS PHOTO ET JUGE RÉGULIÈREMENT LES TRAVAUX DES EXAMENS DE FIN D'ÉTUDES DE DIVERSES ACADÉMIES. ■

WOODY PIRTLE

History tells us that in Victorian England, steam (and later electricity and gasoline) fueled the engines that transformed a rural, agricultural society into a frenetic, mechanized urban one. The Industrial Revolution was born in the wake of fundamental technological change, bringing with it a different way of life. Specialization, increased competition and the need for mass communication in a rapidly changing society altered the nature of visual information. □ Jobbing printers equipped with the latest technology but lacking in esthetic sensibilities were producing material laden with extraneous ornamentation borrowed from the past and eccentricities of contemporary architecture and fashion. In the frenzy of rapid change, designers and printers shared a prevailing confusion regarding the fundamental differences between style, design and content. □ Sound familiar? □ After contemplating the pivotal events that highlight the past 25 years of life on this planet, one feels an acute sense of déjà vu. I guess it supports the theory that history does repeat itself. Just since the late '60s we have witnessed profound social, political, economic and technological developments too numerous to list here. Some have fundamentally altered the way we live our lives and do our work. □ No single development in recent history, however, has had a more profound or pervasive impact on each of us than the advancements made in microchip technology. Some

(ABOVE) PENTAGRAM PAPERS #18 "SKELETON CLOSET"

manifestation of the computer now touches almost every stratum of our existence. From the moment we open our eyes in the morning —struggling to decipher the LED readout on the clock-radio—to the time we retire in the evening, with the latest movie in the VCR, we are constantly confronted with the legacies of the electronics explosion. For emerging generations of information-hungry human beings, the acronyms of the moment—MAC, VCR, ATM, PC, DC, DOS, ROM and RAM—have become the alphabet soup of the times. Every decade, in our quest to assimilate, collate and transmit, we are doubling the volume of information we must digest. □ And look at what has transpired in our own industry. Beginning with our first taste of digitized typography in the '1960s, a series of developments has rocked the design industry. As a result, we are seeing the emergence of a generation of designers whose work seems to reflect the confusion of a world spinning at an ever-accelerating pace, suffering from an acute case of information overload. Legions of designers graduating from art schools enter the work force every year equipped with mind-boggling tech-

nical knowledge, but apparently with a limited understanding of the history of art, architecture, typography or graphic design. Furthermore, a growing percentage of the work produced in recent years appears to reveal more about the latest technological bells and whistles than it reveals about the ideas and messages these same tools were designed to help convey. Aren't we in the business of communication? Are we so enamored of the technological toy box that we've lost sight of the purpose of our profession? To use a colloquialism, it looks as though the tail is wagging the dog. □ Good design isn't about slicing, dicing, stretching and manipulating a message beyond legibility just because it happens to be the current fashion. We've let the clarity, intelligence and personality of man's expression become overshadowed by that of the machine. □ Given the fact that our society is confronted with an ever-growing volume of information, and that time seems to have become one of our most valuable commodities, I believe that we as designers have an even greater responsibility to be more thoughtful about what we choose to say, and more succinct in how we say it. ■

WOODY PIRTLE STUDIED ARCHITECTURE AND FINE ART. IN 1988 HE BECAME A PARTNER IN PENTAGRAM'S NEW YORK OFFICE. HE IS ON THE DESIGN ADVISORY BOARDS OF SEVERAL CORPORATIONS AND IS CONSULTANT TO IBM, CHAMPION INTERNATIONAL AND PANTONE, INC. HIS WORK HAS BEEN EXHIBITED WORLDWIDE, AND IS REPRESENTED IN THE PERMANENT COLLECTIONS OF THE COOPER HEWITT MUSEUM IN NEW YORK AND THE NEUE SAMMLUNG MUSEUM IN MUNICH. ■

Aus der Geschichte wissen wir, dass die mit Dampf (später mit Strom und Kraftstoff) betriebenen Maschinen die bäuerliche Gesellschaft des viktorianischen Englands in eine frenetische, mechanisierte, urbane Gesellschaft verwandelten. Die industrielle Revolution wurde aus einer fundamentalen technischen Entwicklung heraus geboren, und sie brachte eine radikale Veränderung der Lebensweise mit sich. Das individuelle Handwerk wurde von der schnellen, anonymen Massenproduktion verdrängt. Spezialisierung, ein härterer Konkurrenzkampf und die Notwendigkeit der Massenkommunikation veränderte auch das Wesen der visuellen Information. Das Buch – bis dahin wichtigstes Medium zur Verbreitung von Information – trat in den Hintergrund, die Werbung in Form von Plakaten, Anschlägen, Handzetteln und andere direktere, wirkungsvollere Mittel für die Verbreitung des gedruckten Wortes traten an seine Stelle. □ Drucker, mit der neusten Technologie ausgestattet, aber ohne sicheres ästhetisches Empfinden, übernahmen in ihren Erzeugnissen Ornamente aus der Vergangenheit und liessen sich von den Auswüchsen der zeitgenössischen Architektur und Mode beeinflussen. Um den wechselnden Anforderungen der Kommunikation gerecht zu werden, wurden die klassischen Antiqua-Schriften radikal abgewandelt, sie wurden dicker und schwärzer, also das, was wir heute als «fett» bezeichnen. Im Strudel der schnellen Veränderungen war die Verwirrung bei Gestaltern und Druckern hinsichtlich der fundamentalen Unterschiede zwischen Stil, Gestaltung und Inhalt gleich gross. Kommt Ihnen das bekannt vor? □ Denkt man an die wichtigsten Ereignisse der letzten 25 Jahre, wird man das Gefühl des Déjà-vu-Erlebnisses nicht los. Das bestätigt wohl die Theorie, dass Geschichte sich wiederholt. Denken Sie darüber nach. Seit den späten sechziger Jahren hat es tiefgreifende soziale, politische, wirtschaftliche und technische Entwicklungen gegeben, die sich hier nicht alle aufzählen lassen. Einige haben unsere Lebensweise und Arbeit grundlegend verändert. Aber keine der Entwicklungen unserer jüngeren Vergangenheit hat eine so nachhaltige Wirkung auf jeden einzelnen von uns gehabt wie die Microchip-Technologie. Auf irgendeine Weise ist jeder Bereich unserer Existenz vom Computer betroffen. Von dem Augenblick an, in dem wir morgens die Augen öffnen – und mühsam versuchen, die Zeit auf der Digitalanzeige des Radioweckers zu entziffern –, bis zu dem Moment, in dem wir uns spät abends mit einem Videofilm zurückziehen, sind wir permanent mit der Elektronik konfrontiert. Telephonbeantworter vertreten uns in unserer Abwesenheit. Optische Scanner buchen unsere Einkäufe an den Kassen in Supermärkten und Kaufhäusern. Unsere Kinder unterhalten sich mit den neusten Computerspielen. Unsere Botschaften und Notizen im Büro werden elektronisch weitergeleitet. Fax-Geräte übermitteln unsere Dokumente sofort von einem Ende der Welt zum anderen. Unmengen von Information werden via Modem von einem Computer zum anderen übertragen etc. etc. etc. Für die heranwachsende Generation informationshungriger Menschen sind die Initialworte MAC, VCR, ATM, PC, DC, DOS, ROM und RAM zur Alphabet-Suppe ihrer Kindheit geworden. Ständig bemüht anzupassen, zusammenzutragen und zu übermitteln, verdoppeln wir alle zehn Jahre das zu verdauende Informationsvolumen. □ Und was ist in unserer eigenen Branche passiert? Angefangen mit dem Vorgeschmack digitalisierter Typographie in den sechziger Jahren, hat die Lawine der Entwicklungen die Designbranche bis in ihre Grundmauern erschüttert. Das Ergebnis ist das Zutagetreten einer Generation von Designern, deren Arbeit den Zustand einer sich immer schneller drehenden Welt wiederzugeben scheint, die an akuter Informationsüberlastung leidet. Legionen junger Designer verlassen die Kunstschulen in aller Welt, die Köpfe vollgestopft mit technischem Wissen, aber ohne rechtes Verständnis der Kunstgeschichte, Architektur, Typographie oder des Graphik-Designs. Zudem lassen immer mehr der in den letzten Jahren entstandenen Arbeiten den neusten Stand der Technologie erkennen, aber kaum Ideen und Botschaften, die eigentlich mit Hilfe dieser Technologie vermittelt werden sollten. Sind wir nicht in der Kommunikationsbranche? Sind wir so sehr in unser technisches Spielzeug verliebt, dass wir vergessen haben, worum es bei unserer Arbeit geht? Es sieht so aus, als sei die Technik zum Selbstzweck geworden. □ Gutes Design hat nichts mit Zerschneiden, Ausdehnen und Manipulieren einer Botschaft bis zur Unlesbarkeit zu tun, nur weil es gerade Mode ist. Wir haben zugelassen, dass die Klarheit, Intelligenz und Persönlichkeit des menschlichen Ausdrucks von der Maschine überschattet wird. Angesichts der Tatsache, dass unsere Gesellschaft mit einem ständig wachsenden Informationsvolumen konfrontiert wird, und dass Zeit zu einem der kostbarsten Dinge geworden ist, glaube ich, dass wir Designer eine noch grössere Verantwortung tragen und genau überlegen müssen, was wir sagen und wie wir es möglichst knapp ausdrücken. ■

WOODY PIRTLE STUDIERTE ARCHITEKTUR UND KUNST AN DER UNIVERSITÄT VON ARKANSAS. SEINE LAUFBAHN ALS GRAPHIK-DESIGNER BEGANN 1969 BEI DER RICHARDS GROUP IN DALLAS, WO ER 1978 EINE EIGENE FIRMA GRÜNDETE. 1988 WURDE ER TEILHABER DES NEW YORKER BÜROS VON PENTAGRAM. IN VERSCHIEDENEN FUNKTIONEN BERÄT ER DIVERSE FIRMEN IN DESIGNFRAGEN. SEINE GRAPHIK-DESIGN-ARBEITEN WURDEN IN ALLER WELT AUSGESTELLT. ■

. . . .

L'histoire nous apprend que dans l'Angleterre victorienne, la vapeur, puis l'électricité et l'essence, firent fonctionner les machines qui allaient transformer une société rurale, agricole, en une société urbaine, mécanisée, toujours plus frénétique. La Révolution industrielle était née des changements technologiques fondamentaux qui devaient radicalement transformer le mode de vie des habitants. Le caractère individuel du savoir-faire artisanal cédait la place à la vitesse et à l'anonymat de la production à la chaîne. La spécialisation, la concurrence accrue et la nécessité d'une communication de masse dans une société qui évoluait rapidement transformèrent la nature de l'information visuelle. Le livre, qui avait été jusqu'alors un instrument privilégié de l'information, fut relégué au second rang derrière la publicité, que ce soit sous forme d'affiches, de dépliants de grand format, prospectus ou autres véhicules de l'information plus immédiats, d'un impact incontestable. □ Des imprimeurs qui s'étaient équipés des dernières nouveautés techniques du moment, mais qui manquaient totalement de sens esthétique, firent une publicité chargée d'ornementations empruntées au passé, qui n'avaient rien à voir avec le produit en question, et qui reflétaient les extravagances de l'architecture et de la mode du moment. Pour répondre aux nouvelles demandes en matière de communication, les caractères romains classiques subirent des modifications impitoyables: ils devinrent ce que nous appelons aujourd'hui des «caractères gras», leurs formes étant plus épaisses et plus noires. Dans l'ardeur du moment, les designers et les imprimeurs participèrent à la confusion générale regardant la différence fondamentale entre le style, le design et le contenu. Cela ne vous rappellerait pas quelque chose? □ Si l'on considère avec attention les événements essentiels qui ont marqué le dernier quart de ce siècle, on éprouve un sentiment très net de déjà vu. Je suppose que cela renforce la théorie selon laquelle l'histoire tend à se répéter. Réfléchissez-y. Depuis la fin des années soixante, nous avons été témoins de développements sociaux, politiques, économiques et technologiques profonds, trop nombreux pour qu'ils puissent être énumérés ici. Quelques-uns ont radicalement transformé notre mode de vie et nos méthodes de travail. Cependant, aucun autre événement de l'histoire récente n'a eu un impact aussi profond et général sur chacun de nous que les progrès faits dans le secteur de la micro-informatique. Chaque niveau de notre existence est pratiquement touché maintenant par l'une ou l'autre manifestation de l'ordinateur. Du moment où nous ouvrons les yeux le matin – nous efforçant de déchiffrer ce qui apparaît sur l'affichage de notre radio-réveil – à l'heure où nous nous retirons le soir, pour regarder le dernier film sur notre magnétoscope, nous sommes constamment confrontés aux répercussions de la révolution électronique. Des répondeurs automatiques enregistrent les appels quand nous sommes obligés de nous absenter. Des scanners optiques enregistrent nos achats aux caisses des supermarchés et des rayons des grands magasins. Nos enfants se distraient avec la dernière version de Nintendo. Au bureau, les agendas informatisés permettent de transcrire vos messages et vos notes. Les télécopieurs envoient immédiatement vos documents d'un bout à l'autre du monde. Les modems transmettent des quantités d'information d'un ordinateur à un autre, etc., etc. Les acronymes du moment – MAC, VCR, ATM, PC, DC, DOS, ROM et RAM – sont devenus l'ABC des générations montantes, assoiffées d'informations. Dans notre effort d'assimiler, de nommer et de transmettre, le volume d'informations qu'il nous faut digérer est en train de doubler tout les dix ans. □ Examinons maintenant ce qui est arrivé dans notre branche. A commencer par notre engouement pour la typographie digitalisée dans les années soixante, les progrès successifs ont profondément ébranlé l'industrie graphique. Le résultat, c'est que nous voyons émerger toute une nouvelle génération de designers dont le travail semble refléter la confusion d'un monde qui file à toute allure, à un rythme toujours plus accéléré, et qui souffre manifestement d'une surcharge d'informations. Des légions de jeunes designers du monde entier, qui viennent de passer leur diplôme dans les écoles d'art, arrivent sur le marché du travail chaque année, armés d'un savoir technique ahurissant, mais disposant d'une compréhension visiblement limitée de l'histoire de l'art, de l'architecture, de la typographie et du design graphique. Qui plus est, au cours de ces dernières années, un pourcentage croissant du travail produit semble être plus révélateur du tapage fait autour des développements les plus récents de la technologie que des idées et messages que les mêmes outils auraient dû transmettre. Travaillons-nous, oui ou non, dans le secteur de la communication? Est-ce que nous serions tellement épris de ces gadgets de la technologie que nous aurions perdu de vue ce qui est l'essence même de notre profession? □ Un «bon design» ne consiste certes pas à couper en tranches ou en dés, à étirer ou manipuler de quelque manière que ce soit un message jusqu'à ce qu'il soit totalement illisible, uniquement parce que c'est à la mode. Nous avons permis à la machine de porter ombrage à la clarté, à l'intelligence et à la personnalité de l'expression humaine. Etant donné que notre société moderne se trouve confronté à un volume toujours plus grand d'informations, et que le temps semble être devenu l'un de nos denrées les plus précieuses, je crois que, nous les designers, nous avons une responsabilité encore plus grande: nous devons être plus attentifs à ce que nous disons et être plus concis dans notre expression. ∎

WOODY PIRTLE EST UN ASSOCIÉ DU BUREAU NEW-YORKAIS DE PENTAGRAM. APRES AVOIR ÉTUDIÉ L'ARCHITECTURE ET LES BEAUX-ARTS, IL COMMENCE SA CARRIERE DE DESIGNER GRAPHIQUE EN 1969. IL FAIT PARTIE DES CABINETS DE CONSEIL EN DESIGN DE PLUSIEURS ENTREPRISES ET EST CONSULTANT AUPRES D'IBM, CHAMPION INTERNATIONAL ET PANTONE, INC. SES CRÉATIONS PERSONNELLES ONT ÉTÉ EXPOSÉES DANS LE MONDE ENTIER. ∎

BARRIE TUCKER

Good design, like good music, transcends language and political barriers. Good design is based on fact, function and relevance, and it must be tailor-made—created specifically to project the personality and qualities of a product to its chosen audience. That is the foremost responsibility of a designer. □ But good design must also have a magic ingredient: a good idea, a surprise element, a touch of humor or "sparkle," something that sets it apart from its competitors and excites and motivates its audience. One could be forgiven for envying those designers who develop one "house" style and use it for every client, but in fact I feel strongly that these people are doing a disservice to the design and commercial world at large. I see little evidence of any depth of thought or real creativity in this type of skin-deep "decoration" design, and because it can be imitated quite easily, it generally reaches "me-too" plague proportions in a very short time and becomes mindless overkill. □ What is shown in Graphis Design 93 is a wondrous array of work created by many designers from all corners of the globe for all manner of clients. Let me recommend, however, that when you receive your next design brief you don't simply turn to the pages of Graphis Design 93 to "borrow" a style or a concept. Think first of the value of the project you have been given, and of the very real trust and responsibility with which the client has honored you as a designer. Please remember also that what may have worked for company X, Y or Z will not necessarily work for client A, B or C. □ Of course, good design always requires thought, energy, dedication, strength of character, imagination and time. But the result will be exciting and satisfying, and so will the success that it will bring to your clients and to you. ∎

BARRIE TUCKER, AN AUSTRALIAN-BORN DESIGNER, HAS WORKED IN ZÜRICH AND LONDON. HE NOW HEADS BARRIE TUCKER DESIGN IN ADELAIDE, SOUTH AUSTRALIA, AND COLOGNE, GERMANY, AND IS WORKING ON PROJECTS IN JAPAN AND SOUTHEAST ASIA. HE IS RECOGNIZED INTERNATIONALLY FOR HIS WINE AND LIQUOR PACKAGING AND HIS THREE-DIMENSIONAL "PUBLIC" DESIGN IMAGERY. HE HAS BEEN A MEMBER OF THE ALLIANCE GRAPHIQUE INTERNATIONALE SINCE 1979, AND IS A FOUNDING MEMBER OF THE AUSTRALIAN ACADEMY OF DESIGN. ∎

Gutes Design – ähnlich wie gute Musik – überwindet alle sprachlichen und politischen Grenzen. □ Gutes Design basiert auf Fakten, Funktion und Relevanz und muss zudem massgeschneidert sein, speziell darauf angelegt, ein Produkt darzustellen und seine Qualitäten einem ausgesuchten Publikum nahezubringen. Das ist die Hauptverantwortung eines Designers. □ Gutes Design ist jedoch nicht nur die Darstellung von Fakten, Funktionen und Informationen. □ Um die Bezeichnung gutes Design zu verdienen, muss der Lösung etwas hinzugefügt werden: die Zauberformel einer guten Idee, ein Überraschungselement, ein Funken von Humor, etwas, das ein gutes Designkonzept von den mittelmässigen Designkonzepten unterscheidet und sein Publikum erfreut und motiviert. □ Es ist verständlich, wenn man insgeheim jene Leute beneidet, die einen typischen «Haus-Stil» entwickelt haben und ihn unbekümmert für alle ihre Kunden anwenden. □ Ich glaube jedoch, dass diese Leute dem Design und der Geschäftswelt im allgemeinen einen schlechten Dienst erweisen. Bei diesem oft rein «dekorativen» Design vermisse ich gedanklichen Tiefgang und wirkliche Kreativität. Diese Art von Design lässt sich leicht nachahmen; man muss dabei nicht viel denken, und so breitet sich solches Design innert kürzester Zeit wie eine Seuche aus und wird zum völlig gedankenlosen Overkill. □ Was in diesem Buch gezeigt wird, ist eine wunderbare Sammlung von Arbeiten vieler Designer aus allen Teilen der Welt für alle möglichen Kunden. □ Lassen Sie sich aber nicht dazu verführen, beim nächsten Auftrag einfach im *Graphis Design* zu blättern und eine «Anleihe» bei einem Stil oder bei einem ganzen Konzept zu machen. Denken Sie in erster Linie an das Projekt, das Ihnen der Kunden anvertraut hat, und an die sehr reale Verantwortung, die der Kunde Ihnen als Gestalter übertragen hat. □ Bitte vergessen Sie nicht, dass eine Designlösung, die in San Francisco, Tokio oder New York für die Firma X, Y oder Z funktioniert haben mag, nicht automatisch auch für Ihren Kunden A, B oder C funktionieren wird. □ Gutes Design verlangt Überlegung, Energie, völlige Hingabe, Charakterstärke, Phantasie und Zeit. Aber es zahlt sich aus. Wenn Sie sich daran halten, werden Sie belohnt durch die aufregende und befriedigende Erfahrung, die mit der Schaffung guten Designs verbunden ist und letztlich durch den Erfolg, den es für ihren Kunden und Sie persönlich bedeutet. □ Gutes Design macht die Welt schöner. ∎

BARRIE TUCKER IST EIN AUSTRALISCHER DESIGNER. IN DEN SPÄTEN SECHZIGER JAHREN ARBEITETE ER IN ZÜRICH UND IN LONDON. ER LEITET HEUTE BARRIE TUCKER DESIGN IN ADELAIDE, AUSTRALIEN, UND IN KÖLN. ZUDEM ARBEITET ER AN PROJEKTEN IN JAPAN UND SÜDOSTASIEN. ER IST VOR ALLEM FÜR SEINE PACKUNGSGESTALTUNG FÜR ALKOHOLISCHE GETRÄNKE UND SEINE DREIDIMENSIONALEN ARBEITEN IM ÖFFENTLICHEN RAUM BEKANNT. SEIT 1979 IST ER MITGLIED DER AGI; AUSSERDEM IST ER GRÜNDUNGSMITGLIED DER AUSTRALIAN ACADEMY OF DESIGN. ∎

(ABOVE LEFT) LIQUOR PACKAGING FOR ZAMBRACCA CAFE, CABERNET SAUVIGNON ■ (ABOVE LEFT) PACKAGING FOR GRAMP'S, CABERNET MERLOT ■ (BELOW) TUCKER'S IMAGE FROM ZANDERS CALENDAR, 1991, FOR THE MONTH OF DECEMBER ■

Le bon design, tout comme la bonne musique, transcende toutes les langues et les barrières politiques. □ Le bon design se base sur la réalité, la fonction et une certaine pertinence. Il doit donc être fait sur mesure, créé spécialement: il s'agit de concevoir un produit afin d'exprimer son caractère et ses qualités à l'intention d'un public choisi. C'est en cela que consiste la responsabilité principale d'un designer. □ Pour qu'une solution mérite le nom de «bon design», il faut qu'elle ait de surcroît les ingrédients magiques qui feront qu'une idée est une bonne idée; il faut pour cela qu'elle comporte un élément de surprise, une touche, ne serait-ce qu'une étincelle d'humour. C'est ce qui permet de distinguer le concept d'un «bon design» des projets concurrents qui, eux, présentent un «design moyen»; c'est cela qui attire et motive le public. □ On pardonnera à ceux qui envient secrètement tous ces gens qui développent un seul style «maison», et l'utilisent indifféremment pour l'un ou l'autre de leurs clients. □ Quoi qu'il en soit, je crois que ces gens rendent un très mauvais service au design et au monde du commerce en général, car je vois peu de traces d'une quelconque profondeur de pensée ou de véritable créativité dans ce genre de design «décoratif» superficiel. Parce qu'il peut être imité assez facile-

SANCTUARY COVE,
YACHT CLUB SIGNAGE

ment, qu'il demande peu de réflexion, il se répand généralement comme une véritable épidémie qui a des effets ravageurs. □ Ce qui est présenté dans ce livre constitue un merveilleux panorama des travaux créés pour toutes sortes de clients par de nombreux designers des quatre coins du monde. □ Oserais-je cependant vous conseiller une chose: quand vous recevrez votre prochaine commande, ne vous contentez pas tout simplement de tourner les pages de Graphis pour «emprunter» un style ou un concept entier. Réfléchissez tout d'abord à la valeur du projet que votre client vous a confié et mesurez la véritable responsabilité dont il vous a honoré en qualité de designer. Et rappelez-vous aussi que ce qui a marché à San Francisco, Tokyo et New York pour la société X, Y ou Z ne marchera pas forcément automatiquement si vous copiez le résultat final pour un client A, B ou C. □ Bien entendu, un «bon design» demande avant tout de la réflexion, de l'énergie, une grande force de caractère, de l'imagination et beaucoup de temps. Cela suppose que l'on s'y consacre complètement. Mais cela étant, quelle satisfaction de produire un «bon design» et de voir qu'il apporte le succès à ses clients, et en dernier ressort, à soi-même! □ C'est grâce à sa magie que le «bon design» embellit le monde. ■

BARRIE TUCKER EST UN DESIGNER NÉ EN AUSTRALIE. A LA FIN DES ANNÉES SOIXANTE, IL A ÉTÉ EMPLOYÉ À ZURICH, PUIS A TRAVAILLÉ EN FREE-LANCE À LONDRES. IL DIRIGE ACTUELLEMENT LA FIRME BARRIE TUCKER DESIGN À ADÉLAIDE, AUSTRALIE, ET À COLOGNE, ALLEMAGNE; IL TRAVAILLE EN OUTRE SUR DES PROJETS AU JAPON ET DANS L'ASIE DU SUD-EST. BARRIE TUCKER EST CONNU DANS LE MONDE ENTIER POUR SES CRÉATIONS DE PACKAGING POUR VINS ET SPIRITUEUX ET SES DESIGNS TRIDIMENSIONNELS POUR LES ESPACES PUBLICS. MEMBRE DE L'ALLIANCE GRAPHIQUE INTERNATIONALE ET MEMBRE FONDATEUR DE L'ACADEMY OF DESIGN D'AUSTRALIE. ■

ADVERTISING

WERBUNG

PUBLICITE

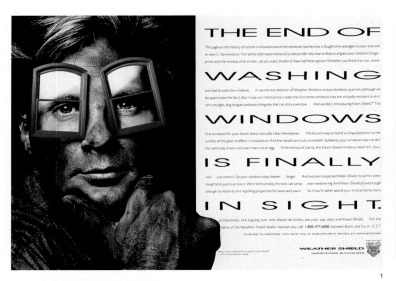

THE END OF WASHING WINDOWS IS FINALLY IN SIGHT.

1

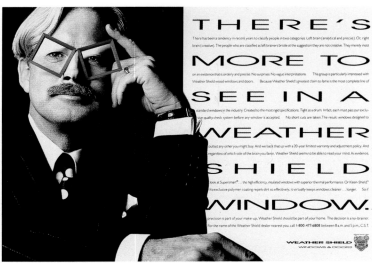

THERE'S MORE TO SEE IN A WEATHER SHIELD WINDOW.

2

THERE'S MORE TO SEE IN A WEATHER SHIELD WINDOW.

3

SEE YOUR WAY COMFORTABLY THROUGH ANY KIND OF WEATHER.

4

1 - 4

ART DIRECTOR:

MIKE WHEATON

DESIGNER:

MIKE WHEATON

PHOTOGRAPHER:

DENNIS MANARCHY

COPYWRITERS:

TOM JORDAN

MIKE WHEATON

REED ALLEN

AGENCY:

HOFFMAN YORK +

COMPTON

CLIENT:

WEATHER SHIELD

WINDOWS & DOORS

5

ART DIRECTOR:
ERIC HOLDEN
PHOTOGRAPHER:
JOHN PARKER
COPYWRITER:
RÉMI NOEL
AGENCY:
DDB NEEDHAM
WORLDWIDE
CLIENT:
VOLKSWAGEN

■ 1-4 ADVERTISING CAMPAIGN DEMONSTRATING THE FINE QUALITIES AND FEATURES OF WEATHER SHIELD WINDOWS. EACH AD CONCERNS A SPECIFIC FEATURE, SUCH AS RESISTANCE TO DIRT, THE COMPLETE LINE OF WINDOWS OFFERED BY THE COMPANY, CUSTOM-MADE WINDOWS FOR EASY REPLACEMENT, AND THERMAL PERFORMANCE. (USA)

■ 5 ONE EXAMPLE FROM A CAMPAIGN FOR THE VOLKSWAGEN GOLF AUTOMOBILE, EMPHASIZING THE DURABILITY OF THE CAR. (FRA)

● 1-4 EINE WERBEKAMPAGNE, IN DER QUALITÄT UND BESONDERE EIGENSCHAFTEN VON WEATHER-SHIELD-FENSTERN ZUM AUSDRUCK KOMMEN SOLL. HIER GEHT ES UM DIE UNEMPFINDLICHKEIT GEGEN SCHMUTZ, DIE GROSSE AUSWAHL VON NORMFENSTERN, DEN PROBLEMLOSEN ERSATZ ALTER FENSTER UND DIE ISOLATIONSQUALITÄTEN. (USA)

● 5 AUS EINER KAMPAGNE FÜR VW GOLF, DEREN THEMA DIE LANGLEBIGKEIT UND ZUVERLÄSSIGKEIT DER MARKE IST. (FRA)

▲ 1-4 EXEMPLES D'UNE CAMPAGNE DE PUBLICITÉ QUI DEVAIT VISUALISER LA QUALITÉ ET LES CARACTÉRISTIQUES DES FENETRES WEATHER SHIELD: LA POUSSIERE N'Y ATTACHE PAS, LE CHOIX DE MODELES STANDARD EST TRES VASTE, ELLES S'ADAPTENT À TOUS LES ENCADREMENTS, LEURS QUALITÉS D'ISOLATION SONT REMARQUABLES. (USA)

▲ 5 EXEMPLE D'UNE CAMPAGNE POUR LA GOLF VW, DONT LE THEME PRINCIPAL EST LA DURABILITÉ DE CETTE VOITURE. (FRA)

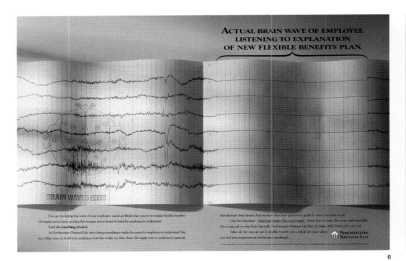

6

7

6, 7

ART DIRECTOR:

JAC COVERDALE

PHOTOGRAPHER:

STEVE UMLAND

COPYWRITER:

JERRY FURY

AGENCY:

CLARITY COVERDALE

RUEFF

CLIENT:

NORTHWESTERN

NATIONAL LIFE

INSURANCE

■ 6, 7 NORTHWESTERN NATIONAL LIFE IN-SURANCE COMPANY ATTACKS THE OVERUSE OF HEALTH-BENEFIT PLANS WITH THIS AD CAMPAIGN, OFFERING COMPANIES BRO-CHURES ON HOW TO SOLVE THE PROBLEM AND HOW TO EXPLAIN A FLEXIBLE BENEFIT PLAN TO EMPLOYEES. (USA)

■ 8-10 ADS FROM A CAMPAIGN FOR FRED VANDERPOEL, A PHOTOGRAPHER. THE FIRST TELLS HOW THE COPY WAS CREATED. THE SECOND SAYS: "ACTUALLY, ALL THE GOOD IMPRESSIONISTS ARE DEAD. EXCEPT VAN-DERPOEL." THE THIRD ONE CLAIMS THAT FRED VANDERPOEL IS A PHOTOGRAPHER WHO CAN LISTEN. (USA)

● 6, 7 «FINDEN SIE, DASS EINIGE ANGE-STELLTE MIT JEDER KLEINIGKEIT ZUM ARZT RENNEN?»; «GEHIRNSTRÖME EINES ANGE-STELLTEN, DER ERKLÄRUNG DES NEUEN FLEXIBLEN KRANKENVERSICHERUNGSPLANS ZUHÖREND». KAMPAGNE EINER VERSICHE-RUNG, DIE ABHILFE ANBIETET. (USA)

● 8-10 BEISPIELE AUS EINER WERBEKAM-PAGNE FÜR DEN PHOTOGRAPHEN FRED VAN-DERPOEL: «WIE MAN DAS MEISTE AUS EINER ANZEIGE HERAUSHOLT», AUS DER SICHT DES TEXTERS (MIT EINGESTREUTEN AUFNAHMEN VON VANDERPOEL); «WIE MAN IM DRUCK GROSSEN EINDRUCK MACHT»; «FRED HAT OHREN UND BENUTZT SIE». (USA)

▲ 6, 7 «TROUVEZ-VOUS QUE CERTAINS EM-PLOYÉS COURENT CHEZ LE MÉDECIN AU MOINDRE PETIT BOBO?» «ENCÉPHALOGRAMME D'UN EMPLOYÉ ÉCOUTANT L'EXPLICATION DU NOUVEAU PLAN FLEXIBLE D'ASSURANCE MAL-ADIE.». UNE ASSURANCE PROPOSE DES BROCHURES D'INFORMATION. (USA)

▲ 8-10 EXEMPLES D'UNE CAMPAGNE DE PUB-LICITÉ POUR LE PHOTOGRAPHE FRED VANDERPOEL: «COMMENT FAIRE DE L'IMPRESSION DANS L'IMPRIMÉ», «COMMENT TIRER PARTI D'UNE PUB» SELON LE RÉDAC-TEUR-CONCEPTEUR (TEXTE ILLUSTRÉ DE PHOTOS DE VANDERPOEL), «FRED A DES OREILLES ET IL LES UTILISE.» (USA)

8-10

ART DIRECTOR:

TOM ROTH

DESIGNER:

TOM ROTH

PHOTOGRAPHER:

FRED VANDERPOEL

COPYWRITERS:

CHRIS WOODBY (8)

MARK LEDERMANN (9)

AGENCY:

ANDERSON & LEMBKE

CLIENT:

FRED VANDERPOEL

HOW TO GET THE MOST OUT OF AN AD.

Vanderpoel

HOW TO GET A GREAT IMPRESSION IN PRINT.

Actually, all the good impressionists are dead. Except Vanderpoel.
Call (415) 621-4405 for Vanderpoel's free printed portfolio.

WHO NEEDS EARS?

A government study has confirmed that of 5.3 billion human beings currently living on earth, over 99% have ears. Our own informal survey, conducted at the Boom Boom Lounge in Lafayette, Miss., reached a similar conclusion.

IMPLICATIONS

The findings leave no doubt: these days, everyone has ears. In fact, the U.S. national average is 2 per person, or 7.2 per household.

But despite the popularity of aural orifices, it is estimated that less than 12% of the public at large are actually proficient at using them. Most people with ears are casual users, including a large subsegment who use them only in conjunction with the audio output on their television sets and car radios.

EAR MASTERS

We set out to find those people truly skilled at ear usage; people whose very livelihoods depend upon the functionality of their auditory sphincters.

Safecrackers. Employees of the larceny and burglary industries use their ears constantly in the line of duty. Trying to hear those numbers fall into place is a demanding aural undertaking, as is listening out for approaching police officers or security guards. (We are, of course, personally opposed to any criminal activity, be it jaywalking or murder or TV evangelism.)

Psychologists. Psychologists make careers out of listening to the problems of confused people and then signing them up to come back again the following week. A psychologist who didn't listen well would soon find his patients confiding in their friends instead of him, and would thus be unemployed. (If you can't afford a psychologist and don't have any friends, we will gladly listen to your problems for $10 an hour plus beer.)

Fred Vanderpoel. Photography is an occupation that we assumed utilized the eyes only, but then we found Fred. Fred has ears. And uses them. Fred's ears, in fact, are as valuable to his trade as lenses and filters.

ABOUT FRED'S EARS

When you hire Fred, you'll see his ears go into action almost immediately. You provide a verbal description of the image you need, and Fred's ears interface with his piles of photographic equipment to produce a visual representation. That's all you have to do. And any effect you can describe, Fred can produce. That's where such trained ears come in handy.

If you need this kind of precision in your productions, as your advisers, we recommend that you call Fred at the first opportunity. And if, God forbid, you aren't willing to take our word for it, call (213) 935-5695 or (415) 621-4405 and ask for Fred's free printed portfolio and a free poster of this photo.

We think you'll like what you see.

After all you're not buying pretty pictures.

You're buying ears.

Vanderpoel.

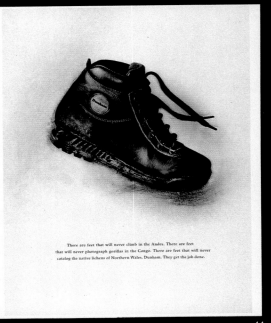

There are feet that will never climb in the Andes. There are feet
that will never photograph gorillas in the Congo. There are feet that will never
catalog the native lichens of Northern Wales. Dunham. They get the job done.

11

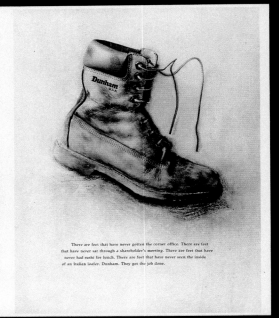

There are feet that have never gotten the corner office. There are feet
that have never sat through a shareholder's meeting. There are feet that have
never had sushi for lunch. There are feet that have never seen the inside
of an Italian loafer. Dunham. They get the job done.

12

There are feet that will never meet the gas pedal of a Range Rover.
There are feet that will never see a condo in Aspen. There are feet that will
never winter in Palm Springs or Palm Beach or Palm anywhere.
Dunham. They get the job done.

13

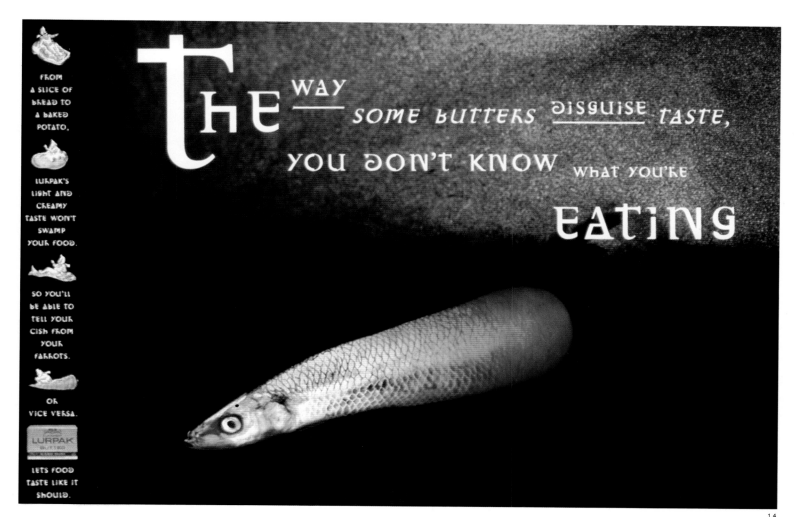

FROM
A SLICE OF
BREAD TO
A BAKED
POTATO,

LURPAK'S
LIGHT AND
CREAMY
TASTE WON'T
SWAMP
YOUR FOOD.

SO YOU'LL
BE ABLE TO
TELL YOUR
CISH FROM
YOUR
CARROTS.

OR
VICE VERSA.

LURPAK

LETS FOOD
TASTE LIKE IT
SHOULD.

THE WAY SOME BUTTERS DISGUISE TASTE, YOU DON'T KNOW WHAT YOU'RE EATING

14

11-13

ART DIRECTOR:
JOHN DOYLE
DESIGNER:
JOHN DOYLE
PHOTOGRAPHER:
NADAV KANDER
COPYWRITER:
ERNIE SCHENCK
STYLISTS:
TIM MITCHELL
JEFF TAPLEY
AGENCY:
DOYLE ADVERTISING
CLIENT:
THE DUNHAM
COMPANY

14

ART DIRECTOR:
KATE STANNERS
PHOTOGRAPHER:
JOHN PARKER
COPYWRITER:
TIM HEARN
AGENCY:
GOLD GREENLESS
TROTT
CLIENT:
MD FOODS

■ 11-13 EXAMPLES FROM AN IMAGE CAM-
PAIGN FOR THE DUNHAM COMPANY, A MAKER
OF LEATHER BOOTS FOR OUTDOOR WORK AND
RECREATIONAL USE. THE ADS GLORIFY THE
WORKING MAN. THE COMPANY'S AIM IS TO
RETAIN ITS PRESENT BASE OF CUSTOMERS
AND AT THE SAME TIME DEVELOP GREATER
AWARENESS AMONG WHITE-COLLAR CON-
SUMERS. (USA)

■ 14 ONE OF SEVERAL ADS FOR LURPAK BUT-
TER, CLAIMING THAT LURPAK LETS FOOD
TASTE THE WAY IT SHOULD. (GBR)

● 11-13 AUS EINER IMAGE-KAMPAGNE FÜR
DIE DUNHAM COMPANY, HERSTELLER VON
STRAPAZIERFÄHIGEN LEDERSTIEFELN. ES
GING DARUM, EINE VERBINDUNG ZWISCHEN
DER ARBEITERKLASSE UND DER PRAGMA-
TISCHEN AUFFASSUNG DER FIRMA HERZU-
STELLEN UND VORHANDENE UND POTEN-
TIELLE KUNDEN AUS ALLEN SCHICHTEN AN-
ZUSPRECHEN. (USA)

● 14 «SO WIE MANCHE BUTTERSORTEN DEN
GESCHMACK VERDECKEN, WEISS MAN NICHT,
WAS MAN ISST.» FÜR EINE BUTTER. (GBR)

▲ 11-13 CAMPAGNE POUR UN FABRICANT DE
BOTTES EN CUIR D'UNE GRANDE SOLIDITÉ.
ON A CHERCHÉ ICI À ÉTABLIR UN RAP-
PROCHEMENT ENTRE LA CLASSE OUVRIERE
ET LA CONCEPTION PRAGMATIQUE QUI A FAIT
LE SUCCES DE CETTE MARQUE. TOUT EN
S'ADRESSANT À LA CLIENTELE ACTUELLE, IL
S'AGISSAIT D'ATTIRER L'INTÉRET DE NOU-
VEAUX CLIENT. (USA)

▲ 14 «CERTAINS BEURRES TRANSFORMENT
TELLEMENT LE GOUT QUE VOUS NE SAVEZ
MEME PLUS CE QUE VOUS MANGEZ.» (GBR)

L'estate ha un gusto unico.

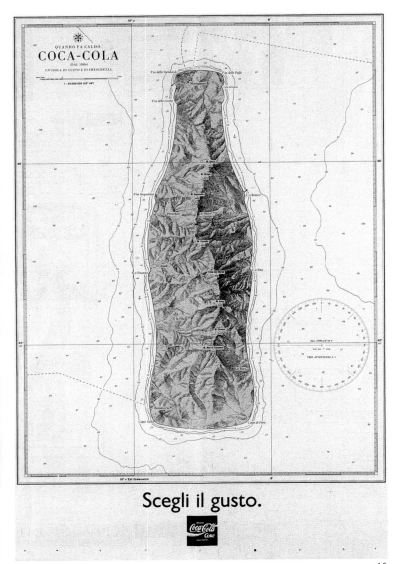

Scegli il gusto.

Scegli il gusto.

15

16

15, 16

CREATIVE DIRECTOR:

FRANCO MORETTI

ART DIRECTOR:

STEFANO COLOMBO

COPYWRITER:

FABRIZIO RUSSO

AGENCY:

MCCANN ERICKSON

CLIENT:

COCA-COLA

17, 18

ART DIRECTOR:

TOMEK LUCZYNSKI

DESIGNER:

DORIS FORSTHUBER

PHOTOGRAPHER:

THOMAS POPINGER

COPYWRITER:

JOHANNES KRAMMER

AGENCY:

DEMNER & MERLICEK

CLIENT:

KURIER

■ 15, 16 "SUMMER HAS A UNIQUE TASTE" AND "WHEN IT IS HOT, COCA-COLA, AN ISLAND OF TASTE AND FRESHNESS," TWO EXAMPLES FROM A NEWSPAPER AD CAMPAIGN FOR COCA-COLA. (ITA)

■ 17, 18 CAMPAIGN FOR THE AUSTRIAN NEWSPAPER KURIER, PROMOTING ITS ADVERTISING SPACE. THE ADVERTISEMENTS ARE ADDRESSED TO SPECIFIC INDUSTRIES, HERE TRAVEL AND REAL ESTATE. (AUT)

● 15, 16 «DER SOMMER HAT EINEN EINZIGARTIGEN GESCHMACK»; «WENN ES HEISS IST, COCA-COLA, EINE INSEL DES GESCHMACKS UND DER FRISCHE». AUS EINER ZEITUNGSKAMPAGNE FÜR COCA-COLA. (ITA)

● 17, 18 AN POTENTIELLE ANZEIGENKUNDEN GERICHTETE KAMPAGNE DER ZEITUNG KURIER. ES WERDEN EINZELNE BRANCHEN ANGESPROCHEN, HIER DIE TOURISTIK- UND DIE IMMOBILIENBRANCHE. (AUT)

▲ 15, 16 «L'ÉTÉ A UN GOUT UNIQUE», «QUAND IL FAIT CHAUD, COCA-COLA, UNE ILE DE GOUT ET DE FRAICHEUR». D'UNE CAMPAGNE D'ANNONCES POUR COCA-COLA PARUE DANS LES JOURNAUX. (ITA)

▲ 17, 18 CAMPAGNE DE PROMOTION DU JOURNAL KURIER. IL S'AGISSAIT D'ATTIRER L'ATTENTION D'ANNONCEURS POTENTIELS DE DIVERSES BRANCHES, ICI LE TOURISME ET LE MARCHÉ IMMOBILIER. (AUT)

19-21

ART DIRECTOR:

MICHAEL
MCLAUGHLIN

PHOTOGRAPHER:

GEORGE SIMHONI

COPYWRITER:

STEPHEN CREET

AGENCY:

MAC LAREN:LINTAS

CLIENT:

NESTLÉ

There's Only One Thing I Admire More Than Myself.

And that's Fancy Feast. Because while I am admirable in oh so many ways, Fancy Feast is perfection itself; unquestionably superior to common cat or real foods. ❦ Fancy Feast contains carefully selected morsels of nothing but real meat or real fish. It comes in three forms: flaked, sliced and paté, in twelve delicious flavours, including two new flaked seafood entrées I am particularly fond of: Sardines, Shrimp and Crab; Tuna and Shrimp. ❦ As evidenced by my lustrous coat, Fancy Feast is superior in nutrition as well as taste because it offers a completely balanced diet and even helps prevent F.U.S. And may I say how much I appreciate those single serving cans which assure me of a fresh meal every time. ❦ Now, as much as I'd like to keep Fancy Feast all to myself, I must confess that it is ideal for every type of cat: cats with pedigrees, cats with stripes, even that uncouth cat across the street. ❦ So if you're as fond of your cat as my two-legged companion is of me, I'd highly recommend Fancy Feast.

There's Nothing Better Than Fancy Feast.

If you'd like to join the Friskies Cat Club or have any questions call 1-800 -843-PETS (7387).

19

There's Only One Thing I Enjoy More Than Playing Hard To Pet.

And that's Fancy Feast. Because while I find it amusing to toy with my human devotees, nothing compares to my favourite cat food. ❦ Fancy Feast is unquestionably superior to common cat foods. It contains carefully selected morsels of nothing but real meat or real fish. It comes in three forms: flaked, sliced and paté, in twelve delicious flavours. ❦ As evidenced by my lustrous coat, Fancy Feast is superior in nutrition as well as taste because it offers a completely balanced diet and even helps prevent F.U.S. And may I say how much I appreciate those single serving cans which assure me of a fresh meal every time. ❦ Now, as much as I'd like to keep Fancy Feast all to myself, I must confess that it is ideal for every type of cat: cats with pedigrees, cats with stripes, even that uncouth cat across the street. ❦ So if you ever want to draw your cat out into the open, I'd highly recommend opening a can of Fancy Feast.

There's Nothing Better Than Fancy Feast.

If you'd like to join the Friskies Cat Club or have any questions call 1-800-843-PETS (7387).

20

There's Only One Thing I Like More Than Getting Into Trouble.

And that's Fancy Feast. Because as much as I enjoy being mischievous and threatening precious objects, nothing's more precious to me than my favourite food. ❦ Fancy Feast is unquestionably superior to common cat foods. It contains carefully selected morsels of nothing but real meat or real fish. It comes in three forms: flaked, sliced and paté, in twelve delicious flavours. ❦ As evidenced by my lustrous coat, Fancy Feast is superior in nutrition as well as taste because it offers a completely balanced diet and even helps prevent F.U.S. And may I say how much I appreciate those single serving cans which assure me of a fresh meal every time. ❦ Now, as much as I'd like to keep Fancy Feast all to myself, I must confess that it is ideal for every type of cat: cats with pedigrees, cats with stripes, even that uncouth cat across the street. ❦ So if you have any intentions of keeping your valuables valuable, I would highly recommend doing what my owner does, and keep your cat happy with Fancy Feast.

There's Nothing Better Than Fancy Feast.

If you'd like to join the Friskies Cat Club or have any questions call 1-800-843-PETS (7387).

21

LAST YEAR, WE GAVE 8 BILLION DOLLARS IN MILITARY AID TO COUNTRIES THAT OUR UNDER-EDUCATED CHILDREN CAN'T EVEN FIND ON A MAP.

If we don't improve the quality of our kids' education, America could find itself in a sad state.

THE CHILDREN'S DEFENSE FUND.

22

IF YOU REALLY WANT TO SEE HOW FAST HE CAN RUN, TELL HIM YOU'RE PREGNANT.

Become pregnant too soon and your whole life can get off track.

THE CHILDREN'S DEFENSE FUND.

23

22, 23

ART DIRECTOR:

DEAN HANSON

PHOTOGRAPHER:

BUCK HOLZMER (23)

COPYWRITER:

DOUG DEGROOD

AGENCY:

FALLON McELLIGOTT

CLIENT:

THE CHILDREN'S
DEFENSE FUND

■ 19-21 THE CLAIM OF THESE ADVERTISE-MENTS—THAT FANCY FEAST CAT FOOD IS SUPERIOR—IS REINFORCED BY THE USE OF THE ELEGANT WHITE CAT AND THE SOPHIS-TICATED LANGUAGE IN THE COPY. THE HEAD-LINES ARE INTENDED TO REMIND CAT OWN-ERS OF THEIR OWN PETS. (USA)

■ 22, 23 THESE AND OTHER ADVERTISEMENTS FOR THE CHILDREN'S DEFENSE FUND ARE MEANT TO HEIGHTEN READERS' AWARENESS OF VARIOUS PROBLEMS. THE FIRST AD DEALS WITH THE QUALITY OF CHILDREN'S EDUCA-TION AND ITS IMPORTANCE FOR THE NA-TION'S FUTURE, THE SECOND WITH EARLY PREGNANCY. (USA)

● 19-21 «NUR EINE SACHE MACHT MIR MEHR SPASS, ALS DIE SCHEUE ZU SPIELEN»; «ES GIBT NUR EINE SACHE, DIE ICH MEHR ALS MICH SELBST BEWUNDERE»; «NUR EINE SACHE MACHT MIR MEHR SPASS, ALS UNSINN ZU MACHEN». ANZEIGEN FÜR FANCY-FEAST-KATZENFUTTER. (USA)

● 22, 23 «LETZTES JAHR GINGEN 8 MILLI-ARDEN DOLLAR ALS MILITÄRHILFE AN LÄN-DER, DIE UNSERE SCHLECHT AUSGEBILDETEN KINDER NICHT MAL AUF DER LANDKARTE FIN-DEN KÖNNEN»; «WENN DU WIRKLICH SEHEN WILLST, WIE SCHNELL ER LAUFEN KANN, SAG IHM, DASS DU SCHWANGER BIST». KAMPAGNE FÜR EIN KINDERHILFSWERK. (USA)

▲ 19-21 «IL Y A UNE SEULE CHOSE QUI ME PLAIT MIEUX QUE DE JOUER À LA TIMIDE.» «IL Y A UNE SEULE CHOSE QUE J'ADMIRE PLUS QUE MOI-MEME» «IL Y A UNE SEULE CHOSE QUE JE PRÉFÈRE AUX BÉTISES.» CAMPAGNE DE PUBLICITÉ POUR UNE MARQUE D'ALIMENTS POUR CHATS. (USA)

▲ 22, 23 «L'ANNÉE DERNIERE, NOUS AVONS FOURNI 8 MILLIARDS DE DOLLARS D'AIDE MILITAIRE À DES PAYS QUE NOS ENFANTS ILLETTRÉS NE SONT MEME PAS CAPABLES DE TROUVER SUR LA CARTE»; «SI TU VEUX VOIR COMME IL COURT VITE, DIS-LUI QUE TU ES ENCEINTE.» POUR UNE ASSOCIATION D'AIDE AUX ENFANTS. (USA)

24, 25

Art Director:

CORDULA ALESSAN-

DRI-EBNER

Designer:

CORDULA ALESSAN-

DRI-EBNER

Artists:

CLAUDIO ALESSAN-

DRI (24)

HANS KUMMER (25)

Copywriter:

BIRGIT HÖTTGES

Agency:

OGILVY & MATHER

MEDICAL

Client:

AUGMENTIN

■ 24, 25 "WE HAVE REGISTERED OUR PENI-CILLIN"; "OUR PENICILLIN IS NOT STRONGER, BUT IT'S MORE INTELLIGENT"—ADS FOR A PENICILLIN WITH SPECIAL QUALITIES. THE TYPOGRAPHY AND LAYOUT WERE USED TO SUPPORT THE CLAIM. (AUT)

● 24, 25 ZWEI FACHANZEIGEN MIT GLEICH-LAUTENDEM LAUFTEXT FÜR EIN GESCHÜTZ-TES PENIZILLIN MIT SPEZIELLEN EIGEN-SCHAFTEN. DIE AUSSAGEN SOLLTEN DURCH DEN EINSATZ DER TYPOGRAPHIE UNTER-STÜTZT WERDEN. (AUT)

▲ 24, 25 «NOTRE PÉNICILLINE EST UNE MAR-QUE DÉPOSÉE»; «NOTRE PÉNICILLINE N'EST PAS PLUS FORTE MAIS PLUS INTELLIGENTE». ANNONCES POUR UNE MARQUE DE PÉNICIL-LINE. LA TYPOGRAPHIE RENFORCE LE MES-SAGE. (AUT)

K

WISSEN SIE, OB IHR ANTIBIOTIKUM TATSÄCH-LICH GEGEN ALLE BAK-TERIENSTÄMME AN-KOMMT, DIE IHR PA-TIENT VIELLEICHT IN SICH TRÄGT? WIE STEHT ES MIT JENEN BAKTE-RIEN, DIE BETA-LAKTA-MASEN BILDEN UND DAMIT RESISTENT SIND GEGEN PENICILLINE UND CEPHALOSPORINE? UNSER PENICILLIN IST NICHT STÄRKER ALS ANDERE. ABER ES HAT EINEN SCHUTZMAN-TEL. DIESER SCHUTZ IST UNSERE GARANTIE FÜR SICHERHEIT: DER AUGMENTIN-CLAVULAN-SÄURE-MANTEL HEMMT DIE WIRKUNG DER BETA-LAKTAMASEN. IRREVER-SIBEL. JETZT FRAGEN WIR UNS NUR NOCH EINES: WARUM VERORDNEN SIE NICHT GLEICH BEIM ERSTEN MAL DAS GE-SCHÜTZTE ANTIBIOTI-KUM - ZUR SICHERHEIT?

SB
SmithKline Beecham
Pharma

UNSER PENICILLIN IST NICHT STÄRKER. **ABER**

Klüger

AUGMENTIN*
DANN KÖNNEN SIE SICHER SEIN.

25

FOR THE BODY, WAX POLISH APPLIED BY HAND.
FOR THE ENGINE,
DETERGENT APPLIED BY THE RIGHT FOOT.

In the days when the D Type cleaned up at Le Mans, the task of cleaning an engine gave little cause for celebration.

One took the whole damned thing apart, decoked it by hand, screwed it back together and wondered what to do with all the bits that were left over.

Not all fuels are the same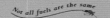

The 'coke' is of course carbon — the ubiquitous by-product of combustion. Rather a lot of which goes on inside the internal combustion engine.

Today, carbon is still as much a threat to classic car engines as it was thirty years ago.

Modern cars are even more sensitive to carbon deposits than their predecessors.

The latest aerodynamics not only reduce drag. They reduce the flow of cooling air to the engine.

Which already runs hotter, because its combustion technology is more efficient.

Extra heat means extra carbon baked onto fuel injectors, carburettors, inlet ports and valves.

Not all fuels are the same

Fuel consumption goes up. Performance goes down, with flat spots disrupting the power curve. Starting becomes more difficult.

So the question of how to combat carbon has become somewhat pressing.

Shell have formulated the answer: a detergent in the fuel that cleans the engine while it's being driven.

(The solution is deceptively simple. Developing it has taken thirty years.)

All Shell Advanced Fuels now contain this extraordinary additive.

It's rather effective. Used regularly, Shell Advanced will keep your engine twice as clean as any other brand.

It also has the power to help remove existing carbon deposits.

Not all fuels are the same

We anticipate an enthusiastic response from the guardians of our motoring heritage.

In a word or three, classic car enthusiasts.

Just think: every time you open the throttle, your right foot could be doing the job that hitherto required two hands, sundry spanners, loads of expertise, and hours of hard labour.

It seems there is something to be said for modern technology after all.

YOU CAN TELL WHEN IT'S SHELL.

26

26

ART DIRECTOR:
CHRISTOPHER GREGORY
PHOTOGRAPHER:
JACK BANKHEAD
COPYWRITER:
CHRISTIAN MARECHAL
AGENCY:
GREENAWAY
BURDETT MARTYN
CLIENT:
SHELL UK

■ 26 EXAMPLE FROM AN ADVERTISING CAMPAIGN FOR SHELL AUTOMOTIVE PRODUCTS, FEATURING SOPHISTICATED CARS. SHOWN HERE IS A D-TYPE JAGUAR. (GBR)

■ 27 PROMOTION PIECE FOR GREAT FACES TYPOGRAPHY DESIGN, MAILED TO ART DIRECTORS AT ADVERTISING AGENCIES THROUGHOUT THE UNITED STATES. (USA)

■ 28 ADVERTISEMENT FROM A CAMPAIGN FOR BMW MOTORCYCLES, FOCUSING ON FREEDOM, SAFETY AND DURABILITY. (USA)

■ 29 DOUBLE-PAGE ADVERTISEMENT INVITING PEOPLE TO VISIT THE NORTH CAROLINA COAST. THE AD SPEAKS OF THE CHARMS OF THE AREA, WHERE, IT SAYS, TIME SEEMS TO HAVE SLOWED DOWN. (USA)

● 26 BEISPIEL AUS EINER WERBEKAMPAGNE FÜR AUTOZUBEHÖR VON SHELL. IN ALLEN ANZEIGEN WIRD MIT ANSPRUCHSVOLLEN AUTOS GEWORBEN, HIER EIN JAGUAR. (GBR)

● 27 ANZEIGE FÜR GREAT FACES TYPOGRAPHY DESIGN: »HÄTTEN SIE LIEBER DEN DANK IHRES BUCHHALTERS ODER EINE AUSZEICHNUNG WIE DIESE?« (USA)

● 28 AUS EINER KAMPAGNE FÜR BMW-MOTORRÄDER. DAS THEMA: FREIHEIT, SICHERHEIT UND ZUVERLÄSSIGKEIT. (USA)

● 29 »BEVÖLKERUNG 5677. OHNE DIE WILDPONIES UND SINGSCHWÄNE.« WERBUNG FÜR DIE KÜSTE NORTH CAROLINAS ALS EIN ERHOLUNGSGEBIET, WO DIE ZEIT STILLZUSTEHEN SCHEINT. (USA)

▲ 26 EXEMPLE D'UNE CAMPAGNE POUR LES ACCESSOIRES AUTOMOBILES DE SHELL: LES ANNONCES PRÉSENTENT DES MODELES DE VOITURES EXCLUSIFS. (GBR)

▲ 27 POUR GREAT FACES TYPOGRAPHY DESIGN: »QU'EST-CE QUE VOUS PRÉFÉREZ? LA GRATITUDE DE VOTRE COMPTABLE? OU UNE RÉCOMPENSE COMME CELLE-LÀ?« (USA)

▲ 28 DEUX ANNONCES POUR LES MOTOS BMW: ON Y MET L'ACCENT SUR LA LIBERTÉ, LA SÉCURITÉ ET LA DURABILITÉ. (USA)

▲ 29 »5677 HABITANTS. SANS COMPTER LES PONEYS SAUVAGES ET LES CYGNES CHANTEURS.« CETTE ANNONCE VANTE LA BEAUTÉ DE LA COTE DE CAROLINE DU NORD, OU LE TEMPS SEMBLE S'ETRE ARRETÉ. (USA)

27

ART DIRECTOR:

SUE CROLICK

DESIGNER:

SUE CROLICK

PHOTOGRAPHER:

KERRY PETERSON

AGENCY:

SUE CROLICK

ADVERTISING +

DESIGN

CLIENT:

GREAT FACES

TYPOGRAPHY

When it comes to typography, which would you rather have?
The undying gratitude of your company comptroller?
Or one of these?

ONE SHOW AWARD

The next time you come up with a headline you love, call Bill Burk at 1-800-222-6798. We can't guarantee your ledger books will win awards. But there's a good chance your ad will. **Great Faces**

27

28

ART DIRECTOR:

ROBERT BILLINGS

DESIGNER:

ROBERT BILLINGS

PHOTOGRAPHER:

TOM TILL

COPYWRITER:

BOB HAIGH

AGENCY:

BURKHARDT &

CHRISTY

ADVERTISING

CLIENT:

BMW MOTORCYCLES

THE HOOK.

THE LINE.

So many roads. So little time.

So let's cut to the chase for motorcycling ideals, not trends. Which are the values of the most intelligent motorcycle gang ever assembled by hand and computer. The BMW K100LT, for example.

Our sporting tour de force. Unlike all the touring blimps on two wheels, it's aerodynamically fat-free. So it confidently shows off curves and straight lines while making the laws of physics extremely comfortable. Moreover, BMW's exclusive ABS is standard.

Which is also a real-world boast of our high-tech masterpiece.

The K1. It's a liquid-cooled, 16-valve, 1000cc super sport machine that accelerates at the values of BMW. Power. Handling. Safety. Durability. Styling. Virtues which also propel the BMW K75S.

A particularly user-friendly machine with 750cc's of uncanny smoothness, a sport suspension and touring ambitions. And our antilock braking system is optional.

Character is inherent, too, in the R100GS or Paris-Dakar 1000cc, ornery independence on or off road.

Note that every BMW motorcycle is also equipped with our 3-year, unlimited-mileage, limited warranty. The BMW Roadside Assistance Plan.™ And free riding school.™

Of course, your time begins with yours. Simply call 1-800-345-4BMW to find your nearest authorized BMW motorcycle dealer. He'll supply the sinker. A thorough test ride?

WORTH THE OBSESSION.

28

29

CREATIVE DIRECTOR:

JOHN RUSSO

ART DIRECTOR:

LARRY BENNETT

PHOTOGRAPHER:

STEVE MURRAY

COPYWRITER:

EMRY MCKINNEY

AGENCY:

MCKINNEY & SILVER

CLIENT:

THE NORTH CAROLINA

DEPARTMENT OF

ECONOMIC & COMMU-

NITY DEVELOPMENT

They say you can't stop time. But along the North Carolina coast, we've at least managed to slow it down.

Come ride a ferry to Hyde County's Ocracoke. Floating twenty-three miles from the mainland, this island is like a tiny piece of seventeenth-century England marooned in an American fishing village. Some locals have even kept a slight Elizabethan accent, saying "hoigh toid" for high tide.

Here, you can still walk barefoot through the center of town, and tell time by the comings and goings of the shrimp boats. On distant dunes, you can see small wild ponies descended from those brought over by explorers four hundred years ago. Since then, so little has changed, the tallest building is still the white-washed lighthouse.

In fact, nearly all our beaches from the Outer Banks to Sunset Beach are islands with wrap-around views of sound and sea, and miles of silky white sand where you can leave the world behind.

POPULATION 5,677.
NOT COUNTING THE WILD PONIES AND WHISTLING SWANS.

Come to beaches like Currituck, Topsail, and Ocean Isle where the wide ocean is perfect for sailing, windsurfing, and fishing. Follow in the footsteps of England's first colonists in wildlife areas and maritime forests that have scarcely changed for centuries. And hear about those early years in our outdoor drama, The Lost Colony.

Across the state are places it seems time forgot. From mountain hamlets where you can buy handmade dulcimers to one-street towns where the soda shops still serve fresh lemonade and homemade pies.

So no matter where you visit, you'll have more time here. Time to watch the sun rise over the ocean and set into the marsh. Time to watch the shadows shift under the piers and the earth revolve beneath the stars. The kind of time that makes it seem your visit will last forever. So come to North Carolina. You'll have the time of your life.

NORTH CAROLINA
The Promised Land.

29

(Pictured: The ultra-lightweight Vacanza Siena.)

COMFORT SINCE 1825.
8 0 0 · 8 4 2 · 9 3 6 4.

© 1991 Clarks of England.

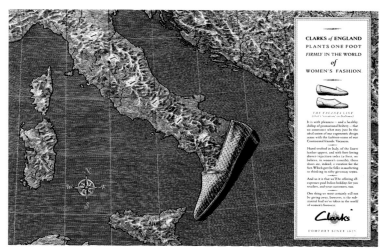

31

32

30-32

ART DIRECTOR:

TRACY WONG

PHOTOGRAPHER:

MICHELE CLEMENT(30)

ARTIST:

GREG DEARTH (31, 32)

COPYWRITER:

CLAY WILLIAMS

AGENCY:

GOODBY, BERLIN &

SILVERSTEIN

CLIENT:

CLARKS OF ENGLAND

■ **30-32** ADVERTISING FOR DIFFERENT LINES OF SHOES FROM CLARKS OF ENGLAND: THE ULTRA-LIGHTWEIGHT VACANZA SIENA, THE WOMEN'S VACANZA LINE, AND BIG GRIPPERS FOR MEN. THE FIRST IS A CONSUMER AD; THE OTHER TWO ARE TRADE SPOTS. (USA)

● **30-32** WERBUNG FÜR VERSCHIEDENE SCHUHE DER MARKE CLARKS OF ENGLAND: DIE ULTRA-LEICHTEN VACANZA SIENA (ZEITSCHRIFTENANZEIGE); DIE VACANZA-LINIE FÜR DAMEN UND DIE «GROSSEN GREIFER» FÜR MÄNNER (FACHANZEIGEN). (USA)

▲ **30-32** PUBLICITÉ POUR LES CHAUSSURES DE LA MARQUE CLARKS OF ENGLAND. LE MODELE VACANZA SIENA, ULTRA-LÉGER; LA LIGNE DE CHAUSSURES POUR FEMMES VACANZA ET LES CHAUSSURES MASCULINES «QUI ACCROCHENT». (USA)

Homers will do that to you. Even when one goes out in mid-game, it stops the story. Nothing *ensues*, for the connective tissue of the game—the men on base, the defensive deployments, the pitcher's struggles, the count, the score—has been snipped, and all our attention falls upon the hero.

THE NEW YORKER

33

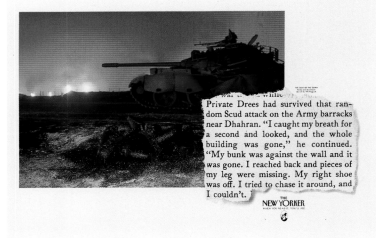

Private Drees had survived that random Scud attack on the Army barracks near Dhahran. "I caught my breath for a second and looked, and the whole building was gone," he continued. "My bunk was against the wall and it was gone. I reached back and pieces of my leg were missing. My right shoe was off. I tried to chase it around, and I couldn't.

THE NEW YORKER

34

Yo! so you thought all sit-down vehicles were for
your old man back home
in his Lay-Z-Boy
until you hit those first waves and your
single-chine deep V-hull
breaks right on through leading to that
major cavitation
where your heart may skip a beat
but your WaveRunner VXR doesn't
'cuz it's stoked
by Yamaha's 633cc 50 hp marine power plant
which means for heart-rending
mind-bending action
your VXR doesn't take a back seat to anyone
**brothers and sisters,
Amen.**

YAMAHA
Fun that won't quit.

Call 1-800-526-4630 for the Yamaha Water Vehicle dealer near you.

35

YAMAHA
Fun that won't quit.

TECHNICALLY SPEAKING, IT'S A RADICAL PIECE OF ENGINEERING.

Yamaha engineers set out to create the most technologically-advanced water vehicle. With design that was revolutionary. Engineering that was state-of-the-art.

Today, Super Jet riders agree we've achieved these goals. But not exactly in those words. Call 1-800-526-6650 for the Yamaha Water Vehicle dealer near you.

36

33, 34

ART DIRECTOR:

RICH SILVERSTEIN

PHOTOGRAPHERS:

WALTER IOOSS (33)

ABBAS/MAGNUM (34)

COPYWRITER:

ANDY BERLIN

AGENCY:

GOODBY, BERLIN &
SILVERSTEIN

CLIENT:

THE NEW YORKER

35, 36

ART DIRECTOR:

CRAIG OPFER

DESIGNER:

CRAIG OPFER

PHOTOGRAPHER:

STEVE UZELL

COPYWRITERS:

MARK CATTERSON

CRAIG OPFER

AGENCY:

HOFFMAN YORK &
COMPTON

CLIENT:

YAMAHA MARINE

■ **33, 34** CAMPAIGN FOR *THE NEW YORKER*, FEATURING QUOTES FROM ARTICLES THAT HAVE APPEARED IN THE MAGAZINE. (USA)

■ **35, 36** TWO ADVERTISEMENTS FOR YAMAHA'S SUPER JET JET-SKI, STRESSING THE EXCITEMENT OF RIDING ONE AND DESCRIBING THE VEHICLE'S QUALITIES AND FEATURES IN THE LANGUAGE OF THE HIP RIDER. (USA)

■ **37-39** IMAGE CAMPAIGN FOR A FURNITURE DEALER, FOCUSING ON THE STORE'S PRICES, WHICH ARE LOWER THAN THE RECOMMENDED ONES. THE HEADLINES READ: "LE CORBUSIER AND OTHERS AVAILABLE AT LOW PRICES," "VIEWS ON DECORATING" AND "BEFORE AND AFTER." (GER)

● **33, 34** KAMPAGNE FÜR *THE NEW YORKER* MIT AUSZÜGEN AUS ARTIKELN, DIE IN DIESER ZEITSCHRIFT ERSCHIENEN SIND. (USA)

● **35, 36** ANZEIGEN FÜR DIE YAMAHA SUPER JET RIDERS (WASSERFAHRZEUGE). IN DER SPRACHE DER AUSGEFLIPPTEN BENUTZER WIRD VON DEM AUFREGENDEN FAHRERLEBNIS BERICHTET UND ÜBER EIGENSCHAFTEN UND TECHNISCHE DETAILS INFORMIERT. (USA)

● **37-39** IMAGEKAMPAGNE FÜR REUTZEL WOHNEN, BEI DER ES VOR ALLEM UM EIN SPEZIELLES PREISANGEBOT BEI BARZAHLUNG GEHT, DAS UNTER DEN EMPFOHLENEN RICHTPREISEN DER HERSTELLER DIESER KLASSIKER UND MARKENEINRICHTUNGS-STÜCKE LIEGT. (GER)

▲ **33, 34** CAMPAGNE DU *NEW YORKER*: DES EXTRAITS D'ARTICLES PARUS DANS CE MAGAZINE ACCOMPAGNENT LES PHOTOS. (USA)

▲ **35, 36** POUR LES SCOOTERS DES MERS YAMAHA. PARODIANT LE LANGAGE BRANCHÉ DES UTILISATEURS, LE TEXTE EXPLIQUE LES DÉTAILS TECHNIQUES. LES VISUELS EXPRIMENT LES SENSATIONS VERTIGINEUSES DES UTILISATEURS. (USA)

▲ **37-39** CAMPAGNE DE PRESTIGE POUR LE MAGASIN D'AMEUBLEMENT REUTZEL; ELLE CONCERNE NOTAMMENT UNE OFFRE SPÉCIALE, CERTAINS CLASSIQUES ÉTANT VENDUS BIEN EN DESSOUS DU PRIX RECOMMANDÉ PAR LE FABRICANT EN CAS DE PAIEMENT COMPTANT. (GER)

37-39

ART DIRECTOR:

PETER HESSLER

PHOTOGRAPHER:

GÜNTER PFANN-
MÜLLER

COPYWRITER:

JOCHEN BEITHAN

AGENCY:

BEITHAN, HESSLER,
MÄTTIG

CLIENT:

REUTZEL WOHNEN

Le Corbusier u.a. preiswert abzugeben.

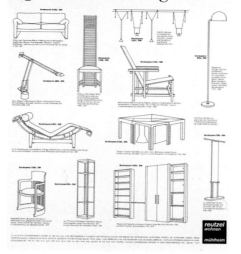

37

Wenn's ums Einrichten geht, ist es mit Lösungen von der Stange nicht getan; nebenbei gesagt, die interessieren mich auch nicht. Die Kunst des Einrichtens ist für mich in erster Linie ein Handwerk. Schließlich gilt es, maßgeschneiderte Wohnkonzepte zu erarbeiten. Konzepte, die sich an persönlichen Wünschen und Bedürfnissen orientieren. Und natürlich an der Wohnsituation. Sperrmüll zu produzieren ist eben nicht mein Ding: Ich suche Lösungen, die auch nach zehn Jahren noch interessant sind. Denn Kundenbetreuung fängt für mich nicht bei den Möbeln an, sondern bei den Menschen. Als Einrichter aus Leidenschaft und Inhaber eines WK-Hauses ist mir die intensive Beratung genauso wichtig wie die perfekte Planung und Ausführung bis ins Detail: Unser Service-Angebot reicht von Innenausbau, Elektro- und Lichtinstallationen über Tapezier- und Näharbeiten bis hin zum Bodenverlegen. Raumgestaltung aus einem Guß. Und in dem finanziellen Rahmen, den der Kunde gesteckt hat. In diesem Zusammenhang ein Kompliment an unsere Kunden. Der Sinn für kreatives Design und Qualität machen es mir leicht, in meinen Konzepten größtmögliche Spannung und Individualität zu verwirklichen. Namen wie WK-Wohnen, deSede, Cassina, Interlübke, Treca (um jetzt nur einige zu nennen) garantieren höchste Flexibilität und Qualität kein Luxus. Und ja auch in der gehobenen Schnäppchen machen. Ich Beispiele für solche Fälle sich dabei um Einzelstellung. Sie sollten also Bevor andere handeln. Ein derangebot und ein Stück von Kill International mit strapazierfähigem BePreisempfehlung des Hermit unserem Barpreis von konkurrieren. Das gleiche

Qualität. So gesehen ist von Fall zu Fall läßt sich nen Einrichtungsklasse ein möchte Ihnen hier ein paar präsentieren: Es handelt stücke aus unserer Ausnicht zu lange überlegen. „klassischer" Fall von Sonfürs Leben: der TV-Sessel Mehrfach verstellbar und zug. Die unverbindliche stellersvon DM 4.056,– kann DM 2.556,– sicher nicht gilt für unser deSede Liegesofa DS 18/16. In Leder natur fügt es sich in jedes Ambiente. Statt der vom Hersteller empfohlenen DM 9.190,– für DM 5.990,– in bar zu haben. Über zwei Meter Sitzkomfort bietet das Sofa von deSede: in rotem Nappa. mit losen, schwarzen Kissen. Die unverbindliche Preisempfehlung des Herstellers von DM 9.760,– unterbieten wir bei Barzahlung mit DM 4.760,–. Zwei Angebote von Cassina: 2 Sofas Modell Maralunga warten auf ihre Besitzer. Das Bezugsdesign ist von Jack Lenor Larssen und die Maße sind bestimmt eine Zusatz-Überlegung wert: zierliche 156 x 85 cm. Statt DM 5.320,– (unverbindl. Preisempf. des Herst.) pro Stück für bare DM 3.820,–. Unser letztes Angebot stammt von Thörmer Exclusiv: ein Liegesofa mit beweglichem Seitenteil und Flechtbezug in feinstem Leder. Die unverbindliche Preisempfehlung des Herstellers beträgt DM 10.112,–, unser Barpreis DM 5.912,–. Und unsere Notizen aus der Provinz sind lange nicht zu Ende: Wir haben noch gut zwei Dutzend äußerst reizvolle „Fall-Beispiele" auf Lager. Wenn Sie sich also in dem einen oder anderen Fall angesprochen fühlen, oder wenn oben nichts für Sie dabei war, sollten Sie einfach mal bei uns vorbeischauen. Bei 2000 qm Ausstellungsfläche und 100 laufenden Metern Schaufenster können Sie sich ein Bild davon machen, was Reutzel Wohnen unter Einrichtungsästhetik versteht. Die Mühe lohnt sich. Soviel sei jetzt schon verraten.

38

Vorher. Nachher.

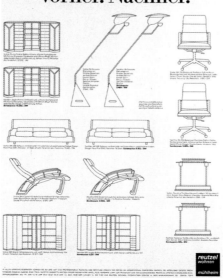

39

As you can see, these new Dunhams are considerably more fashionable than the original pair.

It's likely that George and Charles Dunham wouldn't have had very much to say about our new Dunham Brothers Collection. It wasn't their style. Not that anything was, mind you.

On a scale of one to 10, George and Charles Dunham's sense of fashion very likely wouldn't have made the scale at all. The simple truth of the matter is that the stories we've heard about the two brothers' disdain for haute couture fairly abound.

Difficult as it is to believe, it's long been rumored that Charles spent the first half of his life thinking a fashion plate was a fancy piece of China. And George. The man didn't even have a closet in his bedroom. Didn't need one. Kept all his clothes in the top drawer of his wife's dresser. A very small drawer.

Needless to say, dedicated followers of fashion the brothers Dunham were most certainly and unequivocally not.

Why then, you ask, would we knowingly take what is far and away the most fashionable line of shoes and boots we've ever offered and name it, of all things, The Dunham Brothers Collection? The answer is very simple.

Because despite their generously waxed leathers, their natural colors, their eminently

rugged, yet sophisticated good looks that are as appropriate for Saturday mornings at the office as they are for Sunday afternoons at the stadium, they are, after all, Dunhams.

So while it's true that our newest line of shoes and boots is unmistakably committed to fashion, it is by no means a slave to it. Which very simply means the Dunham Brothers Collection is made as only the Dunham Brothers themselves knew how to make casual shoes and boots.

(And if you know anything at all about Dunham, you know exactly the sort of thing that we are talking about.)

Durable to a fault. Fastidiously and meticulously sewn together, stitch by stitch by painstaking stitch. And with a level of comfort that knows no parallel. An attribute due, in no small part, to thoughtful things like removable cushion insoles and dual-density, shock absorbing outsoles.

The Dunham Brothers Collection. We strongly urge you to see your nearest Dunham retailer at your earliest convenience. We think our latest Dunhams are really something to behold. Which is more than we can say for our first pair.

The Dunham Company   *Brattleboro, Vermont*

Dunham Brothers Founded 1885

40

Thank you for smoking.

Smiden & Son. Undertakers.

41

40

ART DIRECTOR:
JOHN DOYLE
DESIGNER:
JOHN DOYLE
PHOTOGRAPHER:
PAUL CLANCY
COPYWRITER:
ERNIE SCHENCK
AGENCY:
DOYLE ADVERTISING
CLIENT:
THE DUNHAM
COMPANY

41

ART DIRECTORS:
RICHARD DENNISON
MARKHAM SMITH
COPYWRITERS:
MARKHAM SMITH
RICHARD DENNISON
AGENCY:
THE SMITH DENNISON
PARTNERSHIP
CLIENT:
ACTION ON SMOKING
AND HEALTH (ASH)

42, 43

ART DIRECTOR:
GARY GOLDSMITH
DESIGNER:
GARY GOLDSMITH
PHOTOGRAPHER:
STEVE HELLERSTEIN
COPYWRITER:
TY MONTAGUE
AGENCY:
GOLDSMITH/JEFFREY
CLIENT:
EVERLAST

■ 40 EXAMPLE FROM AN ADVERTISING CAMPAIGN FOR DUNHAM BOOTS, CLAIMING THAT THE BOOTS, WHICH HAVE LONG BEEN KNOWN FOR BEING DURABLE AND COMFORTABLE, ARE NOW FASHIONABLE AS WELL. (USA)

■ 41 PRINT ADVERTISEMENT FOR ACTION ON SMOKING AND HEALTH (ASH), A BRITISH ANTISMOKING GROUP. (GBR)

■ 42, 43 TWO EXAMPLES FROM A HUMOROUS ADVERTISING CAMPAIGN PROMOTING A LINE OF BASIC CLOTHING. THE GARMENTS ARE MADE BY USA CLASSIC INC. AND ARE MARKETED UNDER THE TRADEMARK OF EVERLAST. (USA)

● 40 «WIE SIE SEHEN, IST DIESES PAAR NEUER DUNHAMS SEHR VIEL MODISCHER ALS DAS ORIGINALPAAR»; BEISPIEL AUS EINER KAMPAGNE FÜR DUNHAM-SCHUHE, DIE FÜR IHRE SOLIDE MACHART BEKANNT SIND. (USA)

● 41 «DANKE, DASS SIE RAUCHEN. SMIDEN & SONS, BEERDIGUNGSINSTITUT.» FÜR EINE BRITISCHE ANTI-RAUCHER-GRUPPE. (GBR)

● 42, 43 «VIELLEICHT HABEN SIE NIE DIE BEINE EINES BODYBUILDERS. GROSSARTIGE SHORTS SIND ABER LEICHT ZU HABEN.» «GUT, DASS DIES KEINE DER DUFTSTOFF-ANZEIGEN IST.» ANZEIGEN FÜR EVERLAST-TEXTILIEN. (USA)

▲ 40 «COMME VOUS POUVEZ LE CONSTATER, CETTE NOUVELLE PAIRE DE DUNHAMS EST BIEN PLUS À LA MODE QUE L'ORIGINAL»; EXEMPLES D'UNE CAMPAGNE DE PUBLICITÉ POUR LES CHAUSSURES DUNHAM. (USA)

▲ 41 «MERCI DE FUMER. POMPES FUNEBRES SMIDEN & SONS.» POUR UNE ASSOCIATION DE LUTTE CONTRE LE TABAGISME. (GBR)

▲ 42, 43 «VOUS N'AUREZ JAMAIS LES JAMBES D'UN ATHLETE. PAR CONTRE, VOUS TROUVEREZ FACILEMENT DES SHORTS FORMIDABLES.» «HEUREUSEMENT QUE CE N'EST PAS UNE DE CES PUBS POUR PARFUM.» POUR LES VETEMENTS EVERLAST. (USA)

You may never have the legs of a body builder. Great shorts, however, are readily available.

This is not one of those scented ads. Good thing.

Even in the worst weather, you can still drop off the kids, do the shopping, pick up the laundry, take the dog to the vet, stop by the bank, pick up the kids, go to the post office and take the kids to piano lessons. Sorry. The Mazda MPV 4WD can rob you of one of your best excuses for staying in all day.

That's just the way it goes when you've got push-button, shift-on-the-fly four-wheel drive coupled with a powerful V6 engine. And a rear-wheel Anti-lock Brake System helps make sure your stops are smooth and controlled.

We also include touches like theater-style seating, optional rear passenger heating and a side door that opens like a car door instead of a van door.

Think about heading down to visit your Mazda Dealer and the Mazda MPV 4WD right now while the weather's good.

That way, you'll be able to visit your grocer, your dry cleaner, your banker or just about anyone else when the weather's bad.

36-MONTH/50,000-MILE WARRANTY No-deductible, "bumper-to-bumper" protection. See your dealer for limited warranty details. For a free brochure on any new Mazda, call toll-free. 1-800-345-3799 MPV 4WD

mazda
IT JUST FEELS RIGHT

47

44-46
ART DIRECTORS:
JOHN DOYLE
DALE EDMONDSON
DESIGNERS:
JOHN DOYLE
DALE EDMONDSON
PHOTOGRAPHER:
PAUL CLANCY
COPYWRITER:
JONATHAN PLAZONTA
AGENCY:
DOYLE ADVERTISING
CLIENT:
CHELSEA PICTURES

47
CREATIVE DIRECTORS:
BRYAN BIRCH
ED COLE
ART DIRECTOR:
LAURA DELLA SALA
PHOTOGRAPHER:
GARRY MCGUIRE
COPYWRITER:
DOUG REEVES
AGENCY:
FOOTE, CONE & BELDING
CLIENT:
MAZDA MOTOR OF AMERICA

■ **44-46** FROM A CAMPAIGN FOR THE CHELSEA PICTURES PRODUCTION COMPANY, MAILED TO ADVERTISING AGENCIES. THE HEADLINES READ: "UNLIKE SOME THINGS THAT COME IN A CAN, WE THINK YOU'LL FIND OUR FILM QUITE TASTY," "ONE WAY DIRECTOR ED BIANCHI WON'T APPROACH YOUR NEXT COMMERCIAL" AND "...IF YOUR IDEAS ARE A BREED APART, CALL US." (USA)

■ **47** A SAFETY MESSAGE FROM MAZDA THAT NEVER USES THE WORD "SAFETY." INSTEAD, THE AD DESCRIBES THE PROPERTIES OF THE CAR IN SUCH A WAY THAT THE CONCLUSION IS OBVIOUS. IN THE BODY COPY OF THE AD, THE CONSUMER IS TREATED AS A TIRELESS DOER OF IMPORTANT THINGS RATHER THAN AS A WORRYWART. (USA)

● **44-46** ANZEIGEN FÜR DIE FILMPRODUKTIONSGESELLSCHAFT CHELSEA PICTURES: «IM GEGENSATZ ZU MANCHEN KONSERVEN WERDEN SIE UNSEREN FILM GANZ SCHMACKHAFT FINDEN»; «AUF DIESE ART WIRD REGISSEUR ED BIANCHI NICHT AN IHREN NÄCHSTEN WERBESPOT HERANGEHEN»; «...WENN SIE IDEEN BESONDERER SORTE HABEN, RUFEN SIE UNS AN». (USA)

● **47** SICHERHEIT IST DIE BOTSCHAFT DIESER MAZDA-ANZEIGE, OHNE DASS DAS WORT SELBST FÄLLT. DIE EIGENSCHAFTEN DES AUTOS SIND SO DARGESTELLT, DASS MAN ZU DIESER SCHLUSSFOLGERUNG KOMMEN MUSS. ZUDEM WIRD DER ANGESPROCHENE ALS AKTIV UND NICHT ALS ÄNGSTLICH DARGESTELLT. (USA)

▲ **44-46** ANNONCES POUR LA SOCIÉTÉ DE PRODUCTION CINÉMATOGRAPHIQUE CHELSEA PICTURES. «AU CONTRAIRE DE CERTAINES CONSERVES, VOUS TROUVEREZ NOS FILMS DE BON GOUT»; «LE METTEUR EN SCENE ED BIANCHI NE VA PAS S'Y PRENDRE COMME ÇA POUR VOTRE PROCHAIN SPOT»; «...SI VOUS AVEZ DES IDÉES D'UNE AUTRE ESPECE, TÉLÉPHONEZ-NOUS.» (USA)

▲ **47** LE MESSAGE DE CETTE ANNONCE POUR LA MAZDA CONCERNE LA SÉCURITÉ, BIEN QUE LE MOT NE SOIT NULLEMENT PRONONCÉ. ON LE DEVINE CEPENDANT RIEN QU'EN REGARDANT LA PHOTO QUI DÉMONTRE LES QUALITÉS DE CETTE VOITURE. ELLE SUPPOSE D'AILLEURS DES CONDUCTEURS AUDACIEUX PLUTOT QUE TIMORÉS. (USA)

DON'T ROUGH IT.

LIVE LIFE IN COMFORT.

48

DON'T ROUGH IT.

LIVE LIFE IN COMFORT.

49

48, 49

ART DIRECTORS:

NICK PARTON

JOHN BAYLEY

PHOTOGRAPHER:

PETER RAUTER

COPYWRITERS:

NICK PARTON

JOHN BAYLEY

AGENCY:

OGILVY & MATHER

CLIENT:

LEVER BROS.

be ware

There's a thief out there who'll grab your page

Invade your space

And once he's stolen that millionth of a second you'll never see photography in the same light again

Kodak professional film

Choice of the world's top photographers

PROFESSIONAL
PHOTOGRAPHY DIVISION

50

50

CREATIVE DIRECTOR:
KAI MUI
ART DIRECTOR:
KAI MUI
PHOTOGRAPHER:
TYEN
COPYWRITER:
ANN HAYDEN
AGENCY:
RUMRILL HOYT
CLIENT:
EASTMAN KODAK
COMPANY

■ **48, 49** DOUBLE-PAGE ADVERTISEMENTS FROM A CAMPAIGN FOR COMFORT, A FABRIC SOFTENER. (GBR)

■ **50** ONE ADVERTISEMENT FROM A LARGE CAMPAIGN FOR KODAK PROFESSIONAL PRODUCTS, FEATURING IMAGES FROM MANY TOP PHOTOGRAPHERS. VERY MUCH AN "IMAGE" ADVERTISEMENT, IT PROMOTES THE MEDIUM OF PHOTOGRAPHY TO ART DIRECTORS AND DESIGNERS. (USA)

● **48, 49** «WARUM EIN RAUHES LEBEN FÜHREN. LEBEN SIE IN KOMFORT.» ANZEIGEN FÜR DEN GEWEBEVEREDLER COMFORT. (GBR)

● **50** BEISPIEL AUS EINER KAMPAGNE FÜR KODAK PROFESSIONAL FILM, IN DER AUFNAHMEN VON TOP-PHOTOGRAPHEN AUS ALLER WELT GEZEIGT WERDEN. DIE PHOTOGRAPHEN WERDEN ERMUTIGT, GRENZEN ZU ÜBERSCHREITEN, ETWAS ZU WAGEN, WEIL SONST ANDERE IHREN PLATZ EINNEHMEN. (USA)

▲ **48, 49** ANNONCES POUR LE REVITALISANT TEXTILE COMFORT, QUI VOUS PERMET DE MENER UNE VIE PLUS CONFORTABLE. (GBR)

▲ **50** EXEMPLE D'UNE CAMPAGNE POUR LA PELLICULE KODAK PROFESSIONAL QUI PRÉSENTE DES IMAGES DES MEILLEURS PHOTOGRAPHES DU MONDE ENTIER. ON Y INCITE LES PHOTOGRAPHES À SE DÉPASSER, À ETRE PLUS AUDACIEUX, AFIN NE PAS SE LAISSER SUPPLANTER PAR LES CONCURRENTS. (USA)

5:48 p.m. Trekking through the Southern Alps, New Zealand.

[For a free color catalog including full details of our lifetime warranty and the location of your nearest North Face dealer call 1-800-654-1751]

Your RENT is LATE, your GOLDFISH is probably DEAD and you think you've LEFT the IRON ON.
YOU couldn't CARE LESS.

 You're checking out a view that makes an Ansel Adams print look like a snapshot from one of those disposable cameras. But maybe the best part is you're 8,000 miles from the nearest Winnebago. ▫ For over twenty years, outdoor gear from The North Face has been helping people go places where people weren't supposed to go. Like scaling the 5.14a "Scarface" route at Smith Rock, Oregon. Or circling the base of Everest on skis. ▫ Which may be why The North Face has been the choice of practically every major expedition of the past two decades. ▫ And like them, you can expect every article of clothing, every tent, pack and sleeping bag we make to be guaranteed for life. ▫ Because, for us, it has always come down to one thing: making clothing and equipment whose performance you can take for granted. ▫ So you can concentrate on why you're out there in the first place.

THE NORTH FACE

51

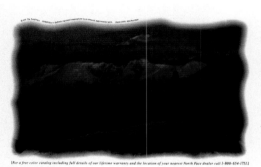

[For a free color catalog including full details of our lifetime warranty and the location of your nearest North Face dealer call 1-800-654-1751]

LAST YEAR you vacationed in Maui. Your OFFICE CALLED EVERY DAY. For some reason, you don't think you'll have that PROBLEM this year.

Annapurna, Nepal. Denali National Park, Alaska. The Vale of Kashmir, India. They're not exactly your ordinary vacation resorts. ▫ It's places like these, however, where you'll find people who use The North Face gear. People more likely to be carrying an avalanche beacon than a pager.

People whose idea of getting away from it all is going somewhere people have never been before. ▫ For over twenty years, The North Face technical outerwear, clothing, packs, and tents have been required equipment on many of the world's toughest expeditions. ▫ Why? Because it works. ▫ That means outerwear with articulated elbows and knees for freedom of movement. Sleeping bags whose inside shell is cut slightly smaller than the outside so the down can loft higher. And packs reinforced with virtually indestructible CORDURA® panels. ▫ It also means everything we make is guaranteed for life. ▫ You see, we don't just design our gear to help you go to these places. ▫ We design it to help you come back.

THE NORTH FACE

52

Suspended sleeping quarters, Salathé Wall, El Capitan.

[For a free color catalog including full details of our lifetime warranty and the location of your nearest North Face dealer call 1-800-654-1751]

It's Dawn. You WAKE UP and start to roll out of bed. Then IT HITS YOU. The FLOOR IS three thousand feet DOWN.

Everybody's gotta sleep. ▫ Only for certain people it happens in some pretty interesting places. Like halfway up El Capitan's Salathé Wall. ▫ It's these people, however, who we keep foremost in our minds when designing The North Face gear. ▫ Not to mention those who may prefer extreme skiing down a 45-degree mountain face in Chamonix.

Or attempting to scale the south-southwest pillar of K2. Or maybe even rowing a boat from South America to Antarctica. ▫ At The North Face, we make a complete line of technical outerwear, clothing, tents, packs and sleeping bags built to overcome situations like these. ▫ Packs with zippers GORE-TEX tested to withstand up to 300 pounds- per-inch of pull. Raingear made with waterproof, breathable Gore-Tex® fabric. And tents whose fabric is meticulously cut along the grainline to insure tautness and proper shape. ▫ All guaranteed for your lifetime. ▫ Why do we go to such lengths to make our gear? ▫ Because out here it can make the difference between life and death. ▫ And we'd hate to lose a customer.

THE NORTH FACE

53

51-53

ART DIRECTOR:

SEAN EHRINGER

PHOTOGRAPHERS:

STOCK (51)

BILL HATCHER (52)

JOHN BURCHAM (53)

HOLLY STEWART

(PRODUCTS)

AGENCY:

MANDELBAUM

MOONEY ASHLEY

CLIENT:

THE NORTH FACE

Setzen Sie die richtigen Akzente.

Der Buchstabe Ç aus der Fairfield 56 in PostScript und PCL 5

Seit immer mehr Personal Computer auf Laser-druckern ausgeben, sind Standard-Typen out. Heute ist auch bei Schriften Individualität angesagt. Die Linotype Library bietet Ihnen über 1500 Schriften, die technisch und typografisch in jeder Hinsicht perfekt sind. Ganz egal, ob Sie Eulen aus Athen ordern, Ihre Kaviarbestellung auf kyrillisch faxen oder beim nächsten Tête-à-tête mit Ihrem französischen Partner ganz neue Akzente setzen.

Linotype
LiBRARY

Mehr kostenlose Infos über Schrift-Fonts und Bezugsquellen per Coupon von Linotype-Hell AG, Abt. SM, Postfach 5660, W-6236 Eschborn. Oder einfach (0 61 96) 98 -29 60 anrufen.

Name _____ PLZ/Ort _____
Straße _____ Ich arbeite mit ☐ Mac ☐ MS-DOS-PC ☐ Unix

54

Wahre Größe zeigt sich im Detail.

Das &-Zeichen aus der Stempel Garamond italic für Macintosh und MS-DOS

Weil immer mehr Schriften auf allen Druckern verfügbar sind, können Sie heute nach Herzenslust mit Hunderten von Schriften jonglieren. Doch schlägt die neue Lust rasch in Frust um, wenn das Handwerkszeug nicht stimmt. Wir von Linotype-Hell wissen, daß gerade kleine Schriftgrößen mit viel Liebe zum Detail entworfen werden müssen. Wenn Sie also für Ihr gutes Geld Perfektion er-warten, sollten Sie auf das Kleingedruckte achten. Wie auch sonst im Leben.

Linotype
LiBRARY

Mehr kostenlose Infos über Schrift-Fonts und Bezugsquellen per Coupon von Linotype-Hell AG, Abt. SM, Postfach 5660, W-6236 Eschborn. Oder einfach (0 61 96) 98 -29 60 anrufen.

Name _____ PLZ/Ort _____
Straße _____ Ich arbeite mit ☐ Mac ☐ MS-DOS-PC ☐ Unix

55

54, 55

ART DIRECTORS:

CHRISTA

SCHWARZWÄLDER

JO SILBER

COPYWRITER:

JOHANNES BRÖCKERS

AGENCY:

CDC CREATIVE &

DESIGN CONSULTANTS

GMBH

CLIENT:

LINOTYPE LIBRARY

■ 51-53 EXAMPLES FROM AN ADVERTISING CAMPAIGN FOR THE NORTH FACE, A MANU-FACTURER OF CLOTHING AND EQUIPMENT. THE ADS CLAIM THAT THE PRODUCTS' PER-FORMANCE CAN BE TAKEN FOR GRANTED—SOMETHING VITAL IN SITUATIONS SUCH AS THOSE PICTURED. (USA)

■ 54, 55 "USE THE RIGHT ACCENT" AND "REAL GREATNESS LIES IN THE DETAILS": ADS FOR COMPUTER FONTS, FOCUSING ON THE FONTS' INDIVIDUALITY AND THE COMPANY'S ATTEN-TION TO DETAIL. (GER)

● 51-53 BEISPIELE AUS EINER ANZEIGEN-KAMPAGNE FÜR NORTHFACE, HERSTELLER VON AUSRÜSTUNG UND BEKLEIDUNG, AUF DEREN QUALITÄT MAN SICH VERLASSEN KANN — UND MUSS, WIE DIE BILDER GEWAGTER EXPEDITIONEN UND SITUATIONEN VERDEUT-LICHEN. (USA)

● 54, 55 BEI DIESEN ANZEIGEN FÜR DIE COMPUTERSCHRIFTFONTS DER LINOTYPE LIBRARY GEHT ES UM DIE INDIVIDUALITÄT DER SCHRIFTEN UND UM DIE LIEBE ZUM DETAIL. (GER)

▲ 51-53 EXEMPLES D'UNE CAMPAGNE D'AN-NONCES POUR NORTHFACE, UN FABRICANT D'ÉQUIPEMENTS ET DE VETEMENTS D'UNE QUALITÉ IRRÉPROCHABLE, QUI RÉSISTENT AUX ENTREPRISES LES PLUS AUDACIEUSES ET AUX SITUATIONS LES PLUS PÉRILLEUSES, AINSI QUE LES PHOTOS LE MONTRENT. (USA)

▲ 54, 55 EXEMPLES D'ANNONCES POUR DES POLICES DE CARACTERES DIGITALISÉS DE LA LINOTYPE LIBRARY: IL Y EST QUESTION DE L'INDIVIDUALITÉ DES LETTRES ET DE L'AMOUR DU DÉTAIL. (GER)

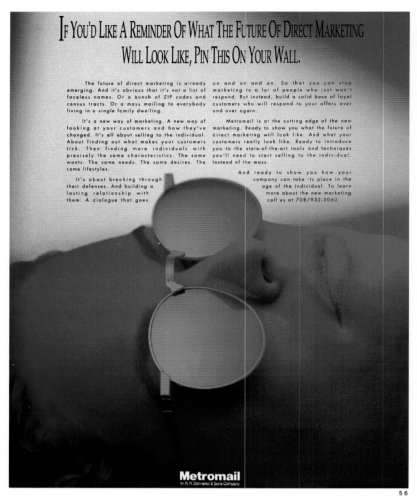

IF YOU'D LIKE A REMINDER OF WHAT THE FUTURE OF DIRECT MARKETING WILL LOOK LIKE, PIN THIS ON YOUR WALL.

The future of direct marketing is already emerging. And it's obvious that it's not a list of faceless names. Or a bunch of ZIP codes and census tracts. Or a mass mailing to everybody living in a single family dwelling.

It's a new way of marketing. A new way of looking at your customers and how they've changed. It's all about selling to the individual. About finding out what makes your customers tick. Then finding more individuals with precisely the same characteristics. The same wants. The same needs. The same desires. The same lifestyles.

It's about breaking through their defenses. And building a lasting relationship with them. A dialogue that goes on and on and on and on. So that you can stop marketing to a lot of people who just won't respond. But instead, build a solid base of loyal customers who will respond to your offers over and over again.

Metromail is at the cutting edge of the new marketing. Ready to show you what the future of direct marketing will look like. And what your customers really look like. Ready to introduce you to the state-of-the-art tools and techniques you'll need to start selling to the individual. Instead of the mass.

And ready to show you how your company can take its place in the age of the individual. To learn more about the new marketing call us at 708/932-3060.

Metromail
An R. R. Donnelley & Sons Company

56

WHILE EVERYONE ELSE IS GETTING BACK TO NATURE, ISN'T IT NICE TO KNOW THAT SOME OF US NEVER LEFT?

Sometimes, discovering new places means acquiring new skills, and vice-versa. To both ends, we offer several Wilderness Outings. If you're just starting, Beginning Backpacking is an ideal first step. In two evenings, you'll learn about equipment, wilderness ethics, camping and hiking techniques, mountain safety, and food. Then, we'll hit the trail on a fun weekend backpacking trip. Other courses include Beginning Rock Climbing, Map and Compass, and Outdoor Photography. For more experienced people, we offer intermediate classes as well. Class schedules are available at any Adventure 16 store.

Where were you in '62? We were in a garage in La Mesa, dreaming of making 16mm adventure films (hence Adventure 16). What we made instead was a backpack using high-grade aluminum and lightweight synthetic fabrics, rather than wood and canvas. It carried weight on the hips, instead of the shoulders. It was comfortable. It was, like the times, revolutionary. And like many revolutionary ideas of that era, it soon became the rule. Explorer Posts, Scout Troops, and other friends gave us much needed feedback. We started making sleeping bags, parkas, and tents based on what they said. And we grew. Much has changed since the early sixties. But the wilderness remains. Some folks are just now getting introduced to it—which we think is terrific. Because we figure the more you enjoy the environment, the more you'll support the environment. So if you have questions, bring them in. Our advice is free. If you want to learn to explore the backcountry with confidence, sign up for one of our Wilderness Outings. You'll get expert guidance from all of our instructors. And you'll get hands-on training in the best

learning environment of all: the environment itself. If you don't have the right stuff, you can borrow ours. We rent all kinds of top-notch outdoor equipment. It's like having a buddy who backpacks, camps, climbs rocks and lends gear. Naturally we sell only serious gear from serious makers, including ourselves. Take our bevy of bivies for example—one-person shelters that set up in seconds. There's our original Bug Bivy, and our new Bivy Shelter, Mesh Bivy Shelter, and Bivy Fly. Like everything we make, they're backed by a lifetime guarantee—plus several lifetimes of experience. So if you're getting back to nature, welcome home. Come join us in our store or in the field. We'll gladly share our knowledge and our gear, both of which you can always count on. After all, we've been here (and there) since 1962. And while trends may wax and wane, we've stayed pretty much the same. Not unlike the wilderness itself.

57

56

ART DIRECTOR:
GORDON HOCHHALTER
DESIGNER:
SCOTT GLICK
PHOTOGRAPHER:
JACK O'GRADY
COPYWRITERS:
BILL KLEIN
TODD CHUBBUCK
GORDON HOCHHALTER

STYLIST:
O'GRADY SALES
PROMOTION
AGENCY:
MOBIUM
CORPORATION
CLIENT:
METROMAIL
CORPORATION

57

ART DIRECTOR:
JOSE SERRANO
DESIGNER:
JOSE SERRANO
PHOTOGRAPHERS:
GALEN ROWELL
CHRIS WIMPEY
COPYWRITER:
JOHN KURAOKA
AGENCY:
MIRES DESIGN, INC.
CLIENT:
ADVENTURE 16

58

CREATIVE DIRECTORS:
MIKE HUGHES
JERRY TORCHIA
ART DIRECTOR:
JELLY HELM
PHOTOGRAPHER:
ROY BOY
COPYWRITER:
RAYMOND MCKINNEY
AGENCY:
THE MARTIN AGENCY
CLIENT:
BERNIE'S TATTOOING

■ 56 THE AIM OF THIS ADVERTISEMENT IS TO REPOSITION A NEWLY REORGANIZED DIRECT-MARKETING COMPANY BY LINKING IT TO CHANGES IN THE INDUSTRY, NEW CHALLENGES AND NEW TECHNIQUES FOR FINDING CUSTOMERS. (USA)

■ 57 ADVERTISEMENT FOR ADVENTURE 16, OUTDOOR AND TRAVEL OUTFITTERS, OFFERING COURSES ON SUBJECTS SUCH AS USING THE COMPANY'S EQUIPMENT, MOUNTAIN SAFETY AND FOOD. (USA)

■ 58 AN ADVERTISEMENT TO PROMOTE A TATTOO PARLOR. THE MODEL IS BERNIE, THE OWNER. (USA)

● 56 «WENN SIE SEHEN MÖCHTEN, WIE DIE ZUKUNFT DES DIRECT MARKETING AUSSEHEN WIRD, HÄNGEN SIE SICH DIES AN DIE WAND.» WERBUNG EINER DIRECT-MARKETING-FIRMA, DIE IHREN KUNDEN NEUE WEGE UND TECHNIKEN AUFZEIGEN WILL. (USA)

● 57 «WÄHREND ALLE ZURÜCK ZUR NATUR WOLLEN, IST ES DOCH GUT ZU WISSEN, DASS EINIGE VON UNS SIE NIE VERLASSEN HABEN.» FÜR EINEN HERSTELLER VON WANDER- UND KLETTERAUSRÜSTUNGEN. (USA)

● 58 WERBUNG FÜR EIN TÄTOWIERUNGS-STUDIO: «ÜBERRASCHEN SIE IHRE FRAU.» DAS MODELL IST DER BESITZER. (USA)

▲ 56 «SI VOUS DÉSIREZ SAVOIR QUEL SERA LE FUTUR DU MARKETING DIRECT, ACCROCHEZ CELA AU MUR.» ANNONCE POUR UNE FIRME DE MARKETING DIRECT QUI ATTIRE L'ATTENTION SUR LES POSSIBILITÉS DE LA TECHNOLOGIE DE POINTE. (USA)

▲ 57 «AU MOMENT OU TOUT LE MONDE PARLE DE RETOUR À LA NATURE, C'EST RASSURANT DE SAVOIR QU'IL Y EN A QUI NE L'ONT JAMAIS QUITTÉE.» POUR UN FABRICANT D'ÉQUIPEMENTS POUR L'ASCENSION. (USA)

▲ 58 «SURPRENEZ VOTRE FEMME.» PUBLICITÉ D'UN STUDIO DE TATOUAGE. LE MODÈLE N'EST AUTRE QUE LE PROPRIÉTAIRE. (USA)

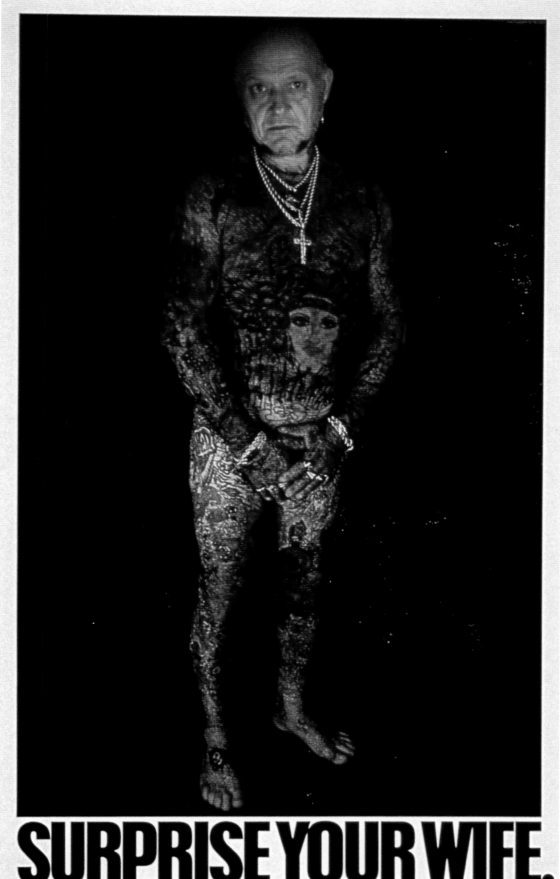

SURPRISE YOUR WIFE.

BERNIE'S TATTOOING

58

NEUERÖFFNUNG

Werbung
Industriedesign
Techn. Dokumentation
Corporate Identity
Art Consulting
Computer Schulung
Firmenfeste
Präsentationen

Durango grafitec gmbh
Reinschmiedstraße 4
8075 Vohburg
Tel. (08457) 2700
Fax. (08457) 7096
Geschäftsführer:
Thomas Neumaier
Cornelia Oechsler

Das Logo ist frei.
Wir haben auch andere.

59

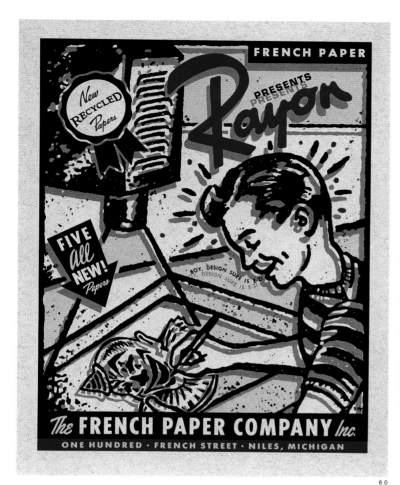

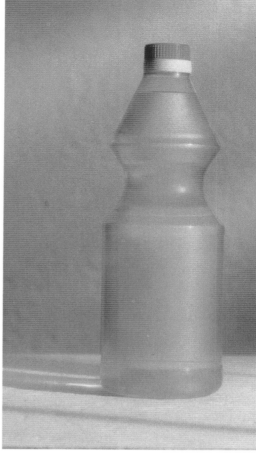

IN THIS AGE OF televangelists who sin, politicians who lie, athletes who cheat, billionaires who evade taxes, movie stars who assault policemen, baseball managers who gamble and teen idols who make home movies...

isn't it nice to know there's still one thing that's completely pure.

Mazola Corn Oil.

No additives.

No preservatives.

No cholesterol.

100% PURE CORN OIL

60

61

60

ART DIRECTORS:
DANIEL OLSON
CHARLES ANDERSON
DESIGNERS:
CHARLES ANDERSON
DANIEL OLSON
ILLUSTRATOR:
RANDALL DAHLK
AGENCY:
C.S. ANDERSON
DESIGN CO.
CLIENT:
FRENCH PAPER CO.

61

ART DIRECTOR:
MICHAEL
MCLAUGHLIN
PHOTOGRAPHER:
RICK MCKECHNIE
COPYWRITER:
STEPHEN CREET
AGENCY:
MAC LAREN:LINTAS
CLIENT:
BEST FOODS

■ 59 "THIS LOGO IS FREE. WE HAVE OTHERS, TOO." NEWSPAPER ADVERTISEMENT ANNOUNCING THE OPENING OF A STUDIO IN GERMANY OFFERING SERVICES IN VISUAL COMMUNICATION. (GER)

■ 60 A MAGAZINE ADVERTISING INSERT, PROMOTING RAYON PAPER FROM THE FRENCH PAPER COMPANY. THIS AD WAS ALSO PUBLISHED AS AN OVERSIZE SILK-SCREEN POSTER. (USA)

■ 61 THE DEEP YELLOW COLOR OF CORN SUGGESTS LIGHT AND PURENESS, REINFORCING THE CLAIM OF THIS ADVERTISEMENT THAT MAZOLA CORN OIL IS COMPLETELY PURE—SOMETHING OF A RARITY THESE DAYS. (USA)

● 59 ZEITUNGSANZEIGE ANLÄSSLICH DER NEUERÖFFNUNG DES STUDIOS DURANGO GRAFITEC, DAS VERSCHIEDENE DIENSTLEISTUNGEN IM BEREICH DER VISUELLEN KOMMUNIKATION ANBIETET. (GER)

● 60 FACHZEITSCHRIFTENBEILAGE ALS WERBUNG FÜR EINE NEUE PAPIERSORTE DER FRENCH PAPER COMPANY. DAS MOTIV ERSCHIEN AUCH ALS RIESIGES SIEBDRUCKPLAKAT. (USA)

● 61 DAS GOLDGELB DES MAISKORNS SUGGERIERT LICHT UND REINHEIT UND UNTERSTREICHT DIE AUSSAGE DIESER ANZEIGE FÜR MAZOLA-MAISÖL, DAS 100 PROZENT REIN IST UND DAMIT EINE SELTENHEIT IN DER HEUTIGEN ZEIT. (USA)

▲ 59 «LE LOGO EST LIBRE. NOUS EN AVONS ENCORE D'AUTRES.» ANNONCE DE L'OUVERTURE D'UN STUDIO QUI PROPOSE DIVERSES PRESTATIONS DANS LE SECTEUR DE LA COMMUNICATION VISUELLE. (GER)

▲ 60 PUBLICITÉ POUR UNE NOUVELLE SORTE DE PAPIER DE LA FRENCH PAPER COMPANY, PARUE DANS DES MAGAZINES PROFES-SIONNELS. CE MOTIF A ÉTÉ REPRIS SUR LES AFFICHES SÉRIGRAPHIQUES GÉANTES. (USA)

▲ 61 LE JAUNE DU MAIS SUGGERE LA LUMIERE ET LA PURETÉ ET VIENT RENFORCER LE MESSAGE DE CETTE ANNONCE POUR L'HUILE MAZOLA, FABRIQUÉE À 100% À PARTIR DE MAIS, CE QUI EST PLUTOT RARE À NOTRE ÉPOQUE. (USA)

何を着ても平気でない人。

服を選ぶときに色や柄だけでなく、
素材にまでこだわってしまうのが正常です。
好みとは違った基本がそこにあるからなんですね。
写真のジャケットは、ラムを70%含んだウール素材。
フィールド・ブラザーズの自信作です。

やさしい・弾性、メリノです。

FIELD BROTHERS

TOKYO 03-436-0411 OSAKA 0727-29-0361 FUKUOKA 092-451-3121

62

It's not easy being in the shoes of a single parent.

Today, one out of four kids is being raised by a single parent. If you're in those shoes, the Y can give you the support you need. We help kids build strong values and develop self-esteem. So join and see how we fit your family. **YMCA. We're family.**

63

62

CREATIVE DIRECTOR:
TOSHIHIRO KIUCHI
ART DIRECTOR:
KAZUHIRO SEKI
DESIGNERS:
KAZUHIRO SEKI
MITSUE MURAKAMI
PHOTOGRAPHER:
SAKAE TAKAHASHI
COPYWRITER:
TOSHIHIRO KIUCHI
AGENCY:
OSAKA YOMIURI
ADVERTISING INC.
CLIENT:
FIELD BROTHERS

63

ART DIRECTOR:
JAC COVERDALE
PHOTOGRAPHER:
JOE MICHAELS/
ARNDT PHOTOGRAPHY
COPYWRITER:
JERRY FURY
AGENCY:
CLARITY COVERDALE
RUEFF
CLIENT:
YMCA

■ **62** EXAMPLE FROM AN ADVERTISING CAMPAIGN FOR FIELD BROTHERS IN JAPAN, FOCUSING ON THE QUALITY OF WOOL IN THE COMPANY'S FABRICS. (JPN)

■ **63** THIS ADVERTISEMENT RECOGNIZES THE CHALLENGES OF BEING A SINGLE PARENT, AND SUGGESTS THAT THE YMCA CAN BE HELPFUL IN COPING. (USA)

■ **64-66** FINNISH SCENERY ILLUSTRATES THIS AD CAMPAIGN FOR FINLANDIA VODKA: THE ARCTIC CIRCLE AT FINNISH LAPLAND, A POOL BELONGING TO A SAUNA ON THE SHORE OF A LAKE, AND FISHING UNDER THE ICE. (USA)

● **62** BEISPIEL AUS EINER ANZEIGENKAMPAGNE FÜR FIELD BROTHERS IN JAPAN, IN DER ES VOR ALLEM UM DIE WOLLQUALITÄT GEHT. (JPN)

● **63** MIT DIESER ANZEIGE SPRICHT DER YMCA DIE GROSSE AUFGABE ALLEINERZIEHENDER ELTERN AN UND VERSPRICHT UNTERSTÜTZUNG. (USA)

● **64-66** FINNISCHE SZENERIEN IN EINER ANZEIGENKAMPAGNE FÜR FINLANDIA-WODKA: AM POLARKREIS IM FINNISCHEN LAPPLAND; EIN POOL, DER ZU EINER AM SEE GELEGENEN SAUNA GEHÖRT; FISCHEN IM WINTER. (USA)

▲ **62** EXEMPLE D'UNE CAMPAGNE D'ANNONCES POUR FIELD BROTHERS AU JAPON, DANS LAQUELLE IL EST QUESTION DE LA QUALITÉ DE LA LAINE. (JPN)

▲ **63** CETTE ANNONCE DE L'YMCA FAIT RÉFÉRENCE AUX PROBLEMES DES FOYERS MONOPARENTAUX, L'ASSOCIATION LEUR OFFRANT DES SOUTIENS. (USA)

▲ **64-66** SCENES DE LA VIE EN FINLANDE ILLUSTRANT CETTE CAMPAGNE POUR LA VODKA FINLANDIA. AU CERCLE POLAIRE, EN LAPONIE; LA PISCINE D'UN SAUNA SITUÉ AU BORD DE LA MER; LA PECHE EN HIVER. (USA)

64-66

ART DIRECTOR:

JEREMY POSTAER

PHOTOGRAPHER:

DUNCAN SIM

COPYWRITER:

ROB BAGOT

AGENCY:

GOODBY, BERLIN &

SILVERSTEIN

CLIENT:

FINNISH NATIONAL

DISTILLERS, INC.

Finlandia. Vodka From The Top Of The World.

64

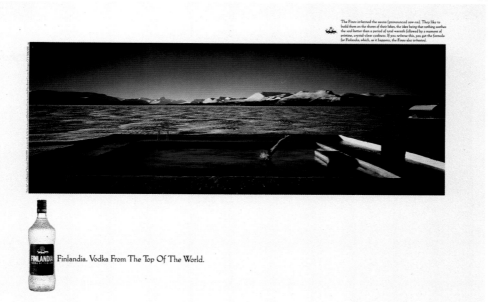

Finlandia. Vodka From The Top Of The World.

65

Finlandia. Vodka From The Top Of The World.

66

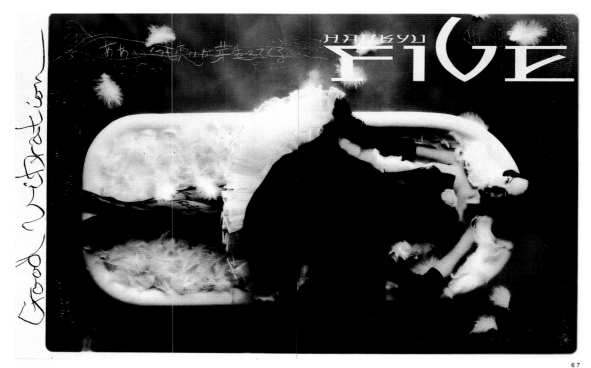

67

68

67, 68

CREATIVE DIRECTOR:
TOSHIHIRO KIUCHI
ART DIRECTOR:
KAZUHIRO SEKI
DESIGNERS:
KAZUHIRO SEKI
MITSUE MURAKAMI
PHOTOGRAPHER:
SAKAE TAKAHASHI

STYLIST:
IIDA KYOKO (68)
COPYWRITER:
TOSHIHIRO KIUCHI
AGENCY:
OSAKA YOMIURI
ADVERTISING INC
CLIENT:
HANKYU FIVE

69

70

69

ART DIRECTOR:

PETER HOLMES

COPYWRITER:

PETER HOLMES

AGENCY:

FRANKLIN DALLAS

CLIENT:

ALPINE/LUXMAN

70

ART DIRECTOR:

JEREMY POSTAER

PHOTOGRAPHER:

TIM BIEBER

DUNCAN SIM

COPYWRITER:

ROB BAGOT

AGENCY:

GOODBY BERLIN &
SILVERSTEIN

CLIENT:

ROYAL VIKING LINE

■ 67, 68 EXAMPLES FROM AN AD CAMPAIGN FOR THE JAPANESE DEPARTMENT STORE HANKYU FIVE, WITH THE GROUP TITLE "GOOD VIBRATIONS." (JPN)

■ 69 ADVERTISEMENT FOR ALPINE CAR AUDIO SYSTEMS, CLAIMING THAT ITS SUSPENSION SYSTEM HELPS AVOID PROBLEMS CAUSED BY BUMPS IN THE ROAD. (CAN)

■ 70 AN AD FOR ROYAL VIKING LINE, INTRODUCING A NEW SHIP. THE ROYAL VIKING QUEEN, SHOWN ON THE RIGHT, IS A SMALLER, MORE INTIMATE VERSION OF THE ROYAL VIKING SUN, SHOWN ON THE LEFT. (USA)

● 67, 68 BEISPIELE AUS EINER ANZEIGEN-KAMPAGNE FÜR DAS JAPANISCHE KAUFHAUS HANKYU FIVE UNTER DER HEADLINE «GUTE SCHWINGUNGEN». (JPN)

● 69 SO SIEHT'S BEI DEN MEISTEN AUTO-CD-SPIELERN BEI EINER UNEBENHEIT DER STRASSE AUS. ALPINE-GERÄTE SIND DURCH EINE FEDERUNG DAGEGEN GESCHÜTZT. (CAN)

● 70 DIE ROYAL VIKING LINE STELLT IN DIESER ANZEIGE IHR NEUES KREUZFAHRT-SCHIFF, DIE ROYAL VIKING QUEEN (RECHTS) VOR. SIE IST EINE KLEINERE, INTIMERE AUS-GABE DER ROYAL VIKING SUN (LINKS). (USA)

▲ 67, 68 EXEMPLES D'UNE CAMPAGNE D'ANNONCES POUR LE MAGASIN JAPONAIS HANKYU FIVE SUR LE THEME DES «BONNES VIBRATIONS». (JPN)

▲ 69 GRACE À UN SYSTEME DE SUSPENSION SPÉCIAL, LES LECTEURS DE C.D. ALPINE, PERMETTENT D'ÉCOUTER DE LA MUSIQUE MEME SUR UNE ROUTE ACCIDENTÉE. (CAN)

▲ 70 LA ROYAL VIKING LINE PRÉSENTE SON DERNIER BATEAU DE CROISIERE, LE ROYAL VIKING QUEEN (À DROITE). C'EST UNE VARI-ANTE, EN PLUS PETIT ET PLUS INTIME, DU ROYAL VIKING SUN (À GAUCHE). (USA)

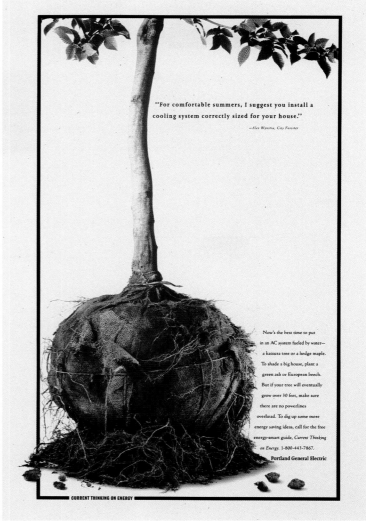

71

72

71, 72

Art Director:

TERRY SCHNEIDER

Photographer:

DOUG PETTY

Copywriter:

GREG EIDEN

Agency:

BORDERS, PERRIN &
NORRANDER

Client:

PORTLAND GENERAL
ELECTRIC

■ **71, 72** UNDER THE UMBRELLA HEADING OF
"CURRENT THINKING ON ENERGY," PORTLAND
GENERAL ELECTRIC DRAWS THE ATTENTION
OF CONSUMERS TO ENERGY-SAVING IDEAS,
SUCH AS PROPER WAYS OF INSULATING
HOUSES AND PLANTING TREES TO PROTECT
HOMES FROM HEAT. (USA)

● **71, 72** UNTER DEM MOTTO «ZEITGEMÄSSES
DENKEN ÜBER ENERGIE» INFORMIERT PORT-
LAND GENERAL ELECTRIC ÜBER MÖGLICHKEI-
TEN, ENERGIE ZU SPAREN, WIE ZUM BEISPIEL
GUTE ISOLIERUNGEN DER HÄUSER UND DAS
PFLANZEN VON SCHATTENSPENDENDEN BÄU-
MEN GEGEN HITZE. (USA)

▲ **71, 72** «RÉFLEXION ACTUELLE SUR L'ÉNER-
GIE»: LA SOCIÉTÉ PORTLAND GENERAL ELEC-
TRIC INFORME DES MOYENS DE FAIRE DES
ÉCONOMIES D'ÉNERGIE, PAR EXEMPLE EN
ISOLANT MIEUX LES MAISONS OU EN PLAN-
TANT DES ARBRES QUI FONT DE L'OMBRE
POUR LUTTER CONTRE LA CHALEUR. (USA)

BROCHURES

BROSCHÜREN

BROCHURES

73

Mary McFadden

In all cultures and eras, grandeur arises from humility, harmony from multiplicity. What is broken is mended into a whole — greater than the sum of its parts.

73, 74
Art Director:
BILL THORBURN
Designer:
BILL THORBURN
Photographer:
SARAH MOON
Hand Tinting:
JEAN HENEY
Copywriter:
AMY FINE COLLINS
Agency:
DAYTON'S HUDSON'S,
MARSHALL FIELD'S
DESIGN
Client:
DAYTON'S
HUDSON'S/IN-HOUSE

74

■ **73, 74** COVER AND SPREAD FROM A SMALL BOOK HELD TOGETHER WITH A SINGLE GOLD THREAD. IT WAS PUBLISHED FOR THE PRESENTATION OF THE 1991 COLLECTION AT DAYTON'S DEPARTMENT STORE, A COLLECTION INSPIRED BY STAINED-GLASS WINDOWS, MOSAICS AND QUILTS. SHOWN IS A DRESS WITH JEWELED-STRAND BACK, DESIGNED BY MARY MCFADDEN. (USA)

■ **75-79** COVER AND SPREADS OF A BROCHURE PROMOTING TIME INC. MAGAZINES AND THE WHOLE FIELD OF ACTIVITIES OF TIME WARNER INC. IT FOCUSES ON THE WIDE VARIETY OF THEMES AMONG TIME INC.'S REGIONAL, NATIONAL AND INTERNATIONAL MAGAZINES, ON THE "POWER OF CHOICE" (THE MOTTO OF THE COVER) AND ON THE "POWER OF PRINT." (USA)

● **73, 74** UMSCHLAG UND DOPPELSEITE AUS EINEM KLEINEN BUCH, DAS NUR VON EINEM GOLDFADEN ZUSAMMENGEHALTEN WIRD UND ÜBER EINE MODESCHAU IM KAUFHAUS DAYTON'S INFORMIERT. DIESE MODE WURDE VON FENSTERN AUS FARBIGEM GLAS, MOSAIKEN UND QUILTS INSPIRIERT. GEZEIGT IST EIN MODELL VON MARY MCFADDEN MIT TRÄGERN AUS GLITZERNDEN STEINEN. (USA)

● **75-79** UMSCHLAG UND DOPPELSEITEN EINER BROSCHÜRE, IN DER DIE PUBLIKATIONEN DER TIME INC. MAGAZINES VORGESTELLT WERDEN, SOWIE AUCH DER GESAMTE TÄTIGKEITSBEREICH DER TIME WARNER INC. ES GEHT HIER VOR ALLEM UM DIE VIELFALT DER THEMEN DER REGIONALEN, NATIONALEN UND INTERNATIONALEN ZEITSCHRIFTEN UND DIE BEDEUTUNG DER DRUCKMEDIEN. (USA)

▲ **73, 74** COUVERTURE ET DOUBLE PAGE D'UN PETIT LIVRE RELIÉ AU MOYEN D'UN FIL DORÉ, PUBLIÉ À L'OCCASION DE LA PRÉSENTATION DE LA COLLECTION 1991 DE DAYTON'S, À LAQUELLE ASSISTAIT MARY MC FADDEN, DONT ON VOIT UN MODÈLE ICI. LES PHOTOS ONT ÉTÉ INSPIRÉES PAR L'ART DU VITRAIL ET DE LA MOSAIQUE, AINSI QUE LES COUVERTURES EN QUILT DES AMISH. (USA)

▲ **75-79** COUVERTURE ET DOUBLES PAGES DU CATALOGUE PRÉSENTANT LES PUBLICATIONS NATIONALES ET INTERNATIONALES DE TIME INC. L'ACCENT EST MIS SUR LA DIVERSITÉ DES THÈMES ET DES PUBLICS VISÉS PAR TOUS SES MAGAZINES, SUGGÉRÉ PAR LE TITRE «LE POUVOIR DU CHOIX» ET LA PREMIÈRE PAGE TYPOGRAPHIÉE: «LE POUVOIR DE L'IMPRIMÉ». (USA)

75

76

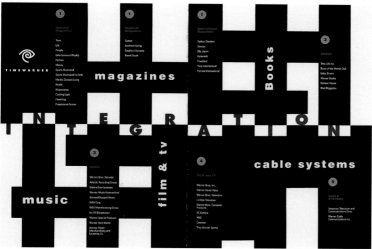

77

78

75-79

CREATIVE DIRECTORS:

AUBREY BALKIND

KENT HUNTER

DESIGNERS:

KENT HUNTER

RUTH DIENER

AGENCY:

FRANKFURT

GIPS BALKIND

CLIENT:

TIME INC.

79

80

81

82

83

80-84

Art Director:

ADRIANO A. BIONDO

Designer:

KAZUKO SHIMADA

Photographer:

ADRIANO A. BIONDO

Copywriter:

RES S.R.L.

Agency:

GUEN COMPANY

Client:

ASCOLI VALIGERIA

S.R.L.

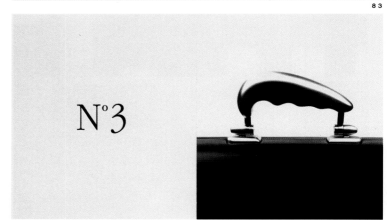

84

■ 80-84 CATALOG FOR THE 1992 COLLECTIONS OF ASCOLI VALIGERIA'S HAND-MADE LEATHER PRODUCTS. NUMBER TWO INTRODUCES THE LINE FOR LADIES, NUMBER THREE PRESENTS THE ONE FOR LADIES AND GENTLEMEN. THE WELL-GROOMED HAND ON THE COVER SERVES AS A SYMBOL FOR BOTH THE HANDCRAFTING OF THE MATERIALS AND THE SOPHISTICATION OF THE USERS. (ITA)

■ 85-87 THESE FACES OF YOUNG CHILDREN ILLUSTRATE THE ANNUAL REPORT OF THE YMCA OF CHICAGO. THE REPORT WAS DESIGNED AS A CONCERTINA FOLDER, AND REFERS IN PARTICULAR TO A PROJECT HELPING CHILDREN FROM DISADVANTAGED FAMILIES AND CRISIS AREAS. SHOWN ARE THE COVER AND TWO INSIDE PAGES. (USA)

● 80-84 GROSSFORMATIGER KATALOG, IN DEM ASCOLI VALIGERIA, HERSTELLER VON ERSTKLASSIGEN, HANDGEMACHTEN LEDER-PRODUKTEN, DIE DREI NEUEN KOLLEKTIONEN FÜR 1992 VORSTELLT. NR. 2 BEZEICHNET DIE NEUE LINIE FÜR DAMEN, NR. 3 DIE FÜR DAMEN UND HERREN. DIE HAND AUF DEM UMSCHLAG DIENT ALS SYMBOL FÜR HANDARBEIT UND HOHE ANSPRÜCHE. (ITA)

● 85-87 DIESE KINDERGESICHTER ILLUSTRIEREN DEN JAHRESBERICHT DES YMCA (CHRISTLICHER VEREIN JUNGER MÄNNER) IN CHICAGO. ER WURDE IN FORM EINES LEPORELLO GESTALTET (VON DEM HIER AUCH EINE INNENSEITE GEZEIGT IST) UND BEZIEHT SICH SPEZIELL AUF HILFSPROGRAMME FÜR BEDÜRFTIGE KINDER. (USA)

▲ 80-84 CATALOGUE GRAND FORMAT PRÉSENTANT LES NOUVELLES COLLECTIONS 1992 D'ASCOLI VALIGERIA, UNE MAISON DE MAROQUINERIE FONDÉE EN 1900 ET SPÉCIALISÉE DANS LA FABRICATION DE SACS ET BAGAGES FAITS MAINS. LE CHAPITRE 2 DÉSIGNE LA LIGNE DE NOUVEAUX PRODUITS POUR LA FEMME, LE CHAPITRE 3 LES NOUVEAUTÉS POUR HOMMES ET FEMMES. (ITA)

▲ 85-87 COUVERTURES ET QUELQUES PAGES DU RAPPORT ANNUEL DE L'YMCA (ASSOCIATION DE JEUNES CHRÉTIENS DE CHICAGO), PUBLIÉ SOUS FORME DE DÉPLIANT EN ACCORDÉON. L'YMCA ORGANISE DES ÉCHANGES OU DES STAGES DE FORMATION POUR DES ENFANTS DE MILIEUX DÉFAVORISÉS ET DE PAYS PAUVRES OU EN GUERRE. (USA)

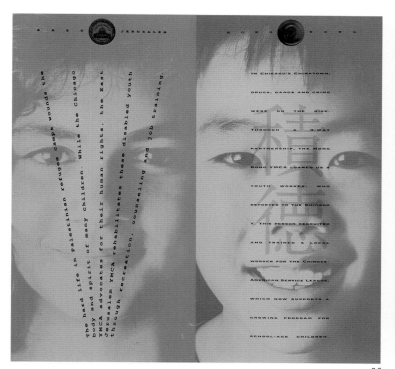

85

86

87

Scott C. Smith ► Chairman
John W. Casey ► President

1991

85-87

ART DIRECTOR:

PAT SAMATA

DESIGNERS:

PAT SAMATA

GREG SAMATA

PHOTOGRAPHER:

MARC NORBERG

COPYWRITER:

PATRICE BOYER

AGENCY:

SAMATA ASSOCIATES

CLIENT:

YMCA CHICAGO

88-91

ART DIRECTORS:
TOM SCHIFANELLA
ROBIN SHEPHERD
DESIGNERS:
TOM SCHIFANELLA
MIKE BARNHART
ILLUSTRATORS:
MIKE BARNHART
CHRIS SMITH
MARTIN SCARROTT
COPYWRITER:
AMANDA TOWNSEND
AGENCY:
ROBIN SHEPHERD
STUDIOS
CLIENT:
UNICORP PAPER
INDUSTRIES

89

88

90

92-97

ART DIRECTORS:
DANIEL OLSON
CHARLES ANDERSON
DESIGNER:
DANIEL OLSON
COPYWRITER:
LISA PEMRICK
AGENCY:
C.S. ANDERSON
DESIGN CO.
CLIENT:
BARBER-ELLIS
FINE PAPERS

91

BROADLY CLASSIFIED, THE 3 main paper grades are: writing paper, printing paper, wrapping paper.

92

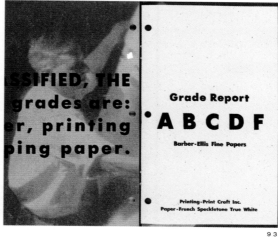

Grade Report

A B C D F

Barber-Ellis Fine Papers

Printing-Print Craft Inc.
Paper-French Speckletone True White

93

THE GRADE REPORT an excellent place to meet mill reps.

A

Excellent

94

THE GRADE REPORT SHOW Thursday, May 2, 1991, 6-10 pm At Harbour Castle Westin Ballroom, Toronto, Ontario, Guest Speaker is Charles S. Anderson

95

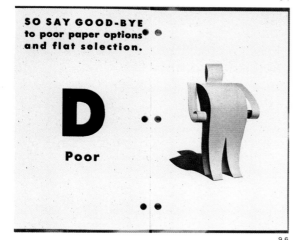

SO SAY GOOD-BYE to poor paper options and flat selection.

D

Poor

96

AND DON'T FAIL TO try the Grade Report. You won't regret it.

F

Failure

R.S.V.P.: Palma Campo or Sandra Ward by phone at (416) 421-8270, or by fax at (416) 421-7278. Seating is limited. Cocktails and Hors d'Oeuvres will be served.

Paper-French Speckletone True White

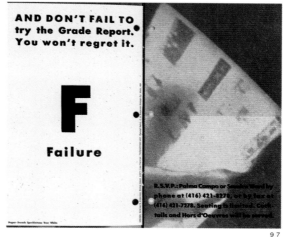

97

■ **88-91** COVER AND SPREADS FROM A BROCHURE DESIGNED TO ILLUSTRATE THE QUALITY AND PERFORMANCE OF VELVET PAPER, MADE BY A CALIFORNIA PAPERMAKER THAT WANTED TO SELL NATIONALLY. THE ORANGE-CRATE LABELS FROM THE PERIOD BETWEEN 1880 AND 1950 WERE CHOSEN AS VISUALS BECAUSE THEY, TOO, TRAVELED FROM COAST TO COAST. (USA)

■ **92-97** COVER AND SPREADS FROM A BROCHURE PROMOTING THE GRADE REPORT SHOW, A PAPERMAKER'S ANNUAL EXHIBITION. THE BROCHURE USES VISUALS REMINISCENT OF SCIENCE TEXTS AND EDUCATIONAL FILMS, WITH TYPE SIMILAR TO THAT OF ELEMENTARY-SCHOOL TEXTBOOKS. (USA)

● **88-91** UMSCHLAG UND DOPPELSEITEN AUS EINER BROSCHÜRE, IN DER EINE IN KALIFORNIEN ANSÄSSIGE FIRMA DIE DRUCKQUALITÄT IHRES VELVET-PAPIERS LANDESWEIT BEKANNT MACHEN MÖCHTE. DIE ILLUSTRATIONEN VON APFELSINENKISTEN AUS DER ZEIT ZWISCHEN 1880–1950 WURDEN GEWÄHLT, WEIL AUCH SIE IM GANZEN LANDE UMHERREISTEN. (USA)

● **92-97** UMSCHLAG UND DOPPELSEITEN AUS EINER PROMOTIONSBROSCHÜRE FÜR DIE JÄHRLICHE AUSSTELLUNG EINES PAPIERHERSTELLERS. DAS KONZEPT BASIERT AUF DEM BEGRIFF QUALITÄT. DIE ILLUSTRATIONEN ERINNERN AN ALTE WISSENSCHAFTLICHE BÜCHER UND UNTERRICHTSFILME. (USA)

▲ **88-91** COUVERTURE ET DOUBLES PAGES DE LA BROCHURE D'UN FABRICANT DE PAPIER, CRÉÉE POUR UN PUBLIC QUI S'ÉTEND DE LA COTE EST À LA COTE OUEST DES ETATS-UNIS. LES MOTIFS DÉCORANT LES CAISSES D'ORANGES DANS LES ANNÉES 1880-1950 ET LE TEXTE ILLUSTRENT LES RELATIONS ENTRE CES DIFFÉRENTES CONTRÉES DU PAYS. (USA)

▲ **92-97** COUVERTURE ET DOUBLES PAGES D'UNE BROCHURE ANNONÇANT L'EXPOSITION ANNUELLE D'UN FABRICANT DE PAPIER. LES QUALITÉS SONT CLASSÉES SUIVANT LE SYSTEME DE NOTATION SCOLAIRE AMÉRICAIN, DE A À F. LES IMAGES RAPPELLENT DE VIEUX LIVRES SCIENTIFIQUES. (USA)

98, 99

Art Director:
SUSAN SLOVER
Designers:
SUSAN HUYSER
KAREN SIMS
Illustrators:
SUSAN HUYSER
KAREN SIMS
Agency:
SUSAN SLOVER
DESIGN
Client:
PARAGON
TYPOGRAPHICS

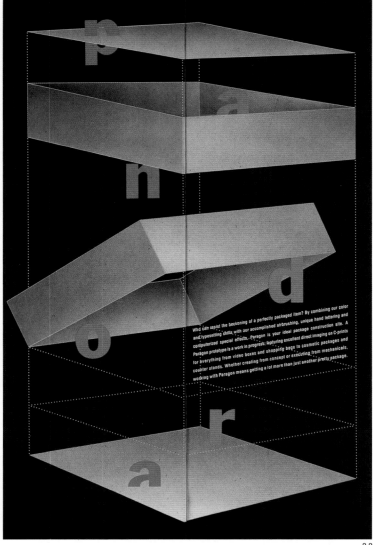

98

99

■ **98, 99** CAPABILITIES BROCHURE FOR PARAGON TYPOGRAPHICS, EACH SPREAD FEATURING ONE OF THE COMPANY'S FIVE DIVISIONS. PANDORA'S BOX IS USED AS A METAPHOR FOR THE COLOR AND TYPESETTING SKILLS APPLIED IN PACKAGING. (USA)

■ **100-107** "BEYOND THE LIMITS OF EXPECTATION"—AN ELONGATED BROCHURE, CONTAINED IN AN ENVELOPE, FOR A COMPANY SPECIALIZING IN RENTING RESORT VILLAS. THE COMPANY PROMISES TO CREATE THE EXCEPTIONAL FOR ITS CLIENTS. (CAN)

● **98, 99** FIRMENBROSCHÜRE FÜR PARAGON TYPOGRAPHICS. JEDEM DER FÜNF BEREICHE DER FIRMA IST EINE DOPPELSEITE GEWIDMET. FÜR SATZ UND DRUCK IM VERPACKUNGSBEREICH (SPRICH VERFÜHRUNG) WIRD DIE BÜCHSE DER PANDORA ZITIERT. (USA)

● **100-107** «ÜBER DIE ERWARTUNGEN HINAUS.» IN EINEM UMSCHLAG ENTHALTENE BROSCHÜRE FÜR EINE FIRMA, DIE VILLEN FÜR BESONDERE ANLÄSSE VERMIETET. SIE VERSPRICHT, FÜR IHRE KUNDEN DAS AUSSERGEWÖHNLICHE ZU SCHAFFEN. (CAN)

▲ **98, 99** BROCHURE DE FORMAT OBLONG POUR PARAGON, UN ATELIER DE TYPOGRAPHIE. CHACUN DES CINQ SECTEURS DE LA FIRME Y EST PRÉSENTÉ. LA BOITE DE PANDORE SYMBOLISE LA SPÉCIALITÉ DE L'IMPRESSION SUR EMBALLAGES (USA)

▲ **100-107** DOSSIER DE FORMAT OBLONG RENFERMANT UNE BROCHURE POUR UNE FIRME QUI LOUE DES VILLAS DE LUXE SITUÉES DANS DES LIEUX PRESTIGIEUX. S'ADRESSANT À UN PUBLIC HAUT DE GAMME, ELLE PROMET L'EXCEPTIONNEL. (CAN)

100

101

102

103

104

105-107

100-107

ART DIRECTOR:

DEL TERRELONGE

DESIGNERS:

DEL TERRELONGE

LESLIE SMITH

PHOTOGRAPHERS:

RON BAXTER SMITH

DAVE WHITACKER

COPYWRITER:

WARREN DUNFORD

AGENCY:

TERRELONGE

DESIGN INC.

CLIENT:

LACURE

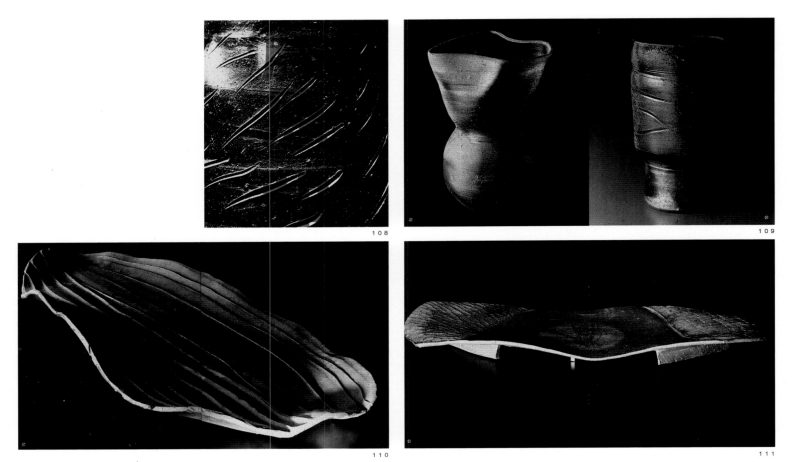

108

109

110

111

108-111

ART DIRECTORS:

ICHIRO MITANI

GAKUSHI TANAKA

DESIGNERS:

ICHIRO MITANI

GAKUSHI TANAKA

PHOTOGRAPHER:

ICHIRO MITANI

AGENCY:

OFFICE G

CLIENT:

TAKASHIMAYA

DEPARTMENT STORE

■ 108-111 COVER AND INTERIOR SPREADS FROM A CATALOG FOR AN EXHIBITION OF CERAMICS BY KAZU FUJIWARA, HELD IN THE GALLERY OF THE TAKASHIMAYA DEPARTMENT STORE IN TOKYO. (JPN)

■ 112-116 COVER AND INTERIOR SPREADS FROM A CATALOG FOR AN EXHIBITION OF DUTCH TYPOGRAPHY, HELD IN THE FRENCH CITY OF VILLEURBANE. (FRA)

● 108-111 UMSCHLAG UND DOPPELSEITEN AUS DEM KATALOG FÜR EINE AUSSTELLUNG DER KERAMIK VON KAZU FUJIWARA IN DER GALERIE DES KAUFHAUSES TAKASHIMAYA IN TOKIO. (JPN)

● 112-116 UMSCHLAG UND DOPPELSEITEN AUS DEM KATALOG FÜR DIE AUSSTELLUNG HOLLÄNDISCHER TYPOGRAPHIE IN DER FRANZÖSISCHEN STADT VILLEURBANE. (FRA)

▲ 108-111 COUVERTURE ET DOUBLES PAGES DU CATALOGUE «LES CÉRAMIQUES DE KAZU FUJIWARA», DONT LE PERE ET LE GRAND-PERE ÉTAIENT DÉJÀ POTIERS, ORGANISÉE À TOKYO EN OCTOBRE 1991. (JPN)

▲ 112-116 COUVERTURE ET QUELQUES DOUBLES PAGES DU CATALOGUE DE L'EXPOSITION «TYPOGRAPHIE HOLLANDAISE», PRÉSENTÉE À VILLEURBANE. (FRA)

112

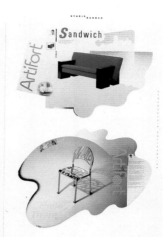

113

112-116

DESIGNER:

HENRIK BARENDS

PHOTOGRAPHER:

PAUL DE NOOIJER

COPYWRITER:

CAREL KUITEN-

BROUWER

AGENCY:

BAUDELAIRE GROEP

CLIENT:

MAISON DU LIVRE,

DE L'IMAGE

ET DU SON

114

115

116

117

118

119

120

117-120

ART DIRECTOR:

MICHAEL MABRY

DESIGNER:

MICHAEL MABRY

PHOTOGRAPHERS:

BRIGITTE LACOMBE

(PORTRAITS)

DAN LANGLEY

(PRODUCTS)

COPYWRITER:

STEVE JOHNSTON

AGENCY:

MICHAEL MABRY

DESIGN

CLIENT:

NIKE

121

RAHEL

121

ART DIRECTOR:

PETRA MERCKER

DESIGNER:

SABINE WAUER

COPYWRITER:

CHARLIE FRAUSCHER

AGENCY:

PHARMA

PERFORMANCE

CLIENT:

SIMONS GMBH

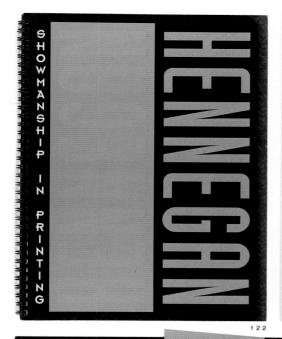

122

123

124

122-124

ART DIRECTORS:
BENJAMIN ROSS
JOHN CARPENTER
DESIGNERS:
BENJAMIN ROSS
JOHN CARPENTER
PHOTOGRAPHER:
OWEN MILBURN
SHAFER
PHOTOGRAPHY
AGENCY:
WOLF BLUMBERG
KRODY, INC.
CLIENT:
HENNEGAN COMPANY

■ **117-120** COVER AND VARIOUS INSIDE SPREADS FROM A CATALOG PRESENTING "SERIOUS CASUAL SHOES" BY NIKE. THE SHADES OF THE TINTED PAGES AND THE SEPIA TONE OF THE BLACK-AND-WHITE PORTRAITS PICK UP ON THE COLORS IN THE LEATHER OF THE SHOES. (USA)

■ **121** CORRUGATED-CARDBOARD COVER OF A BROCHURE MAILED TO BEAUTY SALONS, CONTAINING INFORMATION ON RAHEL, A MEDICATION FOR HAIR AND NAILS. (GER)

■ **122-124** COVER AND SPREADS FROM A SPIRAL-BOUND BROCHURE FOR THE HENNEGAN PRINTING HOUSE. THE MILESTONES IN THE HISTORY OF THIS COMPANY ARE THE THEME OF THIS BOOK. (USA)

● **117-120** UMSCHLAG UND DREI DOPPEL-SEITEN AUS EINEM KATALOG FÜR «ERNSTHAFTE» SPORTSCHUHE VON NIKE. DIE TÖNE DER FARBIGEN SEITEN UND DER SEPIATON DER SCHWARZWEISSPORTRÄTS NEHMEN DIE FARBEN DER GEZEIGTEN LEDERSCHUHE WIEDER AUF (USA)

● **121** WELLKARTONUMSCHLAG EINER AN KOSMETIKERINNEN GERICHTETEN BROSCHÜRE, IN DER ÜBER EIN HAAR- UND NÄGELPRÄPARAT INFORMIERT WIRD. (GER)

● **122-124** UMSCHLAG UND DOPPELSEITEN AUS EINER SPIRALGEBUNDENEN BROSCHÜRE FÜR DIE DRUCKEREI HENNEGAN. DIE WICHTIGEN EREIGNISSE IN DER GESCHICHTE DES UNTERNEHMENS SIND DAS THEMA. (USA)

▲ **117-120** COUVERTURE ET DOUBLES PAGES DU CATALOGUE POUR UNE LIGNE DE CHAUSSURES SPORT DE NIKE. LES TEINTES DES PAGES INTÉRIEURES ET LA COLORATION SÉPIA DES PHOTOS EN NOIR ET BLANC RAPPELLENT LE TON DU CUIR DES CHAUSSURES PRÉSENTÉES. (USA)

▲ **121** COUVERTURE EN CARTON ONDULÉ D'UNE BROCHURE INFORMANT LES ESTHÉTICIENNES D'UN NOUVEAU PRODUIT POUR LES CHEVEUX ET LES ONGLES. (GER)

▲ **122-124** COUVERTURE ET DOUBLES PAGES DE LA BROCHURE D'UNE IMPRIMERIE. L'HISTOIRE DE L'ENTREPRISE EST RETRACÉE ICI, ILLUSTRÉE PAR LES PRODUITS QUI ONT MARQUÉ SON DÉVELOPPEMENT. (USA)

125

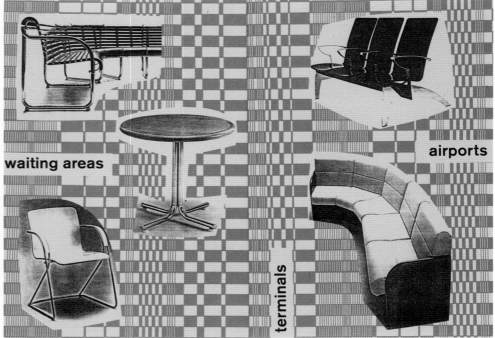

126

127

125-127

ART DIRECTOR:
GABOR PALOTAI
DESIGNER:
GABOR PALOTAI
PHOTOGRAPHER:
GABOR PALOTAI
AGENCY:
GABOR PALOTAI
DESIGN
CLIENT:
VEMO MÖBEL AB

■ 125-127 COVER AND DOUBLE-PAGE SPREADS FROM A BROCHURE FOR A SWEDISH FIRM THAT PRODUCES FURNITURE FOR PUBLIC PLACES. (SWE) ·

■ 128-131 A BROCHURE FOR A HUNTING AND FISHING CAMP IN QUEBEC. HEAVYWEIGHT STOCK AND TIPPED-IN PHOTOS WERE USED TO CREATE THE SENSE OF A PHOTO ALBUM. LETTERPRESS PRINTING, A LEATHER-TANG BINDING AND REAL DUCK FEATHERS HELP CAPTURE THE FEELING OF THIS "WILDERNESS LODGE." (CAN)

■ 132 COVER OF A BROCHURE PRESENTING "HOLLYWOOD PARAMOUNT PRODUCTS," A COLLECTION OF BEDDING, DINNERWARE, ACCESSORIES AND APPAREL DESIGNS INTENDED TO CAPTURE THE ESSENCE OF HOLLYWOOD'S PAST. (USA)

● 125-127 UMSCHLAG UND DOPPELSEITEN AUS DER BROSCHÜRE EINES SCHWEDISCHEN HERSTELLERS VON MÖBELN FÜR DEN ÖFFENTLICHEM RAUM. (SWE)

● 128-131 BROSCHÜRE FÜR EIN JAGD- UND FISCHRESERVAT IN KANADA, DIE WIE EIN UNIKAT WIRKT. DIE BILDER SIND WIE BEI EINEM ALBUM IN PHOTOECKEN GESTECKT, UND ES WURDE SCHWERES PAPIER VERWENDET. TIEFDRUCK, EIN LEDERBAND UND EINE ENTENFEDER UNTERSTÜTZEN DAS GEFÜHL VON NATURNÄHE. (CAN)

● 132 UMSCHLAG EINER BROSCHÜRE, IN DER DIE HOLLYWOOD-PARAMOUNT-PRODUKTE VORGESTELLT WERDEN: BETTWÄSCHE, GESCHIRR, NIPPES UND KLEIDUNGSSTÜCKE. MIT DENEN AN DIE GROSSE VERGANGENHEIT HOLLYWOODS ERINNERT WIRD. (USA)

▲ 125-127 D'UNE BROCHURE POUR UN FABRICANT DE MEUBLES SUÉDOIS, SPÉCIALISÉ DANS LES TABLES ET CHAISES DESTINÉS AUX LIEUX PUBLICS. (SWE)

▲ 128-131 BROCHURE DE PUBLICITÉ POUR UNE RÉSERVE DE CHASSE ET DE PECHE AU CANADA. IMITANT LES VIEUX ALBUMS DE CARTES POSTALES, ELLE PRÉSENTE LE SITE ET LES INSTALLATIONS DE CE LIEU DE VILLÉGIATURE. LA PLUME DE CANARD ET LES LIENS DE CUIR DE LA RELIURE METTENT L'ACCENT SUR LA NATURE. (CAN)

▲ 132 D'UNE BROCHURE PRÉSENTANT LES PRODUITS PORTANT LA MARQUE DU STUDIO PARAMOUNT: UNE COLLECTION DE PARURES DE LIT, COUVERTS, OBJETS ET VETEMENTS QUI RAPPELLENT LA GRANDE ÉPOQUE D'HOLLYWOOD. (USA)

128

129

130

131

128-131

ART DIRECTORS:

BOB HAMBLY

BARB WOOLLEY

DESIGNERS:

BARB WOOLLEY

BOB HAMBLY

AGENCY:

HAMBLY &

WOOLLEY INC.

CLIENT:

CAMPEAU

CORPORATION

132

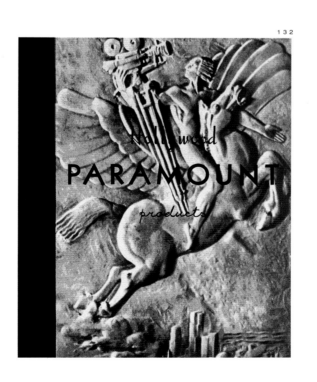

132

ART DIRECTORS:

DANIEL OLSON

CHARLES ANDERSON

HALEY JOHNSON

DESIGNER:

DANIEL OLSON

AGENCY:

C.S. ANDERSON

DESIGN CO.

CLIENT:

PARAMOUNT

PICTURES

133

133

ART DIRECTOR:

STEFAN SAGMEISTER

DESIGNERS:

ANDREW POGSON

PETER RAE

ILLUSTRATOR:

ANDREW POGSON

AGENCY:

LEO BURNETT LTD.

CLIENT:

LEO BURNETT LTD.

■ **133** THIS CONFERENCE MATERIAL, CON- TAINED IN A BOX, WAS CREATED FOR AN INTERNATIONAL MEETING OF LEO BURNETT EXECUTIVES IN HONG KONG IN 1991. (HKG)

■ **134-138** DOUBLE-PAGE SPREADS FROM THE JOHNSON *TABLE SOURCEBOOK*. THE COM- PANY OFFERS TABLES RANGING FROM THE BASIC TO THE EXOTIC. (USA)

● **133** DIESES IN EINER SCHACHTEL ENTHAL- TENE KONFERENZMATERIAL WAR FÜR EIN TREFFEN DER GESCHÄFTSFÜHRER DER LEO- BURNETT-AGENTUREN BESTIMMT. (HKG)

● **134-138** DOPPELSEITEN AUS EINEM KATA- LOG, IN DEM TISCHE ALLER ARTEN VORGE- STELLT WERDEN, DIE DEM KUNDEN VIELE MÖGLICHKEITEN OFFEN LASSEN. (USA)

▲ **133** CETTE BOITE ET CE CARNET DE NOTES ONT ÉTÉ CRÉÉS POUR UNE RÉUNION DES ADMINISTRATEURS DE L'AGENCE LEO BUR- NETT À HONG KONG. (HKG)

▲ **134-138** DOUBLES PAGES D'UN CATALOGUE D'UN FABRICANT DE TABLES, DONT LES MOD- ELES SONT CONÇUS SUIVANT DES PRINCIPES DE FONCTIONNALITÉ. (USA)

134

134-138

ART DIRECTOR:

JEFF BARNES

DESIGNER:

JEFF BARNES

PHOTOGRAPHER:

BILL TUCKER

COPYWRITER:

PAM RUBIN

AGENCY:

BARNES DESIGN

OFFICE

CLIENT:

JOHNSON

INDUSTRIES

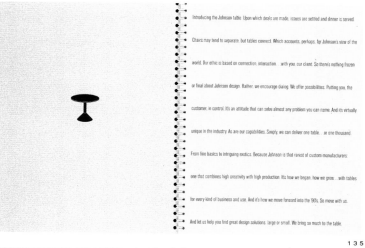

135

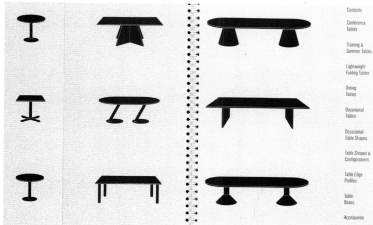

136

137

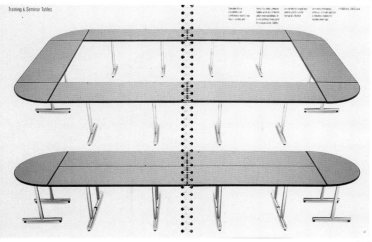

138

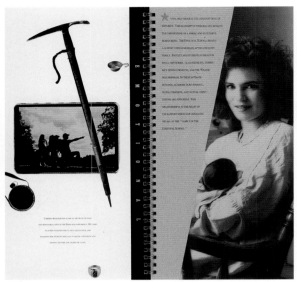

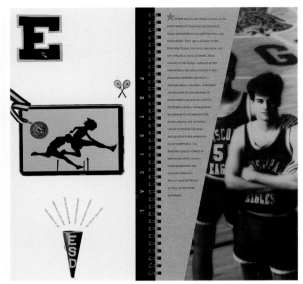

139

140

141

139-141
ART DIRECTOR:
BRIAN BOYD
DESIGNER:
BRIAN BOYD
PHOTOGRAPHER:
ALLAN COOK
AGENCY:
RBMM/THE
RICHARD GROUP
CLIENT:
EPISCOPAL SCHOOL
OF DALLAS

142

142
ART DIRECTOR:
VICKY METZGER
DESIGNER:
VICKY METZGER
PHOTOGRAPHER:
CLAUDE GUERRA
AGENCY:
S.G. STUDIO
CLIENT:
INFITEX

Design: Egon Franck / Sabine Brandenburg-Franck

143

EINMALIG-VIELSEITIGE

SCHMUCKVISIONEN. MAL

HAUCHFEIN. MAL MAR-

KANT. MAL ELEGANT.

MAL EXTRAVAGANT. PRO-

FILE AUS PLATIN. FÜR

FRAUEN UND MÄNNER

MIT EIGENSCHAFTEN.

144

143-145

ART DIRECTOR:

BRUNO HAAG

DESIGNER:

CLAUDIA BRUST-

SCHWING

PHOTOGRAPHER:

MANE WEIGAND

COPYWRITER:

SONJA BISSBORT

AGENCY:

BRUNO HAAG

CLIENT:

PLATIN GILDE

INTERNATIONAL

Design: S. Becker

145

■ **139-141** THIS VIEWBOOK FOR THE EPIS-COPAL SCHOOL OF DALLAS WAS MEANT TO CAPTURE THE SPIRIT AND PHILOSOPHY OF THE SCHOOL. THE SHAPE OF THE PENNANT GLUED TO THE COVER IS REPEATED ON THE INSIDE PAGES. (USA)

■ **142** COVER OF A CATALOG FOR LIYANG MOUNTAIN BIKES. (SPA)

■ **143-145** COVER AND INSIDE SPREADS FROM A BROCHURE PROMOTING PLATINUM JEWELRY CREATED BY VARIOUS DESIGNERS. (GER)

● **139-141** DIESE SPIRALGEBUNDENE INFOR-MATIONSBROSCHÜRE EINER KONFESSIONS-GEBUNDENEN PRIVATSCHULE SOLLTE DEN GEIST DES INSTITUTS WIDERSPIEGELN. DIE FORM DES WIMPELS DES SCHUL-SPORTTEAMS DIENT ALS GRAPHISCHES ELEMENT. (USA)

● **142** UMSCHLAG EINES KATALOGS FÜR LIYANG-MOUNTAIN-BIKES. (SPA)

● **143-145** UMSCHLAG UND DOPPELSEITEN AUS EINER BROSCHÜRE ÜBER SCHMUCK AUS PLATIN. (GER)

▲ **139-141** D'UNE BROCHURE PUBLIÉE PAR L'ECOLE ÉPISCOPALE DE DALLAS. IL S'AGIS-SAIT DE RENDRE L'ESPRIT DE CETTE ÉCOLE RELIGIEUSE. LA FORME DE L'EMBLEME DU CLUB SPORTIF A ÉTÉ REPRISE POUR LES PAGES DE TEXTE. (USA)

▲ **142** COUVERTURE D'UN CATALOGUE POUR LES «MOUNTAIN-BIKES» LIYANG. (SPA)

▲ **143-145** COUVERTURE ET DOUBLES PAGES D'UNE BROCHURE PRÉSENTANT DES BIJOUX DE PLATINE. (GER)

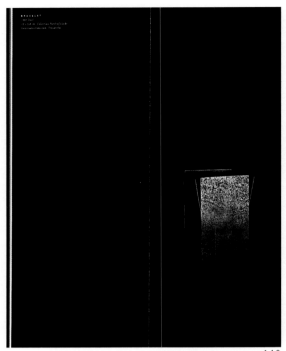

146

147

148

149

■ 146-149 CATALOG FOR AN EXHIBITION OF JEWELRY MADE BY TONE VIGELAND OF OSLO. IN MANY OF HER WORKS, VIGELAND USES A COMBINATION OF PRECIOUS AND NON-PRECIOUS METALS, SUCH AS IRON AND GOLD OR STEEL AND SILVER. (NOR)

■ 150-153 A FOLDER OF SWATCHBOOKS FROM FOX RIVER PAPER. ALL THE PAPERS ARE GREEN-CROSS CERTIFIED AND CONTAIN 50 PERCENT RECYCLED MATERIAL. (USA)

● 146-149 KATALOG FÜR EINE AUSSTELLUNG VON SCHMUCK DER NORWEGISCHEN GOLD-SCHMIEDIN TONE VIGELAND. SIE VERWENDET HÄUFIG KOMBINATIONEN VON EDLEN UND UNEDLEN METALLEN, Z.B. EISEN MIT GOLD, STAHL UND SILBER. (NOR)

● 150-153 MAPPE FÜR PAPIERMUSTER-BÜCHER VON FOX RIVER PAPER. ALLE QUALI-TÄTEN BESTEHEN ZU 50 PROZENT AUS WIE-DERVERWERTETEM MATERIAL. (USA)

▲ 146-149 COUVERTURE ET DOUBLES PAGES D'UN CATALOGUE PUBLIÉ À L'OCCASION D'UNE EXPOSITION DE LA CRÉATRICE DE BIJOUX TONE VIGELAND. ELLE COMBINE SOU-VENT DES MÉTAUX PRÉCIEUX À DES CLOUS ET DES PLAQUES DE MÉTAL. (NOR)

▲ 150-153 POCHETTE DE PRÉSENTATION DES ÉCHANTILLONS DE LA PAPETERIE FOX RIVER PAPER. LES QUALITÉS PROPOSÉES SONT À 50% COMPOSÉES DE PAPIER RECYCLÉ. (USA)

FOX RIVER PAPER CO.

Traditional, time-tested colors you can trust.

Has no added specks, fibers strands, spots, or blotches. Here's a paper with a clear difference.

F PAPER **R**

SWATCHES

EARLY AMERICAN

11 COLORS

Text and Cover weights

Early American paper is Green Cross Certified to contain 50% recycled material and 25% post-consumer waste.

150

FOX | RIVER PAPER CO

CONFETTI

RECYCLED

GREEN CROSS CERTIFIED 50%

25% post-consumer waste

151

DISTINCTIVELY SMOOTH PAPERS
SEVEN RECYCLED SHEETS AVAILABLE
21 COLORS AND 4 BASIS WEIGHTS

SELECT

SWATCHBOOK OF BOND, TEXT, AND COVER WEIGHTS.

Circa Select recycled papers have been **GREEN CROSS CERTIFIED** to contain 50% recycled material and 15% post-consumer waste. Inside, you'll find Circa Select recycled papers identified by double ** asterisks.

FOX RIVER PAPER CO.

200 East Washington Street,
P.O. Box 2215, Appleton, WI 54913.

FOR SAMPLES, CALL 800-543-SMPL

152

153

FOX RIV
ER PAPER
designers, printers
quick printers, and Mather knob.
We make paper to meet the needs of graphic

COMPANY

PAPER SAMPLES

146-149
ART DIRECTOR:
WALTER GRONLI
DESIGNER:
WALTER GRONLI
PHOTOGRAPHERS:
HANS JORGEN ABEL
FRODE PEDERSEN
CLIENT:
GALLERI F-15

150-153
ART DIRECTOR:
SHARON WERNER
DESIGNER:
SHARON WERNER
COPYWRITER:
CHUCK CARLSON
AGENCY:
THE DUFFY
DESIGN GROUP
CLIENT:
FOX RIVER
PAPER CO.

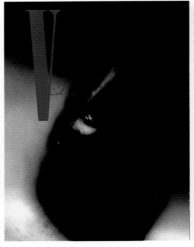

154

155

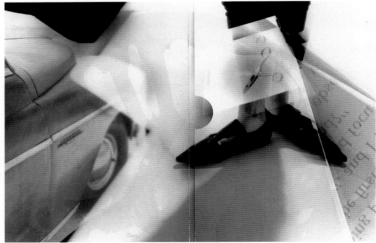

156

157

154-157

Art Director:
TOM STERLING
Designer:
TOM STERLING
Photographer:
GALLEN MEI
Stylist:
TOM STERLING
Copywriter:
MARK KIELAR
Agency:
PINKHAUS
DESIGN CORP.
Client:
WJMK

158

Art Directors:
BILL THORBURN
DEBRA HERDMAN
Designer:
BILL THORBURN
Photographer:
GLENN ERLER
Copywriter:
AMIE VALENTINE
Agency:
DAYTON'S HUDSON'S
MARSHALL FIELD'S
Client:
DAYTON'S HUDSON'S
MARSHALL FIELD'S

■ 154-157 EXAMPLES OF SPREADS AND THE COVER OF A BROCHURE FOR WJMK, A FIRM IN THE AUDIO-VISUAL PRODUCTION INDUSTRY. THE FIRM'S ACTIVITIES ARE SYMBOLIZED BY THE CLOSE-UP SHOTS OF THE EYE, EAR AND CAMERA. THE INSIDE BACK COVER FORMS A POCKET TO HOLD ADDITIONAL MATERIALS. (USA)

■ 158 POSTER ANNOUNCING FALL/WINTER FASHION SHOWINGS AT DAYTON'S MINNEAPOLIS DEPARTMENT STORE. (USA)

● 154-157 BEISPIELE DER DOPPELSEITEN UND UMSCHLAG EINER BROSCHÜRE FÜR WJMK, EINE AUDIO/ VIDEO-PRODUKTIONSFIRMA. IHRE TÄTIGKEIT WIRD HIER DURCH GROSSAUFNAHMEN EINES AUGES UND EINES OHRS SOWIE EINER KAMERA SYMBOLISIERT. DIE VIERTE UMSCHLAGSEITE IST ALS TASCHE GESTALTET. (USA)

● 158 EINLADUNG ZU EINER HERBSTMODESCHAU IM KAUFHAUS DAYTON'S. GEZEIGT IST DIE VORDERSEITE. (USA)

▲ 154-157 COUVERTURE ET EXEMPLES DE DOUBLES PAGES DE LA BROCHURE DE WJMK, UNE SOCIÉTÉ DE PRODUCTION AUDIO-VIDÉO. SES ACTIVITÉS SONT SYMBOLISÉES PAR LES GROS-PLANS DE L'ŒIL ET DE L'OREILLE, AINSI QUE LA CAMÉRA. L'INTÉRIEUR DE LA DERNIERE PAGE COMPORTE UNE POCHETTE POUR DOCUMENTS. (USA)

▲ 158 ANNONCE DE LA PRÉSENTATION DE LA COLLECTION AUTOMNE/HIVER 1991 DES GRANDS MAGASINS DAYTON'S. (USA)

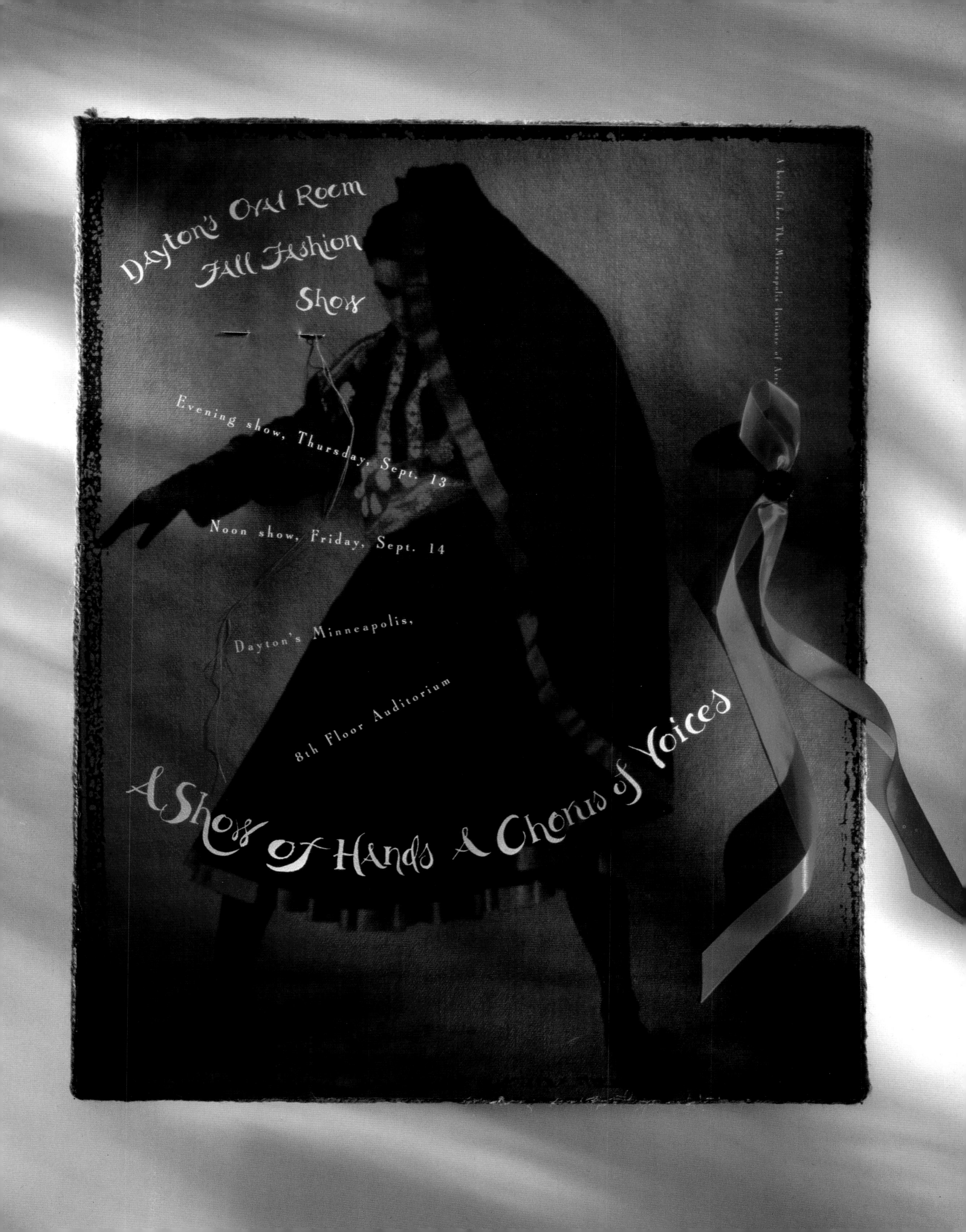
Dayton's Oval Room
Fall Fashion
Show
Evening show, Thursday, Sept. 13
Noon show, Friday, Sept. 14
Dayton's Minneapolis,
8th Floor Auditorium
A Show of Hands A Chorus of Voices
A benefit for The Minneapolis Institute of Arts

159-161

ART DIRECTOR:
GABOR PALOTAI
DESIGNER:
GABOR PALOTAI
ILLUSTRATOR:
GABOR PALOTAI
AGENCY:
GABOR PALOTAI
DESIGN
CLIENTS:
VEMO MÖBEL AB,
SVERIGES
REKLAMFÖRBUND,
INTERIÖRHUSET
MÖBLER ETCETERA

159

160

161

162

163

164

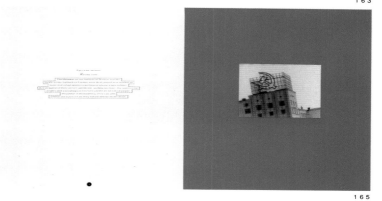

165

166

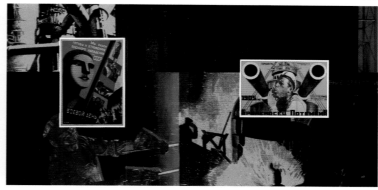

167

162-167

ART DIRECTOR:

JOHN VAN DYKE

DESIGNER:

JOHN VAN DYKE

ARTISTS:

VARIOUS

COPYWRITER:

JON BELL

AGENCY:

VAN DYKE COMPANY

CLIENT:

MEAD CORPORATION

■ 159-161 THREE INVITATION CARDS FOR DIFFERENT CLIENTS. TWO ARE FOR FURNITURE MAKERS, AND ONE IS THE ANNOUNCEMENT OF A BOOK ON ADVERTISING AGENCIES IN SWEDEN. (SWE)

● 159-161 DREI EINLADUNGSKARTEN FÜR VERSCHIEDENE KUNDEN: ZWEI BETREFFEN MÖBELAUSSTELLUNGEN, EINE DAS ERSCHEINEN EINES BUCHES ÜBER SCHWEDISCHE WERBEAGENTUREN. (SWE)

▲ 159-161 TROIS CARTES D'INVITATION, RESPECTIVEMENT POUR LA PARUTION D'UN LIVRE SUR LES AGENCES DE PUBLICITÉ EN SUEDE ET POUR DEUX MAGASINS DE MEUBLES. (SWE)

■ 162-167 COVER AND EXAMPLES OF THE SPREADS FROM A BROCHURE PROMOTING SIGNATURE PAPER. THE SUBJECT OF THE BROCHURE IS RUSSIA. (USA)

● 162-167 UMSCHLAG UND DOPPELSEITEN AUS EINER DER PROMOTIONSBROSCHÜREN FÜR DIE PAPIERQUALITÄT «SIGNATURE». HIER IST DAS THEMA RUSSLAND. (USA)

▲ 162-167 COUVERTURE ET DOUBLES PAGES TIRÉES DE L'UNE DES BROCHURES RÉALISÉES POUR LA PROMOTION DU PAPIER «SIGNATURE». ICI, LA RUSSIE. (USA)

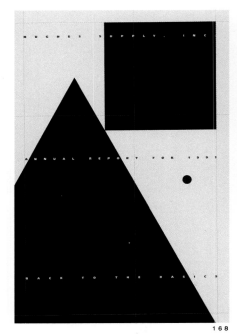

168

169

170

171

168-171

ART DIRECTOR:

ALAN URBAN

DESIGNER:

ALAN URBAN

PHOTOGRAPHER:

RUSTY FLYNN

COPYWRITER:

STEVE ZEPF

DESIGN STUDIO:

URBAN TAYLOR +

ASSOC.

CLIENT:

HUGHES

SUPPLY, INC.

172-174

ART DIRECTOR:

JEFFREY MILSTEIN

DESIGNER:

JEFFREY MILSTEIN

CLIENT:

PAPER HOUSE

PRODUCTIONS

172

173

174

■ **168-171** "BACK TO THE BASICS" CONCEPT FOR THE ANNUAL REPORT OF HUGHES SUPPLY, INC., A DISTRIBUTOR OF PRODUCTS FOR THE CONSTRUCTION TRADE. BASIC GEOMETRIC SHAPES AND ONLY TWO COLORS WERE USED. THE TYPOGRAPHY ADDS LIFE AND INTEREST. (USA)

■ **172-174** LINE OF GREETING CARDS DESIGNED ENTIRELY ON A MACINTOSH COMPUTER. THE CARDS FOLD IN VARIOUS WAYS, BECOMING SMALL, THREE-DIMENSIONAL, FANTASY ARCHITECTURAL FACADES. (USA)

● **168-171** «ZURÜCK ZUR BASIS» IST DAS KONZEPT FÜR DEN JAHRESBERICHT EINES VERTEILERS VON BAUMATERIALIEN. ES WURDEN EINFACHE GEOMETRISCHE FORMEN UND NUR ZWEI FARBEN VERWENDET, WÄHREND MIT DEM EINSATZ DER TYPOGRAPHIE SPANNUNG ERZEUGT WIRD. (USA)

● **172-174** DIESE SERIE VON GRUSSKARTEN WURDE VOLLKOMMEN MIT HILFE VON MACINTOSH-GERÄTEN HERGESTELLT. DIE KARTEN LASSEN SICH IN DREIDIMENSIONALE ARCHITEKTONISCHE GEBILDE FALTEN. (USA)

▲ **168-171** COUVERTURE ET DOUBLES PAGES DU RAPPORT ANNUEL 1991 D'UNE FIRME SPÉCIALISÉE DANS LA DISTRIBUTION DE MATÉRIEL DE CONSTRUCTION. LA MISE EN PAGES EST SIMPLE, N'UTILISANT QUE DEUX COULEURS SUR PAPIER RECYCLÉ ET DES CARACTERES DIGITALISÉS. (USA)

▲ **172-174** CETTE SÉRIE DE CARTES DÉCOUPÉES A ÉTÉ RÉALISÉE SUR UN ORDINATEUR MACINTOSH. CES ARCHITECTURES PLEINES DE FANTAISIE PEUVENT ETRE DÉVELOPPÉES EN MODELES TRIDIMENSIONNELS. (USA)

175

176

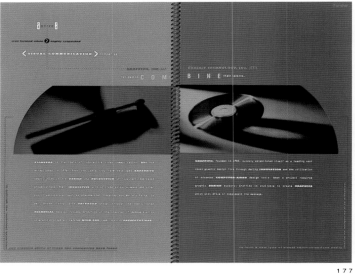

177

178

175-179

ART DIRECTORS:

MORTON JACKSON

TIM THOMPSON

DESIGNERS:

MORTON JACKSON

TIM THOMPSON

JOE PARISI

PHOTOGRAPHERS:

TARAN Z

HOWARD EHRENFELD

ED WHITMAN

MORTON JACKSON

COPYWRITER:

TONY MAFALE

STUDIO:

GRAFFITO

CLIENT:

ACTIVE8

Everyone is trying to say something.
Eyes and ears have become
jaded. Traditional means of
communication
are worn and ineffectual. Amidst the
great profusion of pictures and
words, how can one be assured that
the message does not fall on
deaf (?) ears

look. listen. react.

ACTIVE8

pursues a new way of seeing and
hearing. Because participation
enhances the reception and retention
of the message, ACTIVE8, through
INTERACTIVE and MULTIMEDIA
presentations, involves the audience.

Visionary technology has given us a
new set of tools to create a new
world of communication. A world in
which the viewer can no longer
remain passive. Where action calls
for reaction. Where response is
elicited. A place where the senses and
the mind are

ACTIVATED

179

■ **175-179** COVER AND SPREADS FROM A SPI-RAL-BOUND BROCHURE FOR ACTIVE8, A COM-MUNICATIONS COMPANY SPECIALIZING IN INTERACTIVE AND MULTIMEDIA PRESENTA-TIONS. TRANSPARENT PAGES HALF THE WIDTH OF REGULAR PAGES CARRY INFORMA-TION ON THE CASE HISTORY PRESENTED ON THE FOLLOWING PAGE. THE BROCHURE COMES IN A CORRUGATED-PLASTIC CASE WITH THE LOGO OF ACTIVE8. (USA)

● **175-179** UMSCHLAG UND BEISPIELE DER DOPPELSEITEN AUS EINER SPIRALGEBUN-DENEN BROSCHÜRE FÜR ACTIVE8, HER-STELLER VON KOMMUNIKATIONSMITTELN. AUF TRANSPARENTPAPIER IN SCHMALEREM SEITENFORMAT WIRD ÜBER DIE DARAUF-FOLGENDEN FALLSTUDIEN INFORMIERT. ALS VERPACKUNG DIENT EIN KOFFER AUS GEWELLTEM PLASTIK MIT DEM LOGO DER FIRMA. (USA)

▲ **175-179** D'UNE BROCHURE À RELIURE SPI-RALE POUR UNE FIRME QUI OFFRE DES PRESTATIONS DANS LE SECTEUR DE LA COM-MUNICATION INTERACTIVE ET DES MULTI-MÉDIAS DE L'AUDIOVISUEL. D'ÉTROITES BANDES DE PAPIER TRANSPARENT Y SONT INSÉRÉES, SUR LESQUELLES SONT PRÉSEN-TÉS DES EXEMPLES CONCRETS DE RÉALISA-TIONS. LA BROCHURE EST PRÉSENTÉE DANS UN COFFRET EN PLASTIQUE ONDULÉ. (USA)

180

181

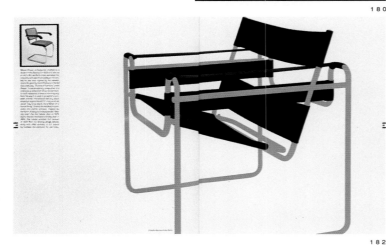

182

183

184

185

■ **180-185** IN *DESIGN & STYLE*, MOHAWK PAPER MILLS AND THE PUSHPIN GROUP PRESENT A YEARLY SURVEY OF PAST DESIGN STYLES AND THEIR INFLUENCE ON CONTEMPORARY GRAPHIC DESIGN. THESE PAGES ARE DEDICATED TO THE BAUHAUS. THE PAGES ARE DESIGNED IN ACCORDANCE WITH THE DESIGN PRINCIPLES OF THIS SCHOOL, AND ARE ILLUSTRATED WITH THE WORKS OF VARIOUS BAUHAUS MEMBERS, SUCH AS A PAINTING BY OSKAR SCHLEMMER (1888–1943), THE TUBULAR CHAIR BY MARCEL BREUER, AND A LAMP DESIGNED BY K.J. JUCKER AND WILHELM WAGENFELD. (USA)

■ **186-188** THIS SMALL BROCHURE IS COVERED IN SOFT LEATHER, WITH PROTECTIVE SILK PAPER SHEETS AND HANDMADE PAPER REINFORCED IN THE BINDING BY A STRIP OF DECORATIVE CLOTH. IT IS BOUND WITH FINE GOLDEN THREADS, AND SERVED AS AN INVITATION TO A CHRISTMAS RECEPTION AT DAYTON'S DEPARTMENT STORE. (USA)

● **180-185** MIT DIESER ZEITSCHRIFT BIETET DER PAPIERHERSTELLER MOHAWK ZUSAMMEN MIT DER PUSHPIN GROUP EINEN JÄHRLICHEN ÜBERBLICK ÜBER EINEN BESTIMMTEN STIL IM GRAPHIK-DESIGN UND SEINEN EINFLUSS AUF HEUTIGES GRAPHIK-DESIGN, HIER DAS BAUHAUS. DIE SEITEN SIND NACH DEN PRINZIPIEN DES BAUHAUSES GESTALTET UND MIT ARBEITEN DER PROTAGONISTEN ILLUSTRIERT, Z.B. MIT EINEM BILD VON OSKAR SCHLEMMER (1888–1943), DEM STAHLROHRSESSEL VON MARCEL BREUER UND DER LAMPE VON K.J. JUCKER UND WILHELM WAGENFELD VON 1923–24. (USA)

● **186-188** IN WEICHES LEDER GEBUNDENE BROSCHÜRE, MIT DECKBLÄTTERN AUS SEIDENPAPIER UND SEITEN AUS HANDGESCHÖPFTEM PAPIER, IM BUND MIT DEKORATIVEN STOFFSTREIFEN VERSTÄRKT UND VON GOLDFÄDEN ZUSAMMENGEHALTEN. SIE DIENT ALS EINLADUNG ZU EINEM WEIHNACHTSEMPFANG IM KAUFHAUS DAYTON'S. (USA)

▲ **180-185** COUVERTURE ET DOUBLES PAGES D'UN MAGAZINE ANNUEL PUBLIÉ PAR LE FABRICANT DE PAPIER MOHAWK PAPER MILLS ET THE PUSHPIN GROUP, CONSACRÉ À UN STYLE PARTICULIER, ICI LE BAUHAUS. LE TEXTE EST PRÉSENTÉ SUIVANT LES PRINCIPES DE LA TYPOGRAPHIE DE CETTE ÉCOLE ET ILLUSTRÉ D'ŒUVRES REPRÉSENTATIVES, PAR EX. UNE PEINTURE D'OSKAR SCHLEMMER (1888–1943), LA CHAISE TUBULAIRE DE MARCEL BREUER OU LA LAMPE DE K.J. JUCKER ET WILHELM WAGENFELD, DE 1923–24. UN ÉLÉMENT MOBILE PERMET D'ANIMER CETTE DERNIERE PAGE. (USA)

▲ **186-188** BROCHURE AVEC COUVERTURE DE CUIR SOUPLE, PAGES DE GARDE EN PAPIER DE SOIE ET FEUILLETS DE PAPIER À LA CUVE RENFORCÉS AU DOS PAR DES BANDES DE TISSU DÉCORATIF ET RELIÉS AU MOYEN DE MINCES FILS DORÉS, POUR UNE INVITATION À UNE RÉCEPTION DES GRANDS MAGASINS DAYTON'S POUR NOEL. (USA)

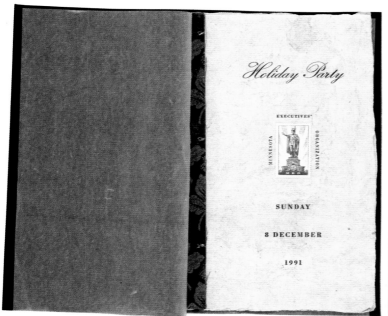

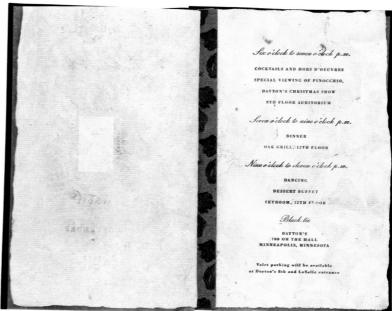

186

187

186-188

Art Director:

ALICIA NAMMACHER

Designer:

ALICIA NAMMACHER

Copywriter:

BETH MELLENDER

Client:

DAYTON'S

HUDSON'S/IN-HOUSE

188

180-185

Art Director:

SEYMOUR CHWAST

Designers:

SEYMOUR CHWAST

ROXANNE SLIMAK

Painting by:

OSKAR SCHLEMMER

Editor:

STEVE HELLER

Client:

MOHAWK PAPER

MILLS

ABOUT FACE ON STRATHMORE

189

190

189

ART DIRECTOR:
MIKE SCRICCO
DESIGNERS:
MIKE SCRICCO
ELIZABETH DZIERSK
PHOTOGRAPHER:
JOHN CASADO
AGENCY:
KEILER DESIGN
CLIENT:
STRATHMORE

190

ART DIRECTOR:
JOEL FULLER
DESIGNERS:
LISA ASHWORTH
MARK CANTOR
PHOTOGRAPHER:
CHUCK MASON
AGENCY:
PINKHAUS DESIGN
CORP.
CLIENT:
CHUCK MASON
PHOTOGRAPHY

■ **189** COVER OF A SPIRAL-BOUND CATALOG FOR STRATHMORE PAPERS. PHOTOGRAPHS BY FIVE DIFFERENT PHOTOGRAPHERS ARE PRINTED ON UNCOATED, TEXTURED, BLACK-AND-WHITE PAPERS. (USA)

■ **190** COVER OF A LARGE-FORMAT MAILER FOR CHUCK MASON, A PHOTOGRAPHER. THE MAILER CONTAINED EXAMPLES OF HIS WORK. MASON'S TELEPHONE NUMBER IS PRINTED IN THE SAME HUGE SIZE ON THE BACK. (USA)

■ **191-194** BLIND-EMBOSSED COVER AND INSIDE SPREADS FROM A LARGE-FORMAT, SPIRAL-BOUND BROCHURE PRESENTING THE ENTIRE LINE OF NEENAH UNCOATED PAPERS. SPECIAL EMPHASIS IS PUT ON THE SUITABILITY OF THIS STOCK FOR ANNUAL REPORTS BY MAKING THE "BOTTOM LINE" THE GENERAL SUBJECT OF THE PROMOTION. (USA)

● **189** UMSCHLAG EINER BROSCHÜRE FÜR EINEN PAPIERHERSTELLER. BILDER VON FÜNF PHOTOGRAPHEN SIND AUF UNGESTRICHENES, STRUKTURIERTES SCHWARZES ODER WEISSES PAPIER GEDRUCKT. (USA)

● **190** UMSCHLAG EINER GROSSFORMATIGEN WERBEMAPPE DES PHOTOGRAPHEN CHUCK MASON, SEINE TELEPHONNUMMER IST EBENSO GROSS WIE DER NAME VORN AUF DER RÜCKSEITE ANGEGEBEN. (USA)

● **191-194** BLINDGEPRÄGTER UMSCHLAG UND DOPPELSEITEN EINER SPIRALGEBUNDENEN BROSCHÜRE, IN DER ALLE UNGESTRICHENEN PAPIERSORTEN VON NEENAH VORGESTELLT WERDEN. THEMA IST DIE EIGNUNG DIESER PAPIERE FÜR JAHRESBERICHTE: «SELBST EIN SCHLECHTES JAHR SIEHT AUF NEENAH-PAPIER GUT AUS.» (USA)

▲ **189** COUVERTURE DU CATALOGUE À RELIURE SPIRALE RENFERMANT UNE SÉLECTION D'IMAGES DE CINQ PHOTOGRAPHES, LITHOGRAPHIÉES EN DEUX COULEURS SUR DES PAPIERS DE TEXTURES DIVERSES. (USA)

▲ **190** COUVERTURE DU DÉPLIANT DU PHOTOGRAPHE CHUCK MASON, PRÉSENTANT UN APERÇU DE SES MEILLEURES RÉALISATIONS. SON NUMÉRO DE TÉLÉPHONE EST INSCRIT EN LETTRES GÉANTES AU VERSO. (USA)

▲ **191-194** COUVERTURE DE PAPIER GAUFRÉ ET DOUBLES PAGES DE LA BROCHURE GRAND FORMAT À RELIURE SPIRALE D'UN FABRICANT DE PAPIER. CHAQUE PAGE PROPOSE DES EXEMPLES D'UTILISATION D'UNE QUALITÉ DE PAPIER. LE SLOGAN: «MÊME UNE MAUVAISE ANNÉE A DE L'ALLURE SUR UN PAPIER NEENAH.» (USA)

Even a bad year looks great on Neenah Paper

191

192

191-194

ART DIRECTORS:

KERRY GRADY

MICHAEL GLASS

DESIGNERS:

KERRY GRADY

MICHAEL GLASS

PHOTOGRAPHER:

GEOF KERN

COPYWRITER:

TODD LIEF

AGENCY:

MICHAEL GLASS

DESIGN, INC.

CLIENT:

NEENAH PAPER

193

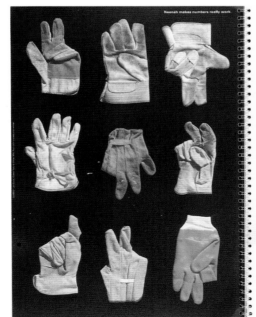

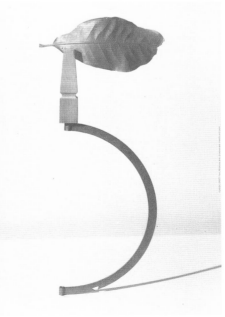

194

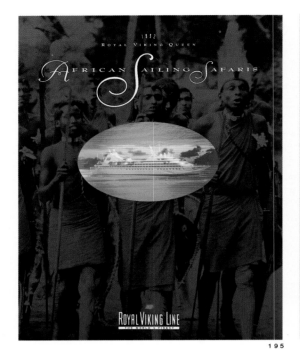

Noël   Runyan Hinsche Associates

195

196

195

ART DIRECTOR:

JOEL FULLER

DESIGNER:

CLAUDIA DECASTRO

AGENCY:

PINKHAUS DESIGN

CORP.

CLIENT:

ROYAL VIKING LINE

196

ART DIRECTOR:

LARRY LONG

DESIGNER:

LARRY LONG

PHOTOGRAPHER:

LARRY LONG

AGENCY:

RUNYAN HINSCHE

ASSOCIATES

CLIENT:

RUNYAN HINSCHE

ASSOCIATES

■ **195** BROCHURE PROMOTING CRUISES TO AFRICA ABOARD THE NEWEST SHIP OF THE ROYAL VIKING LINE. (USA)

■ **196** "A SPECTACULAR VIEW OF ONE OF OUR NATION'S MOST BELOVED LANDMARKS." A CHRISTMAS CARD FROM THE RUNYAN HINSCHE ASSOCIATES DESIGN STUDIO. (USA)

■ **197, 198** THE PROTECTIVE JACKET AND CENTERFOLD SPREAD FROM A BLACK-AND-WHITE BROCHURE SHOWING THE LATEST DESIGNS BY PORSCHE DESIGN. (AUT)

■ **199-201** THIS BOOK, *THE HEART SUTRA*, WAS PUBLISHED IN A LIMITED EDITION OF 30 COPIES. IT WAS PRINTED ON A VANDERCOOK PROOF PRESS USING GARAMOND BOOK CONDENSED TYPE AND SILKSCREEN PRINTING ON RICE PAPER. (USA)

● **195** UMSCHLAG EINER BROSCHÜRE ÜBER AFRIKAKREUZFAHRTEN MIT DEM NEUSTEN SCHIFF DER ROYAL VIKING LINE. (USA)

● **196** «EIN UMWERFENDER BLICK AUF EINES DER BELIEBTESTEN WAHRZEICHEN UNSERES LANDES.» WEIHNACHTSKARTE EINES DESIGN-STUDIOS. (USA)

● **197, 198** SCHUTZUMSCHLAG UND EINE AUS-KLAPPBARE DOPPELSEITE AUS EINER BRO-SCHÜRE MIT DEN NEUSTEN KREATIONEN VON PORSCHE DESIGN. (AUT)

● **199-201** DIESES BUCH MIT DEM TITEL «DAS SUTRA DES HERZENS» IST IN EINER AUFLAGE VON 30 EXEMPLAREN ERSCHIENEN. ES WUR-DE AUF EINER VANDERCOOK-ABZIEHPRESSE, IN GARAMOND-BUCH SCHMAL UND SIEBDRUCK AUF REISPAPIER GEDRUCKT. (USA)

▲ **195** D'UNE BROCHURE OU L'ON PROPOSE DES CROISIERES POUR L'AFRIQUE SUR UN PAQUEBOT DE LA ROYAL VIKING LINE. (USA)

▲ **196** «UN REGARD SPECTACULAIRE SUR L'UN DES SYMBOLES PRÉFÉRÉS DE NOTRE PAYS.» CARTE DE NOËL. (USA)

▲ **197, 198** COUVERTURE À RABATS AVEC STRUCTURE GAUFRÉE ET RECTO DES RABATS DE LA DOUBLE PAGE CENTRALE D'UNE BRO-CHURE PRÉSENTANT LES DERNIERES CRÉA-TIONS DE PORSCHE DESIGN. (AUT)

▲ **199-201** CE LIVRE INTITULÉ «LE SUTRA DU CŒUR» A ÉTÉ PUBLIÉ EN ÉDITION LIMITÉE NUMÉROTÉE ET ILLUSTRÉ DE SÉRIGRAPHIES. IL A ÉTÉ INPRIMÉ SUR PAPIER DE RIZ EN CARACTÈRES GARAMOND SUR UNE PRESSE VANDERCOOK. (USA)

197

198

199

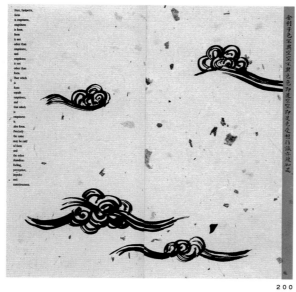

200

201

197, 198

ART DIRECTOR:

CHRISTIAN SATEK

DESIGNER:

SABINE KUNZMANN

PHOTOGRAPHER:

HERB RITTS

COPYWRITER:

RONALD KOLACZEK

AGENCY:

GGK WIEN

CLIENT:

PORSCHE DESIGN

199-201

ART DIRECTOR:

SANG YOON

DESIGNER:

SANG YOON

ILLUSTRATOR:

SANG YOON

CLIENT:

MOONLIGHT EXPRESS

202

203

202, 203

ART DIRECTORS:

ICHIRO MITANI

GAKUSHI TANAKA

DESIGNERS:

ICHIRO MITANI

GAKUSHI TANAKA

PHOTOGRAPHER:

GAKUSHI TANAKA

AGENCY:

OFFICE G

CLIENT:

MIWA KAZUHIKO

204-206

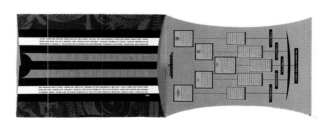

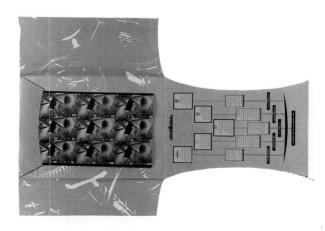

204-206

ART DIRECTOR:

BILL CAHAN

DESIGNER:

STUART FLAKE

AGENCY:

CAHAN &

ASSOCIATES

CLIENT:

NEENAH PAPER

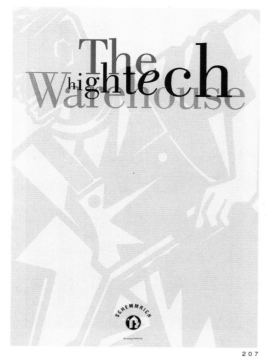

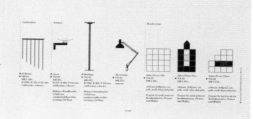

Der folgende Einrichtungsgegenstand wurde nicht für den *Gare de Lyon* erfunden, sondern für den *Gare de Robe* und ist wesentlich stärker als dieser Witz. Sie können eine Makrele dran **hä**n**ge**n oder einen Thunfisch. Sie können aber auch Ihre Kleider weiterhin auf einem Bürostuhl ab**le**g**e**n und mit den gesparten Mäusen gleichzeitig wie Klaus Kinski eine Nacht im 4 Jahreszeiten ver**b**r**i**ngen.

207

208

207, 208

ART DIRECTOR:

STEFAN CAESAR

ARTISTS:

STEFAN CAESAR

OLAF SCHULZ

COPYWRITER:

HANS NEFF

AGENCY:

HESSE

DESIGNAGENTUR

CLIENT:

SCHEMMRICH KG

■ **202, 203** COVER AND AN INSIDE SPREAD FROM THE CATALOG FOR AN EXHIBITION OF POTTERY BY KAZUHIKO MIWA. (JPN)

■ **204-206** "PAPER AT WORK." THE ENVELOPE IS SHOWN CLOSED AND OPENED WITH ITS CONTENTS: PRINTED SAMPLES OF NEENAH PAPER. THE IDEA WAS TO CREATE A USEFUL TOOL THAT IS WORTH KEEPING, A PIECE WITH BOTH A VISUAL LURE AND A PRACTICAL USE. (USA)

■ **207, 208** COVER AND INSIDE SPREAD FROM A LARGE-FORMAT BROCHURE FOR STEEL OFFICE FURNITURE. THE ILLUSTRATIONS ARE PAIRED WITH HUMOROUS COPY. (GER)

● **202, 203** UMSCHLAG UND DOPPELSEITE AUS DEM KATALOG FÜR EINE KERAMIKAUSSTELLUNG VON KAZUHIKO MIWA. (JPN)

● **204-206** «PAPER BEI DER ARBEIT.» GESCHLOSSENE UND GEÖFFNETE MAPPE MIT DEN BEDRUCKTEN MUSTERN VON NEENAHPAPIER. DIE IDEE WAR, EINE NÜTZLICHE DOKUMENTATION ZU BIETEN, DIE GERNE AUFGEHOBEN WIRD – TECHNISCHE INFORMATION ANSPRECHEND VERPACKT. (USA)

● **207, 208** UMSCHLAG UND DOPPELSEITE EINES KATALOGS FÜR BÜROMÖBEL AUS STAHL. DIE ABBILDUNGEN SIND VON HUMORVOLLEN TEXTEN BEGLEITET. (GER)

▲ **202, 203** COUVERTURE ET DOUBLE PAGE DU CATALOGUE D'UNE EXPOSITION DE CÉRAMIQUES DE KAZUHIKO MIWA. (JPN)

▲ **204-206** «LE PAPIER AU TRAVAIL». COUVERTURE DE LA POCHETTE RENFERMANT LES ÉCHANTILLONS DU FABRICANT DE PAPIER NEENAH ET LA POCHETTE OUVERTE AVEC SON CONTENU. L'ASPECT UTILITAIRE A DÉTERMINÉ LE CONCEPT, QUI PRIVILÉGIE L'INFORMATION TECHNIQUE. (USA)

▲ **207, 208** D'UNE BROCHURE GRAND FORMAT PRÉSENTANT LES PRODUITS D'UN FABRICANT DE MEUBLES DE BUREAUX QUI ALLIENT FONCTIONNALITÉ ET STYLE. (GER)

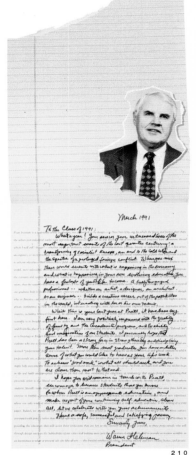

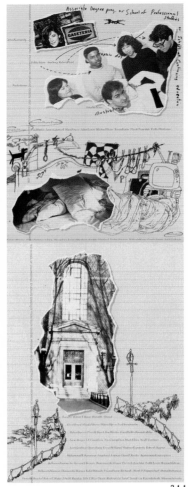

209   210   211   212

209-212

ART DIRECTOR:

GEORGE CHENG

DESIGNERS:

GEORGE CHENG

VINCENT LACAVA

ILLUSTRATOR:

CYNTHIA IGNACIO

CLIENT:

S.G.A. OF PRATT

INSTITUTE

■ **209-212** THE PRATT INSTITUTE'S 1991 YEARBOOK RESEMBLES THE YELLOW NOTEPADS USED BY COLLEGE STUDENTS. THE HANDWRITTEN PRESIDENT'S LETTER, THE SKETCHES AND THE FRAGMENTS OF PHOTOGRAPHS ADD TO THE SPONTANEOUS CHARACTER OF THIS "YEARBOOK." (USA)

■ **213-217** SPREADS AND COVER FROM A MAIL-ORDER CATALOG FOR THE FALL/WINTER 1991 CLOTHING COLLECTION OF THE GRAPHIC DESIGNER MICHAEL CRONAN. "CLOTHING DESIGNED FOR MEN, REMARKABLY WEARABLE BY WOMEN." (USA)

● **209-212** DAS «JAHRBUCH 1991» DES PRATT INSTITUTE IST EIN GELBER NOTIZBLOCK, WIE ER VON DEN AMERIKANISCHEN STUDENTEN VERWENDET WIRD. DER HANDGESCHRIEBENE «BRIEF DES DIREKTORS», DIE SKIZZEN UND AUSGERISSENEN PHOTOS UNTERSTREICHEN DIE SPONTANEITÄT DES «BUCHES». (USA)

● **213-217** DOPPELSEITEN UND UMSCHLAG EINES MODEVERSANDKATALOGS FÜR DIE KOLLEKTION HERBST/WINTER 1991 DES GRAPHIK-DESIGNERS MICHAEL CRONAN. DAS MOTTO LAUTET: «MODE FÜR MÄNNER, DIE AUCH FRAUEN GUT STEHT.» (USA)

▲ **209-212** LE «LIVRE DE L'ANNÉE 1991» DU PRATT INSTITUTE IMITE LE BLOC-NOTES JAUNE UTILISÉ PAR LES ÉTUDIANTS. LA «LETTRE DU DIRECTEUR», ÉCRITE À LA MAIN, LES ESQUISSES ET L'EFFET DES FRAGMENTS DE PHOTOS DÉCHIRÉES CONFERENT À CETTE BROCHURE UNE NOTE SPONTANÉE. (USA)

▲ **213-217** DOUBLES PAGES ET COUVERTURE DU CATALOGUE DE VENTE PAR CORRESPONDANCE DE LA COLLECTION AUTOMNE-HIVER 1991 DU DESIGNER MICHAEL CRONAN, LE SLOGAN: «UNE MODE MASCULINE QUI VA AUSSI AUX FEMMES.» (USA)

213

214

215

216

217

W A L K I N G   M A N

213-217

ART DIRECTOR:

MICHAEL CRONAN

DESIGNERS:

MIKE BOROSKY

MICHAEL CRONAN

PHOTOGRAPHER:

TERRY LORANT

AGENCY:

CRONAN DESIGN, INC.

CLIENT:

CRONAN ARTEFACT

MICHAEL CRONAN

218

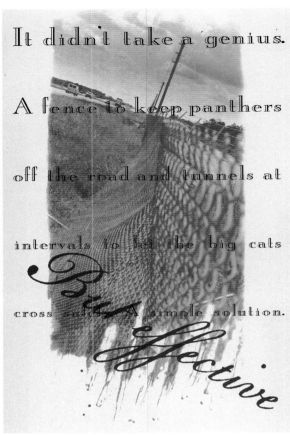

It didn't take a genius.

A fence to keep panthers

off the road and tunnels at

intervals to let the big cats

cross safely. A simple solution.

219

220

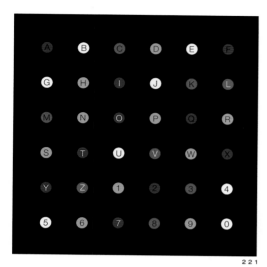

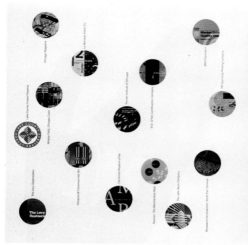

221

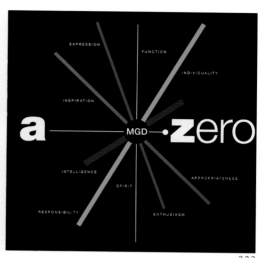

222

218-220

ART DIRECTORS:

JOEL FULLER

MARK CANTOR

TOM STERLING

DESIGNERS:

TOM STERLING

JOEL FULLER

PHOTOGRAPHER:

GALLEN MEI

COPYWRITER:

FRANK CUNNINGHAM

STYLIST:

TOM STERLING

AGENCY:

PINKHAUS

DESIGN CORP.

CLIENT:

GILBERT PAPER

221, 222

ART DIRECTOR:

MICHAEL GLASS

DESIGNER:

MICHAEL GLASS

AGENCY:

MICHAEL GLASS

DESIGN, INC.

CLIENT:

MICHAEL GLASS

DESIGN, INC.

223, 224

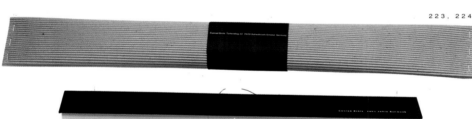

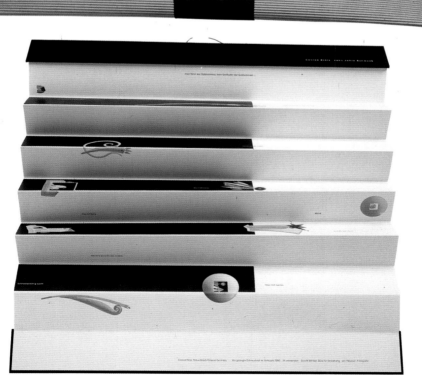

223, 224

ART DIRECTORS:

GÜLER SISA

EBERHART WINKLER

DESIGNERS:

GÜLER SISA

EBERHART WINKLER

PHOTOGRAPHER:

CHRISTOPH VON

HAUSSEN

COPYWRITERS:

EBERHART WINKLER

CONRAD STÜTZ

AGENCY:

SISA UND WINKLER

BÜRO FÜR

GESTALTUNG

CLIENT:

CONRAD STÜTZ

225

225

ART DIRECTOR:

TED FABELLA

DESIGNERS:

TED FABELLA

MATT STRELECKI

PHOTOGRAPHER:

KEVIN IRBY

AGENCY:

BARNSTORM

CLIENT:

CREATIVE CLUB

OF ATLANTA

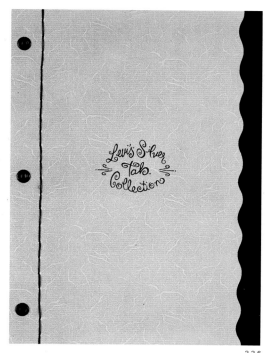

226

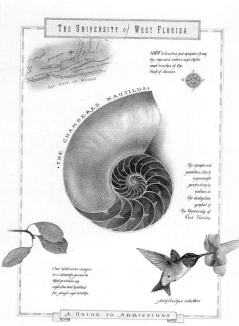

227

228

226

ART DIRECTOR:

JENNIFER MORLA

DESIGNER:

JENNIFER MORLA

AGENCY:

MORLA DESIGN

CLIENT:

LEVI STRAUSS & CO.

227

ART DIRECTOR:

ANTHONY RUTKA

DESIGNER:

MATTHEW DAVIS

ILLUSTRATOR:

ANATOLY

COPYWRITER:

JOAN WEADOCK

AGENCY:

RUTKA WEADOCK

DESIGN

CLIENT:

UNIVERSITY OF

WEST FLORIDA

228

ART DIRECTOR:

JOHN DUNN

DESIGNER:

JOHN DUNN

AGENCY:

DUNN AND RICE

DESIGN, INC.

CLIENT:

ASHBY PARK

COLLECTION

■ **225** *EGO*, A MAGAZINE PUBLISHED BY THE CREATIVE CLUB OF ATLANTA. (USA)

■ **226 THE** COVER OF A CATALOG PRESENTING LÉVI'S SILVER TABS COLLECTION TO RETAIL BUYERS. PHOTOGRAPHY PRINTED IN SILVER AND BLACK SUPPORTS THE DESIRED IMAGE. (USA)

■ **227** BROCHURE FOR THE UNIVERSITY OF WEST FLORIDA, FOCUSING ON THE FACT THAT THE CAMPUS IS A WILDLIFE PRESERVE CLOSE TO THE GULF OF MEXICO. (USA)

■ **228** THIS FOLDER PROMOTING ASHBY PARK, A FIRM SPECIALIZING IN GIFT BASKETS AND BOXES, IS PRESENTED AS IF A GIFT, IN BLIND-EMBOSSED STOCK, WITH A RAFFIA RIBBON AND HANGER. (USA)

● **225** UMSCHLAG VON *EGO*, EINEM MAGAZIN DES CREATIVE CLUB OF ATLANTA. (USA)

● **226** UMSCHLAG EINES KATALOGS, IN DEM DIE SILVER TABS KOLLEKTION VON LEVIS VORGESTELLT WIRD. LIFESTYLE-PHOTOS IN SILBER UND SCHWARZ ENTSPRECHEN DEM GEWÜNSCHTEN IMAGE. (USA)

● **227** UMSCHLAG EINER INFORMATIONS-BROSCHÜRE DER UNIVERSITY OF WEST FLORIDA, DEREN CAMPUS EIN NATURRESER-VAT IST, NAH AM GOLF VON MEXIKO. (USA)

● **228** DIESE WERBEMAPPE FÜR ASHBY PARK, EINE AUF GESCHENKARTIKEL SPEZIALI-SIERTE FIRMA, IST WIE EIN GESCHENK GE-STALTET: KARTON MIT BLINDPRÄGEDRUCK, EINEM BASTBAND UND ANHÄNGER. (USA)

▲ **225** COUVERTURE D'*EGO* PUBLIÉE PAR LE CREATIVE CLUB OF ATLANTA. (USA)

▲ **226** COUVERTURE DU CATALOGUE DE LA COLLECTION LEVI'S SILVER TABS, DESTINÉ AUX DÉTAILLANTS, QUI COMPORTE DES PHO-TOS EN IMPRESSION ARGENT DE CETTE NOU-VELLE LIGNE DE JEANS. (USA)

▲ **227** COUVERTURE DE LA BROCHURE D'IN-FORMATION PUBLIÉE PAR LA UNIVERSITY OF WEST FLORIDA, SITUÉE DANS LE CADRE D'UNE RÉSERVE NATURELLE. (USA)

▲ **228** LE DÉPLIANT PUBLICITAIRE POUR ASHBY PARK SE PRÉSENTE ENVELOPPÉ COMME UN PAQUET CADEAU DANS UN PAPIER GAUFRÉ NOIR, MAINTENU PAR UN LIEN DE RAPHIA AVEC ÉTIQUETTE. (USA)

229

230

229, 230

ART DIRECTORS:

JOEL FULLER

MARK CANTOR

DESIGNERS:

MARK CANTOR

JOEL FULLER

PHOTOGRAPHER:

ERIC MEOLA

COPYWRITER:

FRANK CUNNINGHAM

AGENCY:

PINKHAUS

DESIGN CORP.

CLIENT:

REX THREE, INC.

231

June 5, 1991

231

ART DIRECTOR:

AMY QUINLIVAN

DESIGNER:

AMY QUINLIVAN

PHOTOGRAPHERS:

GEOF KERN

DAVID MEUNCH

COPYWRITER:

SARAH MCNEAL

AGENCY:

AMY QUINLIVAN

DESIGN

CLIENT:

TARGET

232-235

ART DIRECTOR:

JIM BERTÉ

DESIGNER:

JIM BERTÉ

PHOTOGRAPHER:

RUSS WIDSTRAND

COPYWRITER:

JOHN TUFFY

AGENCY:

MORAVA OLIVER

BERTÉ

CLIENT:

LOGICON

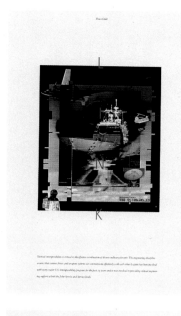

232

233

234

235

■ **229, 230** COVER OF A BROCHURE, SHOWN BOTH FULLY OPENED AND CLOSED WITH THE FLAP IN THE SLIT PROVIDED. A PROMOTIONAL PIECE FOR A PRINTER, IT DEMONSTRATES THE CLIENT'S COLOR PRINTING THROUGH REPRODUCTIONS OF THE COLORFUL IMAGES OF THE PHOTOGRAPHER ERIC MEOLA. (USA)

■ **231** COVER OF A BROCHURE FOR THE UNITED EARTH INAUGURATION CEREMONY, AN EVENT PROMOTING RESPONSIBILITY FOR BOTH NATURE AND HUMANITY, HELD IN COOPERATION WITH THE UNITED NATIONS ENVIRONTMENT PROGRAM. (USA)

■ **232-235** COVER AND SPREADS FROM THE 1991 ANNUAL REPORT OF LOGICON, A COMPANY SUPPLYING ADVANCED TECHNOLOGY SYSTEMS (SUCH AS RADAR CONTROL SYSTEMS) AND SERVICES FOR GOVERNMENTAL, CIVIL AND INDUSTRIAL PURPOSES. (USA)

● **229, 230** UMSCHLAG EINER BROSCHÜRE, HIER GANZ GEÖFFNET UND GESCHLOSSEN MIT DER LASCHE IM VORGESEHENEN SCHLITZ GEZEIGT. SIE DIENT ALS WERBUNG EINER DRUCKEREI, DIE iHRE FARBDRUCKQUALITÄT ANHAND DER PHOTOGRAPHIEN VON ERIC MEOLA DEMONSTRIERT. (USA)

● **231** BROSCHÜRE FÜR DIE «UNITED EARTH»-ERÖFFNUNGSZEREMONIE, EIN PROGRAMM, MIT DEM DAS VERANTWORTUNGSBEWUSST-SEIN FÜR MENSCH UND NATUR GEFÖRDERT WERDEN SOLL, IN ZUSAMMENARBEIT MIT DEM UNO-UMWELTPROGRAMM. (USA)

● **232-235** UMSCHLAG UND DOPPELSEITEN AUS EINEM JAHRESBERICHT FÜR LOGICON, EINE FIRMA, DIE TECHNOLOGIE UND DIENST-LEISTUNGEN FÜR MILITÄRISCHE, INDUSTRI-ELLE UND ZIVILE ZWECKE ANBIETET, WIE Z.B. RADARKONTROLLSYSTEME. (USA)

▲ **229, 230** COUVERTURE DE LA BROCHURE D'UN IMPRIMEUR CÉLEBRE POUR LA QUALITÉ DE SES IMPRESSIONS EN COULEURS. ELLE RENFERME DE SPECTACULAIRES PHOTOS D'ERIC MEOLA ET SE FERME COMME UN DOS-SIER, S'OUVRANT SUR UN RABAT ILLUSTRÉ DE L'IMAGE DE COUVERTURE. (USA)

▲ **231** BROCHURE ÉDITÉE À L'OCCASION DE LA CÉRÉMONIE D'INAUGURATION DU PRO-GRAMME DES NATIONS-UNIES POUR L'ENVI-RONNEMENT. ON Y PRÉSENTE DES PER-SONNALITÉS QUI ŒUVRENT EN FAVEUR DE LA PROTECTION DE LA NATURE. (USA)

▲ **232-235** COUVERTURE ET DOUBLES PAGES DU RAPPORT ANNUEL 1991 DE LOGICON, UNE FIRME SPÉCIALISÉE DANS LA TECHNOLOGIE DE POINTE APPLIQUÉE À LA SÉCURITÉ CIVILE ET MILITAIRE, PAR EXEMPLE AUX SYSTEMES DE CONTROLE RADAR. (USA)

236

237

238

239

236-239

DESIGNER:

MICHAEL MABRY

ILLUSTRATOR:

GUY BILLOUT

AGENCY:

MICHAEL MABRY

DESIGN

CLIENT:

GATX CAPITAL

LEASING

■ 236-239 COVER AND SPREADS FROM THE 1990 ANNUAL REPORT FOR GATX CAPITAL LEASING. THE IMAGES REFER TO THE COMPANY'S INVENTIVE SPIRIT AND THE INDUSTRIES THE COMPANY SERVES. (USA)

■ 240, 241 COVER, SHOWN CLOSED AND OPENED, OF THE 1990 ANNUAL REPORT FOR THE DES MOINES METROPOLITAN AREA SOLID WASTE AGENCY. THE TORN EDGE OF THE CORRUGATED CARDBOARD IS INTENTIONAL, AS IS THE KELLOGG'S IMPRINT ON THE INSIDE. THEY EMPHASIZE THE AGENCY'S COMMITMENT TO RECYCLING. (USA)

■ 242, 243 INVITATION TO AN EXHIBITION ON "RUSSIAN GRAPHIC DESIGN: 1880-1917," HELD AT ART CENTER COLLEGE OF DESIGN IN PASADENA, CALIFORNIA. WHEN THE INVITATION IS OPENED, A WORK FROM THE EXHIBITION APPEARS; THE EXHIBIT SPECIFICS ARE PRESENTED ON THE OUTSIDE OF THE ENVELOPE. (USA)

● 236-239 UMSCHLAG UND DOPPELSEITEN AUS DEM JAHRESBERICHT 1990 FÜR GATX FINANZIERUNGEN. DIE ILLUSTRATIONEN BEZIEHEN SICH AUF DIE INDUSTRIEZWEIGE, DIE ZU DEN KUNDEN DER FIRMA GEHÖREN. (USA)

● 240, 241 GESCHLOSSENER UND GEÖFFNETER UMSCHLAG DES JAHRESBERICHTES 1990 EINES STÄDTISCHEN ABFALLVERWERTUNGSBETRIEBES. DIE ABGERISSENE ECKE DES WELLKARTONS IST BEABSICHTIGT. WIE DER KELLOG'S AUFDRUCK AUF DER INNENSEITE UNTERSTÜTZT SIE DAS THEMA WIEDERVERWERTUNG. (USA)

● 242, 243 EINLADUNG ZU EINER AUSSTELLUNG ÜBER RUSSISCHES GRAPHIK-DESIGN VON 1880–1917 IM ART CENTER COLLEGE OF DESIGN. ÖFFNET MAN DIE EINLADUNG, WIRD EINE ZUR AUSSTELLUNG GEHÖRENDE SCHOKOLADENVERPACKUNG SICHTBAR, WÄHREND EINZELHEITEN ÜBER DIE AUSSTELLUNG AUSSEN ANGEGEBEN SIND. (USA)

▲ 236-239 COUVERTURE ET DOUBLES PAGES DU RAPPORT ANNUEL 1990 DE GATX, UN INSTITUT DE FINANCEMENT. LES IMAGES ILLUSTRENT LES STRATÉGIES DE CETTE SOCIÉTÉ ET SON ESPRIT INVENTIF. (USA)

▲ 240, 241 COUVERTURE ET DOUBLE PAGE DU RAPPORT ANNUEL 1990 D'UN ORGANISME OFFICIEL CHARGÉ DES PROBLEMES DE RECYCLAGE. IL A ÉTÉ IMPRIMÉ SUR PAPIER RECYCLÉ ET ON A UTILISÉ DES CARTONS D'EMBALLAGE USAGÉS DE CORN FLAKES KELLOGG'S POUR LES PLATS DE LA COUVERTURE À RELIURE SPIRALE. (USA)

▲ 242, 243 CARTE D'INVITATION POUR UNE EXPOSITION DE DESIGN GRAPHIQUE RUSSE (1880-1917). EN DÉPLIANT L'ENVELOPPE, ON DÉCOUVRE UN EXEMPLE DU CONTENU DE L'EXPOSITION, L'IMAGE D'UN EMBALLAGE DE TABLETTE DE CHOCOLAT, L'ANNONCE DE L'ÉVÉNEMENT FIGURANT SUR L'EXTÉRIEUR DE L'ENVELOPPE. (USA)

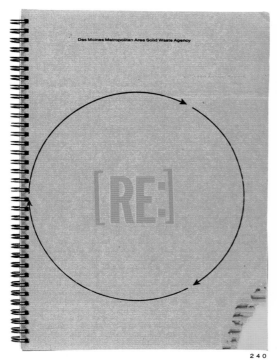

Des Moines Metropolitan Area Solid Waste Agency

[RE:]

240

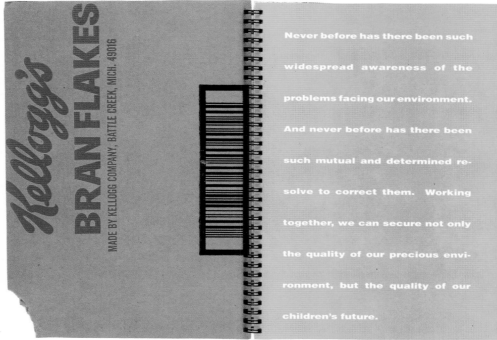

Never before has there been such widespread awareness of the problems facing our environment. And never before has there been such mutual and determined re-solve to correct them. Working together, we can secure not only the quality of our precious envi-ronment, but the quality of our children's future.

241

240, 241
ART DIRECTOR:
STEVE PATTEE
DESIGNERS:
STEVE PATTEE
KELLY STILES
TIM SCHUMANN
COPYWRITER:
MIKE CONDON
AGENCY:
PATTEE DESIGN
CLIENT:
METRO SOLID
WASTE AGENCY

242, 243

242, 243
ART DIRECTOR:
REBECA MENDEZ
DESIGNER:
REBECA MENDEZ
STUDIO:
ART CENTER DESIGN
OFFICE
CLIENT:
ART CENTER
COLLEGE OF DESIGN

244-249

ART DIRECTOR:
MASSIMO OSTI
DESIGNER:
MASSIMO OSTI
PHOTOGRAPHERS:
IRVING UNDERHILL
(COVER)
DANIELA
FACCHINATO
AGENCY:
STUDIO POLI
CLIENT:
C.P. COMPANY

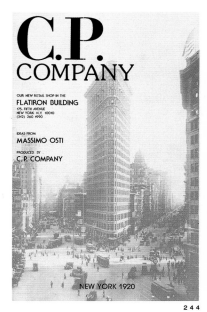

244

245

Massimo Osti: la memoria e il futuro

Nelle vecchie copie d'archivio delle stampe per le T-shirt che Osti disegnava nei primi anni '70 si individuano chiaramente quei segnali che hanno distinto il suo modo di porsi verso il "vestire": sono disegni che richiamano alla memoria il cosmo della Pop Art, segni che catturano l'attenzione della gente immediatamente, come immediati erano nei primi anni '70 i messaggi che gli Stati Uniti inviavano, dalle ribellioni giovanili alle rivoluzioni artistiche.

La primissima fase della carriera di Massimo Osti puntò principalmente sull'immagine/disegno e sulla grafica poi, come naturale evoluzione, sul perfezionamento dell'abito inteso come oggetto d'uso, senza per questo rinunciare al piacere estetico, così il destino di un capo era legato alla funzione che doveva assolvere: in un giaccone da lavoro venivano trasportate le deformità strutturali, come immediate quelle del gomito dovute alla tensione costante, proprie di un capo usato.

Il termine "storico" è una parola chiave nello sviluppo del lavoro di Osti, sia perché le migliaia di vestiti vecchi che ha raccolto in tutto il mondo rappresentano il punto di partenza quando si accinge a progettare una nuova collezione, sia perché il desiderio di creare vestiti sempre più confortevoli e simili, nella loro funzionalità, all'usato da cui traeva spunto, lo hanno spinto a continue ricerche nel campo dei tessuti, arrivando a rivoluzionare questo settore produttivo.

Dalla smerigliatura e gommatura delle lane e dei cotoni, fino all'Ice Jacket, un tessuto a cristalli liquidi termosensibili che

246

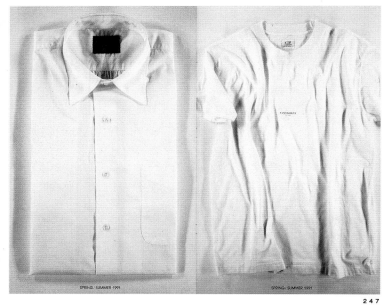

247

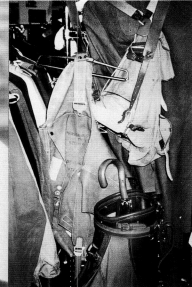

248

tale lavoro.

Sui pannelli-lavoro campeggiano i bozzetti della Vespa progettata da Osti nel 1989 per la Piaggio e che l'elaborazione al computer grafico mostra realisticamente definita; in un altro corner è testimoniato il "Progetto Sci", uno studio che ha condotto nell'intento di modificare l'attuale tendenza del settore, votata all'uso esagerato di capi e materiali che [...] casi: il "moon [...] tessuto [...] colore a seconda della temperatura, e [...] privilegia la funzione [...] piuttosto [...] l'adeguamento alle [...]

In qu[...]io, a volte condizionati [...] e dai mate[...] affollano, Osti diseg[...] sempre [...] questi segnali che [...] a volte [...] a volte superflui [...] to, ma che [...] aiutano a formulare [...]ni.

[...] questi anni di serrate sperim[...] devono essere [...]ordati alcuni episodi legati a [...] di nuove ideazioni, ad [...]ello di un materiale giapponese [...] stud[...] [...]ziali, usato da O[...] come interno [...] one, che i[...] di sotto di una certa temperatura, o il più recente caso di tessuto di lana spalmato in gomma, che col tempo irrigidisce perché cambia la composizione della spalmatura. Sono casi che dimostrano come in una incessante ricerca possano verificarsi fatti imputabili ai tempi strettissimi del ciclo-moda,

i quali, a volte, non lasciano spazio ad un collaudo definitivo. Dopo tutti questi anni di lavoro è maturata la decisione di approdare al mercato americano.

Il negozio di New York nasce con l'int[...] recuperare e restituire alla città, attraverso il restauro [...]eno del Flatiron Building, una delle sue più [...] architettoniche.

Il [...] di questo spazio, occupat[...] C.P. Com[...] è [...] punto avanti seguendo il [...]o"; un [...] navigare tra passato [...] have metropolitana entro la quale è possibile [...] agini della nostra memoria alle tecnologie [...] ttagli tecnic[...] dei capi.

Nel negozio si possono [...] specifiche ricerche curate [...] del design applicato alle [...] epoca, e che danno la possibilità di [...] urope[...] In un apposito spazio, chi volesse continuar[...] consultare una selezione di libri di design e [...] gita dalla "Feltrinelli International". Chi lo d[...] acquistare direttamente presso le rispettive sedi editori[...] volumi in [...]rto.

Vi è anche un a[...] occupato da una selezione discografica di cantautori e musicis[...] italiani.

Non sarà un negozio [...]tto, ai capi saranno affiancati una serie di accessori frutto [...] specifica ricerca che spazia tra gli oggetti complementari al "vestito" ritenuti più adatti

249

ZUKUNFT. EINTRITT FREI.

250

251

DIE NADEL FÜR AUFGEBLASENE WERBER.

Wir führen uns nicht auf wie die Gockel und nehmen uns nicht übertrieben wichtig. Dafür aber um so mehr unsere Arbeit und unsere Kunden.

252

FASSS...STATT PLATZ.

069-6031051 STATT LUFTNUMMERN.

253

254

250-254

ART DIRECTOR: AGENCY:
MATTHIAS SIMON   STUBENRAUCH
DESIGNER: & SIMON
RÜDIGER GÖTZ   CLIENT:
COPYWRITER: STUBENRAUCH
JOCHEN HÄMEL   & SIMON

■ 244-249 COVER AND SPREADS FROM A LARGE-FORMAT CATALOG FOR THE C.P. COMPANY, EVOKING THE PERSONALITY OF THE CREATOR OF THIS LINE OF PRACTICAL GARMENTS, MASSIMO OSTI, AND DETAILING IMPORTANT STEPS IN THE COMPANY'S DEVELOPMENT. IT WAS PUBLISHED ON THE OCCASION OF THE OPENING OF A STORE IN NEW YORK'S FLATIRON BUILDING. (ITA)

■ 250-254 COVER AND SPREADS FROM A BLACK-AND-WHITE BROCHURE FOR A GERMAN ADVERTISING AGENCY THAT DESCRIBES ITSELF AS BITING, COURAGEOUS, STRAIGHTFORWARD AND LOYAL—JUST LIKE THE DOG THAT THE COMPANY CHOSE AS ITS SYMBOL. ILLUSTRATIONS AND COPY REFER TO OTHER QUALITIES OF THE AGENCY IN THE SAME HUMOROUS SPIRIT. (GER)

● 244-249 UMSCHLAG UND DOPPELSEITEN EINES KATALOGS DER C.P. COMPANY, MIT DEM AN DEN DESIGNER DIESER LINIE PRAKTISCHER BEKLEIDUNG, MASSIMO OSTI, SOWIE AN DIE VERSCHIEDENEN ETAPPEN DER FIRMENGESCHICHTE ERINNERT WIRD. ER WURDE ZUR ERÖFFNUNG EINES LADENS IN NEW YORKS FLATIRON (BÜGELEISEN) GEBÄUDE HERAUSGEGEBEN. (ITA)

● 250-254 UMSCHLAG UND DOPPELSEITEN AUS DER IMAGEBROSCHÜRE (IN SCHWARZWEISS) EINER DEUTSCHEN WERBEAGENTUR, DIE SICH ALS BISSIG, MUTIG, DIREKT UND LOYAL DARSTELLT – GANZ DEM HUND ENTSPRECHEND, DER IHR SYMBOL IST. ÄHNLICH HUMORVOLL BESCHREIBEN ALLE ILLUSTRATIONEN UND TEXTE DIE VORTEILE DIESER AGENTUR. (GER)

▲ 244-249 COUVERTURE ET DOUBLES PAGES DU CATALOGUE GRAND FORMAT DE LA C.P. COMPANY, QUI ÉVOQUE LA PERSONNALITÉ DU FONDATEUR DE CETTE LIGNE DE VETEMENTS PRATIQUES, MASSIMO OSTI, ET LES ÉTAPES IMPORTANTES DU DÉVELOPPEMENT DE LA FIRME. IL A ÉTÉ ÉDITÉ À L'OCCASION DE L'OUVERTURE DU MAGASIN DE NEW YORK, SITUÉ DANS LE «FLATIRON BUILDING». (ITA)

▲ 250-254 COUVERTURE ET DOUBLES PAGES DE LA BROCHURE EN NOIR ET BLANC D'UNE AGENCE DE PUBLICITÉ ALLEMANDE QUI ALLIE LE MORDANT ET L'HUMOUR AU SÉRIEUX ET À L'EFFICACITÉ EN MATIERE DE COMMUNICATION. LES ILLUSTRATIONS, DANS L'ESPRIT DU SIGLE DE LA FIRME, ACCOMPAGNÉES DE COMMENTAIRES LAPIDAIRES, ILLUSTRENT LA CRÉATIVITÉ DE CETTE AGENCE. (GER)

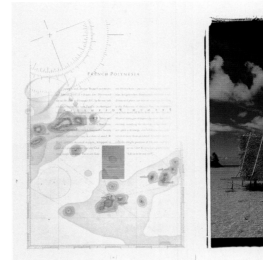

255

256

257

258

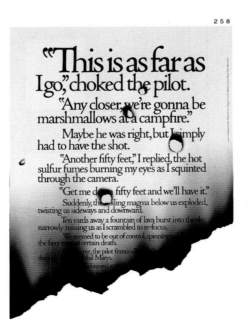

255-257

ART DIRECTOR:
JACK ANDERSON
DESIGNERS:
JACK ANDERSON
DENISE WEIR
PAULA COX
ILLUSTRATOR:
BRUCE MORSER
AGENCY:
HORNALL ANDERSON
DESIGN WORKS
CLIENT:
WINDSTAR CRUISES

258

ART DIRECTOR:
SUE CROLICK
DESIGNER:
SUE CROLICK
PHOTOGRAPHER:
KERRY PETERSON/
DUBLIN PHOTOGRAPHY
STYLISTS:
MINNEFEX
JACK MOLLOY
COPYWRITER:
TOM MCELLIGOTT
AGENCY:
SUE CROLICK
ADV.+ DESIGN
CLIENT:
SCIENCE MUSEUM
OF MINNESOTA

259-261

ART DIRECTOR:

KIT HINRICHS

DESIGNERS:

KIT HINRICHS

BELLE HOW

ARTISTS:

BOB ESPARZA

BARBARA BENTHIAN

WILL NELSON

COPYWRITER:

DELPHINE HIRASUNA

AGENCY:

PENTAGRAM

CLIENT:

GRAPHIC ARTS

CENTER

259

260

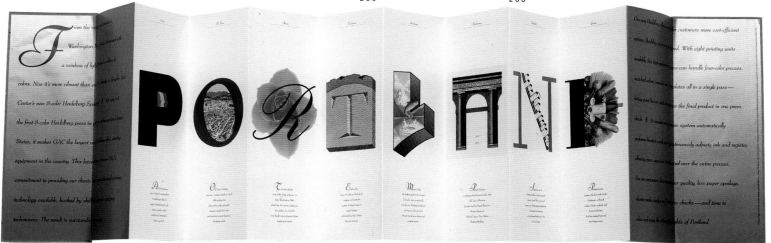

261

■ **255-257** THIS BROCHURE FOR WINDSTAR CRUISES CONTAINED THE SAILING SCHEDULE FOR 1992, AND HAD TO GET ACROSS THE BEAUTY OF THE SHIPS, THEIR COMFORT AND SERVICE, AND THE LINE'S DESTINATIONS. SHOWN ARE THE COVER AND TWO INSIDE SPREADS. (USA)

■ **258** DIRECT-MAIL PIECE FOR THE SCIENCE MUSEUM OF MINNESOTA. IT AIMED TO ATTRACT NEW MEMBERS BY PROMOTING THE MUSEUM'S NEW MOVIE ON VOLCANOES. THE BURNT SECTIONS ARE AN ALLUSION TO THE SUBJECT. (USA)

■ **259-261** CONCERTINA FOLDER WITH REINFORCED FRONT AND BACK, CONTAINED IN A BLACK ENVELOPE. CREATED FOR THE GRAPHIC ARTS CENTER, A PRINTING COMPANY, THE BROCHURE DISCUSSES THE FIRM'S NEW EIGHT-COLOR HEIDELBERG PRESS AND ITS HOME CITY OF PORTLAND. (USA)

● **255-257** DIESE BROSCHÜRE FÜR WINDSTAR-KREUZFAHRTEN MIT DEM PROGRAMM FÜR 1992 SOLLTE DIE SCHÖNHEIT DER SCHIFFE, IHREN KOMFORT UND SERVICE SOWIE DIE EINZIGARTIGEN DESTINATIONEN ZEIGEN. ABGEBILDET SIND DER UMSCHLAG UND ZWEI DOPPELSEITEN. (USA)

● **258** DIREKTWERBUNG FÜR DAS WISSENSCHAFTSMUSEUM VON MINNESOTA. DURCH SEINEN NEUEN FILM ÜBER VULKANE WILL DAS MUSEUM NEUE MITGLIEDER WERBEN. DIE BRANDLÖCHER SIND EINE ANSPIELUNG AUF DAS VULKANTHEMA. (USA)

● **259-261** LEPORELLO MIT VERSTÄRKTEN VORDER- UND RÜCKSEITEN. ER WIRD IN EINEM SCHWARZEN UMSCHLAG VERSCHICKT UND INFORMIERT ÜBER DIE NEUE 8-FARBEN-HEIDELBERGER-DRUCKPRESSE EINER DRUCKEREI SOWIE ÜBER PORTLAND, WO DIE FIRMA IHREN SITZ HAT. (USA)

▲ **255-257** COUVERTURE ET DOUBLES PAGES DE LA BROCHURE PRÉSENTANT LE PROGRAMME 1992 DES CROISIERES WINDSTAR. ON Y MONTRE LA BEAUTÉ ET LE CONFORT DES BATEAUX, LES SERVICES PROPOSÉS, AINSI QUE LES DESTINATIONS UNIQUES OFFERTES PAR CETTE COMPAGNIE. (USA)

▲ **258** PUBLICITÉ POUR LE MUSÉE DE LA SCIENCE DE MINNESOTA. IL S'AGISSAIT DE PROMOUVOIR UN FILM SUR LES VOLCANS ET D'ATTIRER DE NOUVEAUX MEMBRES. LES TRACES DE BRULURE ONT ÉTÉ IMITÉES AFIN DE VISUALISER LE SUJET DU FILM. (USA)

▲ **259-261** DÉPLIANT EN ACCORDÉON À COUVERTURE RIGIDE POUR UNE IMPRIMERIE DE PORTLAND. AU RECTO, CHACUNE DES LETTRES SYMBOLISE UN ASPECT PROPRE À CETTE VILLE. L'ENTREPRISE EMPLOIE UNE PRESSE HEIDELBERG, QUI PERMET D'IMPRIMER EN HUIT COULEURS. (USA)

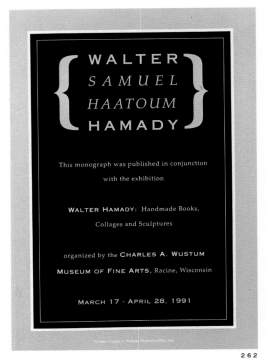

262

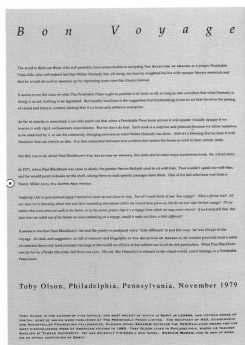

263

264

262-264

ART DIRECTORS:
KEVIN WADE
DANA LYTLE
DESIGNERS:
DANA LYTLE
KEVIN WADE
PHOTOGRAPHER:
MIKE REBHOLZ
AGENCY:
PLANET DESIGN CO.
CLIENT:
CHARLES A. WUSTUM
MUSEUM OF FINE
ARTS

■ **262-264** COVER AND SPREADS FROM A CATALOG FOR A RETROSPECTIVE EXHIBITION OF HANDMADE BOOKS, COLLAGES AND SCULPTURES BY WALTER HAMADY. THE TYPE WAS MEANT TO ENHANCE HIS WORK RATHER THAN COMPETE FOR ATTENTION. (USA)

■ **265-268** COVER AND INSIDE SPREADS FROM THE CATALOG FOR A POTTERY EXHIBITION HELD IN TOKYO'S TAKASHIMAYA DEPARTMENT STORE. (JPN)

■ **269** THIS CATALOG PRESENTS THE COLLIER CAMPBELL LABEL HOME-FURNISHINGS COLLECTION FOR J.P. STEVENS/WEST POINT PEPPERELL. THE LABEL IS ATTACHED WITH A PIECE OF STRING. (USA)

● **262-264** AUS DEM KATALOG FÜR EINE RETROSPEKTIVE DER HANDGEMACHTEN BÜCHER, COLLAGEN UND SKULPTUREN VON WALTER HAMADY. DIE ZURÜCKHALTENDE TYPOGRAPHIE UNTERSTÜTZT DIE WIRKUNG DER ABBILDUNGEN. (USA)

● **265-268** UMSCHLAG UND DOPPELSEITEN AUS DEM KATALOG FÜR EINE KERAMIKAUSSTELLUNG IN DER KUNSTGALERIE DES KAUFHAUSES TAKASHIMAYA IN TOKIO. (JPN)

● **269** DAS COLLIER-CAMPBELL-ETIKETT IST MIT EINER KORDEL AM UMSCHLAG BEFESTIGT UND IDENTIFIZIERT SEINE HEIMTEXTILIEN-KOLLEKTION FÜR J.P. STEVENS/WEST POINT PEPPERELL. (USA)

▲ **262-264** COUVERTURE ET PAGES DU CATALOGUE PUBLIÉ À L'OCCASION DE L'EXPOSITION «WALTER HAMADY: LIVRES FAITS À LA MAIN, COLLAGES ET SCULPTURES». ON A OPTÉ POUR UNE TYPOGRAPHIE DISCRETE, QUI NE CONCURRENCE PAS L'IMAGE. (USA)

▲ **265-268** COUVERTURE ET DOUBLES PAGES TIRÉES DU CATALOGUE D'UNE EXPOSITION DE CÉRAMIQUES DANS LA GALERIE DU GRAND MAGASIN TAKASHIMAYA À TOKYO. (JPN)

▲ **269** L'ÉTIQUETTE DU COLLIER CAMPBELL EST FIXÉE À LA COUVERTURE PAR UN CORDON ET SERT À L'IDENTIFICATION VISUELLE DE LA COLLECTION DE VETEMENTS DE J.P. STEVENS/WEST POINT PEPPERELL. (USA)

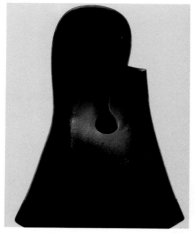

265

266

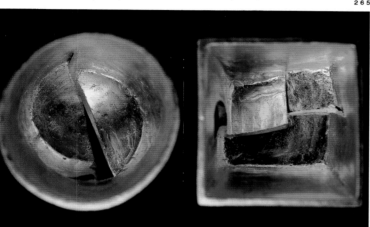

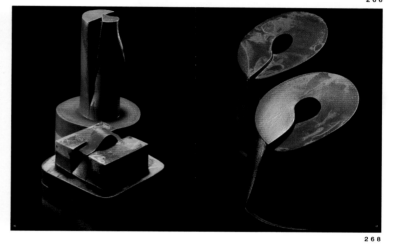

267

268

265-268

ART DIRECTORS:

ICHIRO MITANI

GAKUSHI TANAKA

DESIGNERS:

ICHIRO MITANI

GAKUSHI TANAKA

PHOTOGRAPHER:

ICHIRO MITANI

AGENCY:

OFFICE G

CLIENT:

TAKASHIMAYA

DEPARTMENT STORE

269

269

ART DIRECTOR:

JEAN MCCARTNEY

DESIGNER:

JEAN MCCARTNEY

AGENCY:

WEST POINT

PEPPERELL, INC./

IN-HOUSE

CLIENTS:

J.P. STEVENS

& CO., INC.

WEST POINT

PEPPERELL, INC.

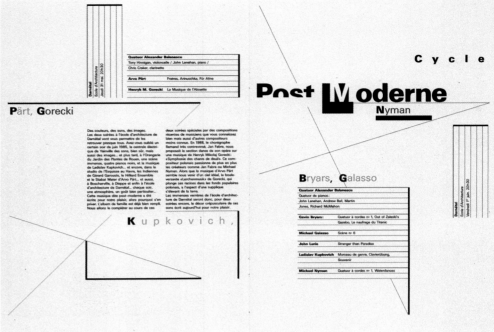

270

271

270, 271

ART DIRECTOR:

PHILIPPE APELOIG

DESIGNER:

PHILIPPE APELOIG

CLIENT:

FESTIVAL D'ÉTÉ DE

SEINE-MARITIME

272, 273

ART DIRECTOR:

GABOR PALOTAI

DESIGNER:

GABOR PALOTAI

AGENCY:

GABOR PALOTAI

DESIGN

CLIENTS:

INTERIÖRHUSET

MÖBLER ETCETERA

272

273

274

275

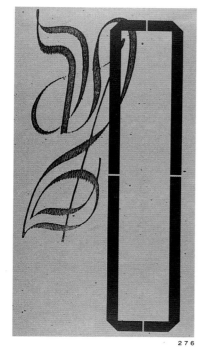

276

274-276

Art Director:

DEL TERRELONGE

Designers:

DEL TERRELONGE

LESLIE SMITH

Photographer:

RON BAXTER SMITH

Agency:

TERRELONGE

DESIGN INC.

Client:

VISUAL PERCEPTION

■ **270, 271** A PROGRAM FOR THE 1991 SUMMER FESTIVAL OF SEINE-MARITIME. EACH SPREAD, DESIGNED IN A SPECIAL WAY, IS DEDICATED TO A DIFFERENT CULTURAL EVENT. THE SUBJECT OF THIS SPREAD IS "POSTMODERN MUSIC." (FRA)

■ **272, 273** CONCERTINA FOLDER SERVING AS THE INVITATION TO A FURNITURE SHOW. SHOWN CLOSED AND OPEN. (SWE)

■ **274-276** SPREADS AND COVER FROM "THE 'YO' BOOK," AN OVERSIZE BROCHURE CREATED AS PART OF A TRAVELING EXHIBITION, "VISUAL PERCEPTIONS." THE DESIGNERS FOR WILSON AND MICHELE WASHINGTON WERE THE CURATORS. "VISUAL PERCEPTIONS" IS DESIGNED TO CHALLENGE GENERALIZATIONS AND STEREOTYPES OF AFRICAN-AMERICANS AS DEPICTED IN THE PRESS. (USA)

● **270, 271** PROGRAMM FÜR DAS SEINE-MARITIME-SOMMER-FESTIVAL 1991. JEDE DOPPELSEITE IST BESONDERS GESTALTET UND INFORMIERT ÜBER DIE VERANSTALTUNGEN, HIER DIE SOGENANNTE POSTMODERNE MUSIK. (FRA)

● **272, 273** GESCHLOSSENER UND GEÖFFNETER LEPORELLO ALS EINLADUNG ZU EINER MÖBELAUSSTELLUNG. (SWE)

● **274-276** GROSSFORMATIGE BROSCHÜRE FÜR EINE AUSSTELLUNG MIT DEM TITEL «VISUELLE WAHRNEHMUNGEN». SIE WURDE VON DER PARSONS SCHOOL OF DESIGN ORGANISIERT, UM DER VERALLGEMEINERNDEN DARSTELLUNG DER AMERIKANER AFRIKANISCHEN URSPRUNGS IN DEN MEDIEN ENTGEGENZUWIRKEN. GEZEIGT SIND DER UMSCHLAG UND ZWEI DOPPELSEITEN. (USA)

▲ **270, 271** COUVERTURE ET PROGRAMME DU FESTIVAL D'ÉTÉ 1991 DE SEINE-MARITIME. CHAQUE SPECTACLE EST PRÉSENTÉ SUR UNE DOUBLE PAGE, FAISANT L'OBJET D'UNE COMPOSITION TYPOGRAPHIQUE À CHAQUE FOIS DIFFÉRENTE. (FRA)

▲ **272, 273** INVITATION À UNE EXPOSITION DE MEUBLES: LE DÉPLIANT UNE FOIS FERMÉ ET OUVERT. (SWE)

▲ **274-276** COUVERTURE ET DOUBLES PAGES D'UNE BROCHURE GÉANTE À RELIURE SPIRALE POUR UNE EXPOSITION INTITULÉE «PERCEPTION VISUELLE». ELLE A ÉTÉ ORGANISÉE PAR LA PARSONS SCHOOL OF DESIGN POUR ESSAYER DE RÉPONDRE AUX CLICHÉS VÉHICULÉS PAR LES MÉDIAS CONCERNANT LA POPULATION D'ORIGINE AFRICAINE AUX ETATS-UNIS. (USA)

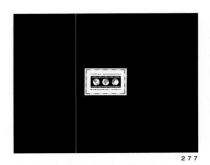

277

278

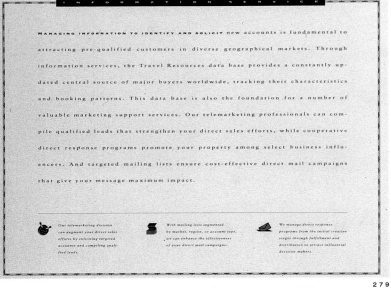

279

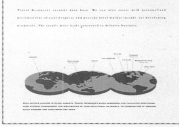

280

281

282

283

277-281

ART DIRECTOR:

PAUL BLACK

DESIGNER:

PAUL BLACK

PHOTOGRAPHER:

ROB DEBENPORT

ILLUSTRATOR:

PAUL BLACK

AGENCY:

THE DESIGN

GROUP–JRSK

CLIENT:

TRAVEL RESOURCES

MANAGEMENT GROUP

282, 283

ART DIRECTOR:

MICHAEL BROCK

DESIGNERS:

MICHAEL BROCK

DAINA HOWARD-KEMP

PHOTOGRAPHER:

ROBERT S. PEAK

ARTIST:

MICHAEL BROCK

AGENCY:

MICHAEL BROCK

DESIGN

CLIENT:

WARNER HOME VIDEO

284

Art Director:
JENNIFER STERLING
Designer:
JENNIFER STERLING
Photographer:
GALLEN MEI
Agency:
COJOTO DESIGN
Client:
FISHBONE STUDIO

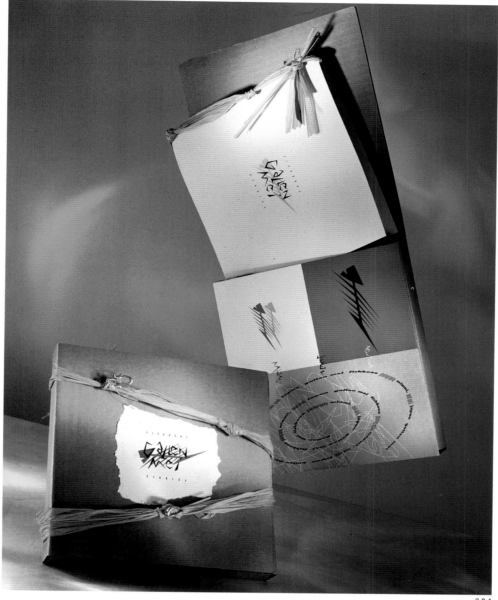

284

■ **277-281** BROCHURE PROMOTING THE TRAVEL RESOURCES MANAGEMENT GROUP, A FIRM SUPPLYING MANAGEMENT SERVICES AND CONSULTING TO THE HOTEL INDUSTRY. EACH SPREAD IS DEDICATED TO A DIFFERENT SERVICE. (USA)

■ **282, 283** PROTECTIVE FOLDER AND COVER OF THE 1991-1992 CATALOG FOR WARNER HOME VIDEOS, FEATURING THE WARNER BROTHERS EMBLEM. (USA)

■ **284** BROCHURE SERIES, PART OF A CORPORATE-IDENTITY PROJECT FOR FISHBONE STUDIOS, A MULTIDISCIPLINE PHOTOGRAPHY STUDIO. THE BROCHURE HAD TO BE ADAPTABLE TO SEVERAL MAILINGS. (USA)

● **277-281** UMSCHLAG UND DOPPELSEITEN EINER BROSCHÜRE FÜR EIN UNTERNEHMEN, DAS DEM HOTELGEWERBE VERSCHIEDENE DIENSTLEISTUNGEN UND BERATUNG ANBIETET. JEDE DOPPELSEITE INFORMIERT ÜBER EINE BESTIMMTE DIENSTLEISTUNG. (USA)

● **282, 283** KARTONHÜLLE UND UMSCHLAG DES WARNER-KATALOGS 1991-1992 FÜR HEIMVIDEOS MIT DEM WARNER-BROTHERS-EMBLEM. (USA)

● **284** EINE REIHE VON BROSCHÜREN ALS TEIL EINES CORPORATE IDENTITY DESIGNS FÜR DAS FISHBONE (FISCHGRÄTEN) PHOTO-STUDIO. SIE MUSSTEN SICH FÜR MEHRERE MAILINGS EIGNEN. (USA)

▲ **277-281** COUVERTURE ET DOUBLES PAGES D'UNE BROCHURE CONÇUE POUR UNE ENTREPRISE QUI PROPOSE DIVERS SERVICES AUX HOTELIERS. CHAQUE DOUBLE PAGE COMPORTE DES INFORMATIONS SUR UNE PRESTATION PARTICULIERE. (USA)

▲ **282, 283** ÉTUI DE CARTON ET COUVERTURE DU CATALOGUE DE VIDÉOS WARNER 1991-1992 ORNÉ DE L'EMBLEME DE LA WARNER-BROTHERS. (USA)

▲ **284** SÉRIE DE BROCHURES FAISANT PARTIE DE L'IDENTITÉ VISUELLE DU STUDIO DE PHOTOGRAPHE FISHBONE (ARETE DE POISSON). ELLES DEVAIENT CONVENIR À PLUSIEURS MAILINGS. (USA)

285

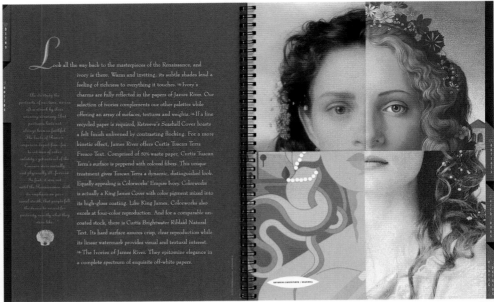

286

285, 286

ART DIRECTOR:
REX PETEET
DESIGNER:
REX PETEET
ARTISTS:
BRYAN LEISTER
REX PETEET
BOBBY BADGER
COPYWRITER:
MARY LANGRIDGE
AGENCY:
SIBLEY/PETEET
DESIGN
CLIENT:
JAMES RIVER CORP.

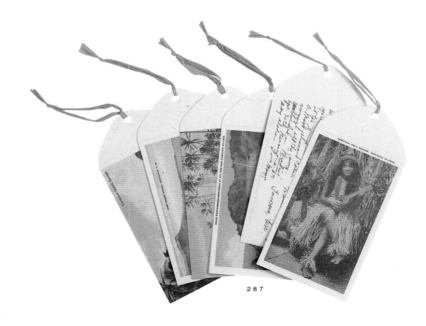

287

287

ART DIRECTOR:
OREN SCHLIEMAN
DESIGNER:
OREN SCHLIEMAN
STUDIO:
INFO GRAFIK
CLIENT:
CANOE CLOTHING
COMPANY

288

289

290

291

288-292

ART DIRECTOR:
GREG SAMATA
DESIGNERS:
PAT SAMATA
GREG SAMATA
ARTIST:
JOHN VAN DYKE
(288, LEFT)
MICHAEL VANDERBYL
(288, RIGHT)
ERIC MADSEN
(289, LEFT)
MCRAY MAGLEBY
(289, RIGHT)

DIANA GRAHAM
(290, LEFT)
APRIL GREIMAN
(290, RIGHT)
SAM SILVIO
(291, LEFT)
JILLY SIMONS
(291, RIGHT)
COPYWRITER:
SAMATA ASSOCIATES
AGENCY:
SAMATA ASSOCIATES
CLIENT:
SAMATA ASSOCIATES

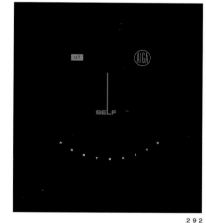

292

■ **285, 286** ALL GRADES OF JAMES RIVER PAPER WERE USED IN THIS BROCHURE, ALLOWING A CUSTOMER TO COMPARE THE GRADES, TEXTURES AND COLORS. THE FACE OF VENUS—A FACE ONE CAN LOOK AT WITHOUT TIRING—WAS CHOSEN AS THE UNIVERSAL FRAME OF REFERENCE. SHOWN ARE THE COVER AND AN INSIDE SPREAD. (USA)

■ **287** THIS SERIES OF LABELS, EACH WITH A RAFFIA RIBBON, WAS USED TO GENERATE PUBLICITY FOR A LINE OF TROPICAL CLOTHES. THE LABELS ARE BASED ON OLD HAND-TINTED HAWAIIAN POSTCARDS. HANDWRITTEN GREETINGS WERE PRINTED ON SEPARATE TRANSPARENT SHEETS ATTACHED TO THE BACKS OF THE CARDS. (USA)

■ **288-292** COVER AND DOUBLE-PAGE SPREADS FROM THE BOOK *92 AIGA SELF-PORTRAITS*, IN WHICH DESIGNERS FROM THE DIFFERENT CHAPTERS OF THE ORGANIZATION LOOK AT WHO THEY ARE. PROCEEDS FROM SALES OF THE BOOK WILL GO TO THE AIGA CHICAGO SCHOLARSHIP FUND FOR PEOPLE INTERESTED IN DESIGN CAREERS. (USA)

● **285, 286** ALLE PAPIERSORTEN VON JAMES RIVER SOLLTEN IN DIESER BROSCHÜRE SO VERWENDET WERDEN, DASS STÄRKEN, STRUKTUR UND FARBEN MITEINANDER VERGLICHEN WERDEN KÖNNEN. DAS GESICHT DER VENUS ERWIES SICH DAFÜR WEGEN SEINES UNIVERSALEN CHARAKTERS UND SEINER SCHÖNHEIT AM GEEIGNETSTEN. (USA)

● **287** DIESE SERIE VON ETIKETTEN, MIT BASTBÄNDERN VERSEHEN, DIENT ALS WERBUNG FÜR EINE KLEIDERLINIE IM TROPENSTIL. ALTE, HANDKOLORIERTE POSTKARTENMOTIVE VON HAWAII DIENEN ALS ILLUSTRATION, HANDGESCHRIEBENE FERIENGRÜSSE WURDEN AUF EIN SEPARATES BLATT TRANSPARENTPAPIER GEDRUCKT. (USA)

● **288-292** UMSCHLAG UND DOPPELSEITEN AUS DEM BUCH «92 SELBSTPORTRÄTS DER AIGA». DESIGNER VERSCHIEDENER AIGA-SEKTIONEN SAGEN IN SELBSTPORTRÄTS, WER SIE SIND. DIE EINNAHMEN AUS DEM VERKAUF DES BUCHES KOMMEN DEM STIPENDIENFOND DER AIGA CHICAGO FÜR GRAPHIK-DESIGN-STUDENTEN ZUGUTE. (USA)

▲ **285-286** CE CATALOGUE PRÉSENTE LES DIFFÉRENTES QUALITÉS DE PAPIER DE JAMES RIVER CORP. LE VISAGE DE VÉNUS A ÉTÉ CHOISI EN RAISON DE SON CARACTERE UNIVERSEL. L'IMAGE VARIE EN FONCTION DES DIVERS SYSTEMES DE SUPERPOSITIONS DES PAGES, AINSI QUE DES TEXTURES ET TEINTES DES PAPIERS EMPLOYÉS. (USA)

▲ **287** CETTE SÉRIE D'ÉTIQUETTES AVEC LIEN EN RAPHIA SERT DE PUBLICITÉ AU FABRICANT D'UNE LIGNE DE VETEMENTS DE STYLE TROPICAL. ON A UTILISÉ D'ANCIENNES CARTES POSTALES COLORÉES ARTISANALEMENT; LE TEXTE ÉCRIT AU VERSO PAR LES TOURISTES A ÉTÉ REPRODUIT SUR UN FEUILLET TRANSPARENT SÉPARÉ. (USA)

▲ **288-292** DU CATALOGUE «92 AUTOPORTRAITS DE L'AIGA»: LES CRÉATEURS DES DIVERSES SECTIONS EXPRIMENT VISUELLEMENT LEUR PERSONNALITÉ SOUS FORME D'AUTOPORTRAITS. LE PRODUIT DE LA VENTE DE CE LIVRE ALIMENTE UN FONDS DE BOURSES DESTINÉES AUX ÉLEVES D'ÉCOLES D'ART GRAPHIQUE. (USA)

293

294

295

■ **293-295** THREE DIRECT-MAIL PIECES ANNOUNCING MUSICAL EVENTS, PRINTED ON CORRUGATED CARDBOARD. (AUT)

■ **296-299** A SERIES OF BROCHURES ILLUS-TRATING THE TECHNICAL SKILLS OF A PRINT-ER. EACH COVER IS PRINTED ON A DIFFER-ENT GRADE AND SHADE OF STOCK, AND GIVES DETAILS ABOUT THE PRINTING OF THE COMPANY SIGN. EACH BROCHURE IS A DEMON-STRATION OF A PRINTING TECHNIQUE, AND EACH PAGE AND EACH PHOTOGRAPH IS ACCOM-PANIED BY DETAILED INFORMATION ON THE PRINTING PROCESS. (USA)

● **293-295** DREI KARTEN AUS WELLKARTON FÜR DIE ANKÜNDIGUNGEN VON MUSIKVERAN-STALTUNGEN. (AUT)

● **296-299** VERSCHIEDENE KLEINE BROSCHÜ-REN, MIT DENEN EINE DRUCKEREI UNTER-SCHIEDLICHE DRUCKVERFAHREN VORSTELLT. FÜR DIE UMSCHLÄGE WURDEN DIVERSE PAPIERQUALITÄTEN VERWENDET, WOBEI AUCH DAS FIRMENZEICHEN AUF VERSCHIE-DENE ART GEDRUCKT WURDE. AUF JEDER SEITE UND NEBEN JEDER ABBILDUNG WER-DEN INFORMATIONEN ÜBER DIE SPEZIELLEN DRUCKTECHNIKEN GEGEBEN. (USA)

▲ **293-295** CARTES ANNONÇANT DIVERS CON-CERTS, IMPRIMÉES SUR DU CARTON ONDULÉ, ENVOYÉES EN PUBLIPOSTAGE. (AUT)

▲ **296-299** SÉRIE DE BROCHURES ILLUS-TRANT LES COMPÉTENCES TECHNIQUES D'UN IMPRIMEUR. CHAQUE COUVERTURE EST RÉA-LISÉE DANS UNE QUALITÉ ET UNE COULEUR DE PAPIER DIFFÉRENTE, LE SIGLE ÉTANT IMPRIMÉ DANS DES COULEURS DIVERSES. CHAQUE BROCHURE EST UNE DÉMONSTRA-TION DE PROCÉDÉS D'IMPRESSION D'UNE HAUTE TECHNICITÉ, AVEC SUR CHAQUE PAGE LES INDICATIONS TECHNIQUES. (USA)

296

297

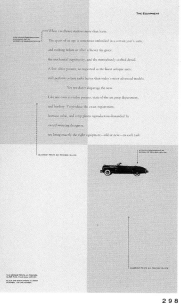

298

299

293-295

Art Director:

KRISTIN KONIAREK

Agency:

ATELIER SCHMÖLZER

Client:

SCHROT + KORN

296-299

Designer:

MICHAEL MABRY

Photographer:

MICHAEL LAMOTTE

Copywriter:

MARCHAND

MARKETING

Studio:

MICHAEL MABRY

DESIGN

Client:

JAMES H. BARRY

COMPANY

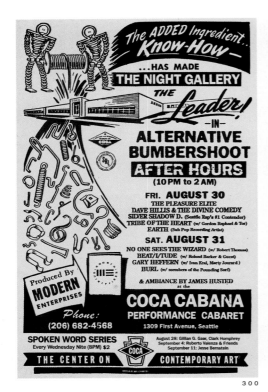

300

301

302

300-302

ART DIRECTOR:

ART CHANTRY

DESIGNER:

ART CHANTRY

CLIENT:

COCA (CENTER OF
CONTEMPORARY ART)

■ 300-302 POSTER-SIZE DIRECT-MAIL FLIERS PRINTED ON NEWSPAPER STOCK, DESIGNED AS A PROMOTION FOR THE CENTER OF CONTEMPORARY ART IN SEATTLE, WASHINGTON. INDUSTRIAL-TOOL NEWSPAPER ADVERTISING FROM THE 1950S WAS TWISTED TO FORM A CYNICAL COMMENT ON AVANT-GARDE CRAZES. (USA)

● 300-302 FÜR DEN POSTVERSAND BESTIMMTE KLEINE PLAKATE AUF ZEITUNGSPAPIER, DIE ALS PROMOTION FÜR VERANSTALTUNGEN VON COCA, EINEM ZENTRUM FÜR ZEITGENÖSSISCHE KUNST, DIENTEN. WERKZEUGWERBUNG AUS DEN FÜNFZIGER JAHREN DIENTE ALS PARODIE AUF EINIGE VERRÜCKTHEITEN DER AVANT-GARDE-KUNST. (USA)

▲ 300-302 SÉRIE DE PETITES AFFICHES DÉPLIANTES SUR PAPIER JOURNAL INVITANT A UNE MANIFESTATION AVANT-GARDISTE, ORGANISÉE PAR LE «COCA», UN CENTRE D'ART CONTEMPORAIN DE SEATTLE, WASHINGTON. ELLES REPRENNENT DES MOTIFS D'ANCIENNES RÉCLAMES DE JOURNAUX DES ANNÉES CINQUANTE. (USA)

EDITORIAL DESIGN

REDAKTIONELLES DESIGN

DESIGN DE PERIODIQUES

303

304

303-305

ART DIRECTOR:

DOUGLAS MAY

DESIGNER:

CANDACE BUCHANAN

AGENCY:

MAY & CO.

CLIENT:

PAGING NETWORK,

INC.

■ 303-305 COVERS OF PAGING NETWORK'S HOUSE ORGAN, *BEEPS & VIBES*. THE ILLUSTRATIONS REFER TO THE COMPANY'S NEW ADDRESS, TO ITS BECOMING THE NATION'S LARGEST PAGING COMPANY, AND TO ITS TENTH ANNIVERSARY. (USA)

● 303-305 UMSCHLÄGE DER HAUSZEITSCHRIFT *BEEPS & VIBES* DER FIRMA PAGING NETWORK. DIE THEMEN: DIE NEUE ADRESSE AN DER WALL STREET; DIE FÜHRENDE POSITION (ELEKTRONISCHE SUCHGERÄTE) UND DAS 10JÄHRIGE BESTEHEN. (USA)

▲ 303-305 COUVERTURES DE BEEPS & VIBES, LE MAGAZINE DE LA FIRME PAGING NETWORK (SYSTEMES DE DÉTECTION ÉLECTRONIQUE). LES SUJETS ÉTAIENT: LA NOUVELLE ADRESSE À WALL STREET, LA POSITION DE LEADER ET LES 10 ANS DE L'ENTREPRISE. (USA)

PAGING NETWORK, INC. VOL. 1 NO. 2

'81

Commemorative Issue

10 Years and

1,000,000

Pagers Sold

INSIDE THIS ISSUE:

MILESTONES:
Terry Scott tallies PageNet's growth

GREAT BEGINNINGS:
George Perrin tells the whole story

TIMEZONES:
Regional scrapbooks

FACES BEHIND THE SCENES:
Who's the girl with the Southern drawl?

THE RANKS:
The race is on for the 2nd Quarter of '91

ON THE MOVE:
Who's climbing the ladder to success

BEEP, BEEP WHO'S THERE?:
The Best of the Beeper Stories

LIFE AFTER 5:
Beeps, Bunts and Bruises

'91

305

ABITO DI VOILE CON POLSI BRODÉ E GONNA A PIÙ STRATI, VALENTINO COUTURE. COLLANT MALERBA; SCARPE LERRE. NELLA PAGINA ACCANTO, CAPPOTTO DI VELLUTO CON REVERS BRODÉ, MARTINE SITBON. CAPPELLO BIANCA E BLU. FASHION EDITOR ALICE GENTILUCCI.

gonne tutù, body brodé: uno stile tra note classiche e ritmi moderni

BALLET

306

306-310

ART DIRECTOR:

LUCA STOPPINI

PHOTOGRAPHERS:

ELLEN VON

UNWERTH (306)

ALFA CASTALDI (307)

BRUNO RINALDI (307)

FARABOLA (308)

TIZIANO MAGNI (309)

BALENCIAGA (310)

CLIENT:

VOGUE ITALIA

PUBLISHER:

EDIZIONE CONDÉ

NAST S.P.A.

■ **306-310** THE SUBJECTS OF THESE SINGLE- AND DOUBLE-PAGE EXAMPLES FROM *VOGUE ITALIA* ARE AS FOLLOWS: FASHION INSPIRED BY THE BALLET; FASHION IN CIRCUS STYLE; GIANNI AGNELLI, "MR. FIAT," AND HIS WIFE; BEACHWEAR; FASHION BY BALENCIAGA. (ITA)

● **306-310** DIE THEMEN DIESER EINZEL- UND DOPPELSEITEN AUS *VOGUE ITALIA* SIND: VOM BALLETT INSPIRIERTE MODE; MODE IM ZIRKUS-STIL; «MR. FIAT» GIANNI AGNELLI UND SEINE FRAU; STRANDMODE; MODE VON BALENCIAGA. (ITA)

▲ **306-310** PAGES DE VOGUE ITALIA ILLUSTRANT LES SUJETS SUIVANTS: UNE MODE INSPIRÉE PAR LA DANSE CLASSIQUE ET LE CIRQUE; «MONSIEUR FIAT» GIANNI AGNELLI ET SA FEMME; LES NOUVEAUX MAILLOTS DE BAIN; LA MODE DE BALENCIAGA. (ITA)

Moda-Circo. Vestirsi da «clown bianco» con i costumi più fastosi, o da «augusto» con i colori e i patterns più irridenti? Nella moda autunno-inverno '91-'92 circola aria di circo. Federico Fellini e Thierry Mugler...

D. P.
di Anna Piaggi

307

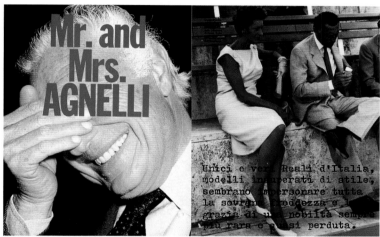

308

*neo-fantasie
per bikini
shorts e
accappatoi*

309

310

311

312

Does it exist — or
do bad things just happen?

200TH ANNIVERSARY

313

314

311, 312

ART DIRECTORS:

RUDOLPH HOGLUND (311)

MIRKO ILIC (312)

DESIGNERS:

ARTHUR HOCHSTEIN (311)

MIRKO ILIC (311)

LOUISE FILI (312)

ARTIST:

MARK SUMMERS (312)

PUBLISHER:

TIME

313, 314

ART DIRECTOR:

PAUL DAVIS

DESIGNERS:

ALEX GINNS (314)

RISA ZAITSCHEK (313)

PHOTOGRAPHER:

ANDREW BRUCKER (313)

ARTIST:

ALEXA GRACE (314)

CLIENT:

WIGWAG

TOM MIX BY DEAN LEONARD HAT SHOP, LUBBOCK; BEAVER, $150

SAN ANTONE BY RESISTOL HATS, GARLAND; STRAW, $60

112 MAY 1991

315

315

ART DIRECTOR:
D.J. STOUT
DESIGNER:
D.J. STOUT
PHOTOGRAPHER:
RAYMOND MEIER
PUBLISHER:
TEXAS MONTHLY

■ 311, 312 TWO VERY DIFFERENT COVERS OF TIME MAGAZINE ON TWO VERY DIFFERENT SUBJECTS: THE QUESTION OF THE EXISTENCE OF EVIL AND THE 200TH ANNIVERSARY OF MOZART'S DEATH. (USA)

■ 313, 314 COVERS OF WIGWAG, A GENERAL-INTEREST MAGAZINE THAT HAS SINCE SUSPENDED PUBLICATION. THE FEBRUARY 1991 ISSUE, WITH ITS VALENTINE'S DAY THEME, WAS THE LAST ISSUE. (USA)

■ 315 SPREAD FROM AN ARTICLE ON HATS IN TEXAS MONTHLY. (USA)

● 311, 312 «EXISTIERT DAS BÖSE, ODER PASSIEREN SCHLECHTE DINGE EINFACH?» UND MOZARTS 200STER GEBURTSTAG IM JAHRE 1991 – THEMEN VON UMSCHLÄGEN DER ZEITSCHRIFT TIME. (USA)

● 313, 314 UMSCHLÄGE FÜR WIGWAG, EIN UNTERHALTUNGSMAGAZIN, DAS NICHT MEHR ERSCHEINT. DIE LETZTE AUSGABE WAR DIE VOM FEBRUAR 1991 MIT DEM VALENTINSTAG-THEMA. (USA)

● 315 DOPPELSEITE MIT HUTMODE AUS TEXAS MONTHLY. (USA)

▲ 311, 312 «LE MAL – EXISTE-T-IL OU LES MAUVAISES CHOSES ARRIVENT-ELLES TOUT SIMPLEMENT?» ET LE 200E ANNIVERSAIRE DE LA NAISSANCE DE MOZART EN 1991: COUVERTURES DU MAGAZINE TIME. (USA)

▲ 313, 314 COUVERTURES DE WIGWAG, UN MAGAZINE QUI A DEPUIS CESSÉ DE PARAITRE. LE DERNIER NUMÉRO, CELUI DE FÉVRIER 1991, ÉTAIT CONSACRÉ AU THEME DE LA SAINT VALENTIN. (USA)

▲ 315 LES NOUVEAUX CHAPEAUX À LA MODE; D'UN ARTICLE DU TEXAS MONTHLY. (USA)

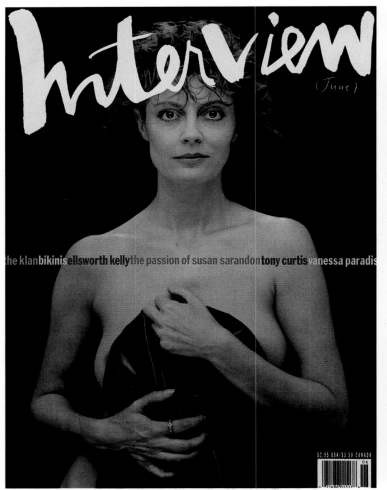

316

317

316, 317

EDITOR:

INGRID SISCHY

CREATIVE DIRECTOR:

TIBOR KALMAN

DESIGNERS:

RICHARD

PANDISCIO (316)

KRISTIN JOHNSON (317)

PHOTOGRAPHERS:

ROBERT

MAPPLETHORPE (316)

STEVEN MEISEL (317)

PHOTO EDITOR:

SUZANNE DONALDSON

PUBLISHER:

INTERVIEW

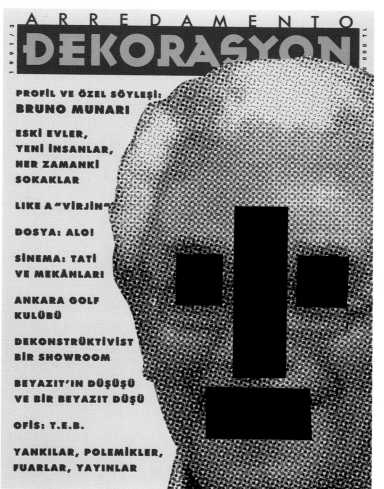

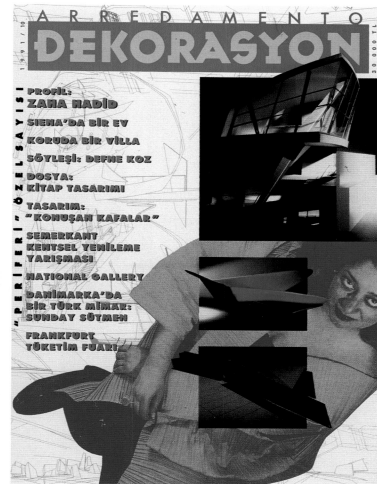

318

319

318, 319
ART DIRECTOR:
BÜLENT ERKMEN
DESIGNER:
BÜLENT ERKMEN
ILLUSTRATOR:
BÜLENT ERKMEN
AGENCY:
REKLAMEVI/YOUNG
& RUBICAM
CLIENT:
DEKORASYON
PUBLISHER:
BOYUT PUBLISHING
GROUP

■ **316, 317** COVERS OF *INTERVIEW* MAGAZINE, WITH PORTRAITS OF SUSAN SARANDON AND LIZA MINELLI. (USA)

■ **318, 319** COVERS OF THE TURKISH DESIGN MAGAZINE *DEKORASYON*, FEATURING ARTICLES ON THE 84-YEAR-OLD ITALIAN DESIGNER BRUNO MUNARI AND THE FEMALE ARCHITECT ZAHA HADID. (TUR)

● **316, 317** UMSCHLÄGE DER ZEITSCHRIFT *INTERVIEW* MIT PORTRÄTS VON SUSAN SARANDON UND LIZA MINELLI. (USA)

● **318, 319** UMSCHLÄGE DER ZEITSCHRIFT *DEKORASYON*. SIE BEZIEHEN SICH AUF BEITRÄGE ÜBER DEN 84JÄHRIGEN ITALIENISCHEN DESIGNER BRUNO MUNARI UND DIE ARCHITEKTIN ZAHA HADID. (TUR)

▲ **316, 317** COUVERTURES DU MAGAZINE *INTERVIEW* AVEC LES PORTRAITS DE SUSAN SARANDON ET LIZA MINELLI. (USA)

▲ **318, 319** COUVERTURES DU MAGAZINE DE DESIGN TURC *DEKORASYON*. ELLES CONCERNENT DES ARTICLES SUR LE DESIGNER ITALIEN BRUNO MUNARI ET L'ARCHITECTE ZAHA HADID. (TUR)

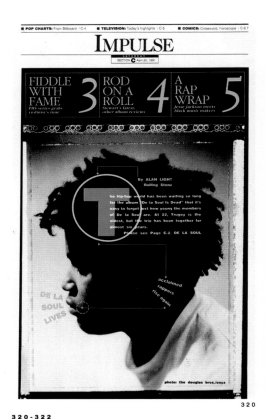

320

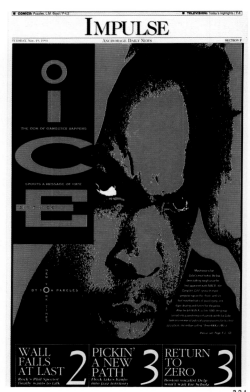

321

322

320-322

ART DIRECTOR:

JEAN-LOUIS GALIE

DESIGNER:

JEAN-LOUIS GALIE

ILLUSTRATOR:

JEAN-LOUIS GALIE

CLIENT:

ANCHORAGE DAILY NEWS

323

ART DIRECTOR:

LUCA STOPPINI

PHOTOGRAPHER:

STEVEN MEISEL

CLIENT:

VOGUE ITALIA

PUBLISHER:

EDIZIONE CONDÉ
NAST S.P.A.

■ 320-322 COVERS FOR IMPULSE, THE ANCHORAGE DAILY NEWS'S ENTERTAINMENT SECTION, DESIGNED TO ATTRACT YOUNGER READERS. (USA)

■ 323 COVER OF A SPECIAL SUPPLEMENT TO VOGUE ITALIA, PRESENTING THE SPRING/SUMMER 1992 COLLECTIONS OF THE MAJOR INTERNATIONAL FASHION HOUSES. (ITA)

● 320-322 UMSCHLÄGE FÜR DIE RUBRIK «IMPULSE», UNTERHALTUNGSTEIL EINER ZEITUNG, DER EINE JÜNGERE LESERSCHAFT ERREICHEN SOLL. (USA)

● 323 UMSCHLAG FÜR EINE SONDERBEILAGE VON VOGUE ITALIA, IN DER ALLE KOLLEKTIONEN DER GROSSEN MODEFIRMEN FÜR FRÜHJAHR/SOMMER 1992 GEZEIGT WERDEN. (ITA)

▲ 320-322 COUVERTURES DE LA RUBRIQUE «IMPULSE», CONSACRÉE AUX LOISIRS, DU ANCHORAGE DAILY NEWS, UN JOURNAL QUI VISE UN PUBLIC JEUNE. (USA)

▲ 323 COUVERTURE D'UN SUPPLÉMENT DE VOGUE ITALIA DANS LEQUEL SONT PRÉSENTÉES TOUTES LES COLLECTIONS PRINTEMPS/ÉTÉ 1992 DES GRANDS COUTURIERS. (ITA)

VOGUE

100 sfilate

COMPLETO RIFAT OZBEK

323

324

325

324, 325

Art Director:

HANS WOLF

Designer:

BAS VAN DER PAARDT

Photographer:

MARC ASCOLI (324)

PETER HERMUS (325)

Illustrator:

MILOU HERMUS (325)

Editor:

RONALD KRAAYEVELD

Client:

BLAD

Publisher:

VNU TIJDSCHRIFTENGROEP

■ **324, 325** COVERS OF *BLAD* MAGAZINE. ONE TOUTS A SPECIAL FASHION PRIZE AWARDED BY THE MAGAZINE, THE OTHER ANNOUNCES A FEATURE ON THE WORK OF THE ILLUSTRATOR AND PAINTER MILOU HERMUS. (NLD)

■ **326-328** THREE COVERS FROM THE SATIRICAL SWISS MAGAZINE *NEBELSPALTER*: "ART SCENE 1991" REFERS TO THE SUPPORT THE MAGAZINE OFFERS ART COLLECTORS IN THE CONFUSING ART MARKET; "NAILING COLORS TO THE MAST" REFERS TO THE COLORS OF POLITICAL PARTIES; THE THIRD COVER IS A NEW VERSION OF "HIS MASTER'S VOICE." (SWI)

● **324, 325** UMSCHLÄGE VON *BLAD*. SIE BEZIEHEN SICH AUF DEN VON DER ZEITSCHRIFT VERGEBENEN MODEPREIS UND AUF EINEN BEITRAG ÜBER DIE ARBEIT DER ILLUSTRATORIN/MALERIN MILOU HERMUS. (NLD)

● **326-328** UMSCHLÄGE DES SATIRISCHEN MAGAZINS *NEBELSPALTER*. «KUNSTSZENE 91» BEZIEHT SICH AUF DEN SCHWIERIGEN KUNSTMARKT UND DIE VON DER ZEITSCHRIFT GEBOTENE ORIENTIERUNGSHILFE; MIT «FARBE BEKENNEN» IST DIE POLITISCHE COULEUR GEMEINT; DIE SPEZIELLE VERSION VON «HIS MASTER'S VOICE» HAT KEINEN DIREKTEN BEZUG ZUM INHALT. (SWI)

▲ **324, 325** COUVERTURES DE *BLAD*. ELLES CONCERNENT LE PRIX DE LA MODE DÉCERNÉ PAR LE MAGAZINE ET UN ARTICLE SUR LES CRÉATIONS DE L'ILLUSTRATRICE ET PEINTRE MILOU HERMUS. (NLD)

▲ **326-328** TROIS COUVERTURES DU *NEBELSPALTER*, UN JOURNAL SATIRIQUE SUISSE. «LA SCENE ARTISTIQUE EN 1991»: POUR UN NUMÉRO OU IL EST QUESTION DE LA DIFFICILE SITUATION DU MARCHÉ DE L'ART ET DES CHOIX QUI S'OFFRENT AUX COLLECTIONNEURS; «ANNONCER LA COU-LEUR» (POLITIQUE); UNE INTERPRÉTATION DE «LA VOIX DE SON MAITRE». (SWI)

326

326-328
ART DIRECTOR:
WERNER MEIER
ARTISTS:
ROUMEN SIMEONOV
(326)
BORISLAV STANKOVIĆ
(327)
JIRI SLIVA(328)
PUBLISHER:
NEBELSPALTER

327

328

329

330

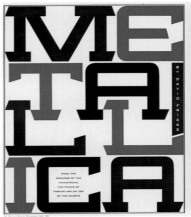

331

332

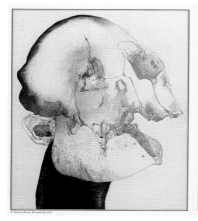
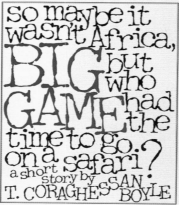
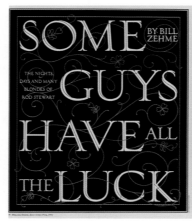

333

334

329-335

ART DIRECTOR:
FRED WOODWARD

PHOTOGRAPHY DIRECTOR:
LAURIE KRATOCHVIL

DESIGNERS:
DEBRA BISHOP (329,
330, 335)
FRED WOODWARD (331)
ANGELA SKOURAS (332)

PHOTOGRAPHERS:
ANDREW ECCLES
(329, 334)

DAN WINTERS (330)
DIEGO UCHITEL (331)
MARK SELIGER (332)
HERB RITTS (335)

ILLUSTRATOR:
ALAN E. COBER (333)

LETTERING:
ANITA KARL (329, 330)

CLIENT:
ROLLING STONE

PUBLISHER:
STRAIGHT ARROW
PUBLISHERS

Men are in crisis,
whereas he is not.
He does not know
the meaning of
"crisis." Or perhaps

MR.

BigSHOT

he does, but he
pretends otherwise.
He is Austrian,
after all, and some

By Bill Zehme

38 · ROLLING STONE, AUGUST 22ND, 1991

PHOTOGRAPH BY HERB RITTS

335

■ **329-335** OPENING SPREADS FOR FEATURE ARTICLES IN *ROLLING STONE* MAGAZINE ON THE RAP STAR VANILLA ICE; FATHER MATTHEW FOX, A CONTROVERSIAL CATHOLIC PRIEST; THE ROCK MUSICIAN ROBBIE ROBERTSON; KIRK HAMMETT, LARS ULRICH, JASON NEWSTED AND JAMES HETFIELD OF THE GROUP METALLICA; AN AFRICAN GAME RANCH IN AMERICA; ROD STEWART; AND THE AUSTRIAN-BORN ACTOR AND DIRECTOR ARNOLD SCHWARZENEGGER. (USA)

● **329-335** AUFMACHERSEITEN ZU BEITRÄGEN IN DER ZEITSCHRIFT *ROLLING STONE*. DIE THEMEN: RAP-STAR VANILLA ICE; EIN KONTROVERSER KATHOLISCHER PFARRER AUS DEN USA; GITARRIST ROBBIE ROBERTSON (THE BAND); KIRK HAMMETT, LARS ULRICH, JASON NEWSTED UND JAMES HETFIELD VON DER GRUPPE METALLICA; EINE KURZGESCHICHTE, DIE IN EINEM SAFARI-PARK IN DEN USA SPIELT; BODYBUILDER UND SCHAUSPIELER ARNOLD SCHWARZENEGGER. (USA)

▲ **329-335** OUVERTURES D'ARTICLES PUBLIÉS DANS LE MAGAZINE *ROLLING STONE*. LA STAR DU RAP, VANILLA ICE; UN PRETRE CATHOLIQUE CONTROVERSÉ AUX USA; ROBBIE ROBERTSON; KIRK HAMMETT, LARS ULRICH, JASON NEWSTED ET JAMES HETFIELD, DU GROUPE METALLICA; UNE NOUVELLE AYANT POUR CADRE UN PARC DE SAFARI DES ÉTATS-UNIS, ARNOLD SCHWARZENEGGER, GRANDE VEDETTE INTERNATIONALE DU CULTURISME ET ACTEUR DE CINÉMA. (USA)

THE URBAN MAGAZINE OF ARCHITECTURE AND DESIGN

METROPOLIS

SEPTEMBER 1991 $4.50

GRAND CENTRAL
INFORMATION
PLASTICS
FURNITURE FAIR

GILLIAM
GOTHAM
& GOD

337

START WITH AN
ASSUMPTION. A
RASH ASSUMPTION·
WE ARE BECOMING
A CULTURE OF THE
PICTURE RATHER
THAN OF THE WORD.
IS IT TRUE OR FALSE?
IS IT GOOD OR BAD? ➜

by Karrie Jacobs

338

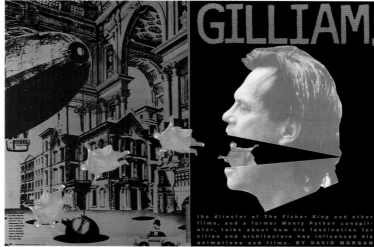

GILLIAM,

the director of *The Fisher King* and other films, and a former Monty Python conspirator, talks about how his fascination for cities and architecture has influenced his animations and films. BY DAVID MORGAN

339

tiny

tokyo's

houses

by naomi pollock

340

saint or
sinner?

louis
kahn

Thanks to a new museum retrospective, Louis I. Kahn has joined the pantheon of architectural greats. As his reputation soars, however, a question arises: should his daunting legacy become today's gospel?

by barbara flanagan

Was it an eyesore or masterpiece? In the late 1960s, while the University of Pennsylvania debated whether to leave or raze or whitewash the ugly Victorian castle brooding over its campus, students filed up stairs to Louis Kahn's studio, high in the building's tower over the old library, to learn to make a timeless architecture that

341

337-341

ART DIRECTORS:
CARL LEHMANN-HAUPT
NANCY COHEN
DESIGNERS:
CARL LEHMANN-HAUPT
NANCY COHEN
PHOTOGRAPHERS:
DAN WINTERS (337, 341)
JAMES HAMILTON (337)
YUTAKA SUZUKI (340)
EDITORS:
MARISA BARTOLUCCI
(339, 341)
SUSAN SZENASY (338, 340)
CLIENT:
METROPOLIS
PUBLISHER:
HORACE HAVEMEYER III

■ **337-341** COVER AND OPENING SPREADS FOR *METROPOLIS* MAGAZINE ON THE CULTURAL EFFECT OF PICTURES AND SYMBOLS; THE DIRECTOR TERRY GILLIAM AND HIS THOUGHTS ON ART, ARCHITECTURE AND HIS FILM *THE FISHER KING*; INNOVATIVE BUILDINGS DESIGNED TO DEAL WITH TOKYO'S DESPERATE SHORTAGE OF SPACE; AND A REEXAMINATION OF LOUIS KAHN'S ARCHITECTURE AND THEORIES. (USA)

● **337-341** UMSCHLAG UND AUFMACHERSEITEN DES ARCHITEKTURMAGAZINS *METROPOLIS*. DIE THEMEN: DIE STILLE SPRACHE VON BILDERN UND SYMBOLEN; REGISSEUR TERRY GILLIAM UND SEINE THEORIEN ÜBER KUNST UND ARCHITEKTUR SOWIE SEIN FILM *THE FISHER KING*; INNOVATIVE GEBÄUDE IN TOKIO, DIE DEM PLATZMANGEL BEGEGNEN; EINE NEUE SICHT DER THEORIEN UND DES WERKES DES ARCHITEKTEN LOUIS KAHN. (USA)

▲ **337-341** DOUBLES PAGES INTRODUISANT DES ARTICLES DANS *METROPOLIS*. LE LANGAGE SILENCIEUX DES IMAGES ET DES SYMBOLES; LE METTEUR EN SCÈNE TERRY GILLIAM, SES THÉORIES SUR L'ART ET L'ARCHITECTURE, ET SON FILM *THE FISHER KING*; LES INNOVATIONS LIÉES AU MANQUE D'ESPACE DANS L'ARCHITECTURE JAPONAISE; L'ŒUVRE ET LES THÉORIES DE L'ARCHITECTE LOUIS KAHN VUES SOUS UN AUTRE ANGLE. (USA)

342

343

342, 343

DESIGNER:

SABINE KRANZ

344-346

ART DIRECTORS:

JEANNE ARNOLD (344)

JIM HINCHEE (345, 346)

DESIGN CONSULTANT:

RON ALBRECHT

PHOTOGRAPHER:

GREG WATERMAN

CLIENT:

LEAR'S

■ 342, 343 STUDENT WORK. THE OPENING AND FOLLOWING SPREAD FOR AN IMAGINARY MAGAZINE FEATURE ON THE SUBJECT OF WALKING. (GER)

■ 344-346 THREE COVERS FROM *LEAR'S*, THE MAGAZINE "FOR THE WOMAN WHO WASN'T BORN YESTERDAY." THE WOMEN, FROM TOP TO BOTTOM, ARE: JERILYNN R. HANSON, A MARKETING DIRECTOR; CHARLOTTE PRITT, A WEST VIRGINIA STATE SENATOR; AND JOAN M. FARKAS, A STOCKBROKER. (USA)

● 342, 343 STUDIENPROJEKT. HIER DIE AUFMACHER- UND EINE DOPPELSEITE FÜR EINEN FIKTIVEN MAGAZINARTIKEL ZUM THEMA «GEHEN». (GER)

● 344-346 DREI UMSCHLÄGE FÜR *LEAR'S*, EINE ZEITSCHRIFT FÜR FRAUEN, «DIE NICHT VON GESTERN SIND». ABGEBILDET SIND (VON OBEN NACH UNTEN): JERILYNN R. HANSON, MARKETING DIREKTORIN; CHARLOTTE PRITT, SENATORIN VON WEST VIRGINIA; JOAN M. FARKAS, BÖRSENMAKLERIN. (USA)

▲ 342, 343 PROJET D'UNE ÉTUDIANTE POUR UN ARTICLE DE MAGAZINE SUR LE THÈME «ALLER», AVEC L'INTRODUCTION ET UNE DOUBLE PAGE. (GER)

▲ 344-346 COUVERTURES DE *LEAR'S*, LE MAGAZINE DESTINÉ AUX FEMMES «QUI NE SONT PAS D'HIER». DE HAUT EN BAS: JERILYNN R. HANSON, DIRECTRICE DE MARKETING; CHARLOTTE PRITT, SÉNATRICE DE LA VIRGINIE DE L'OUEST; JOAN M. FARKAS, AGENTE À LA BOURSE. (USA)

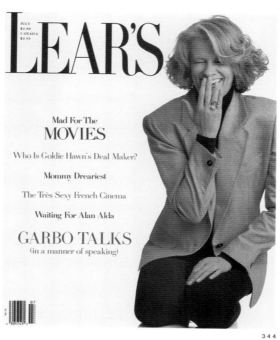

JULY
$2.00
CANADA
$3.95

LEAR'S

Mad For The
MOVIES

Who Is Goldie Hawn's Deal Maker?

Mommy Dreariest

The Très Sexy French Cinema

Waiting For Alan Alda

GARBO TALKS
(in a manner of speaking)

344

The Non-Nuke   APRIL   Jessica Tandy:
$3.00
Family: What   CANADA   What Drives
$3.95
the Law Allows # LEAR'S   the Real Daisy?

Intimate Scenes from an   Playing the Global

Eccentric Marriage   Market Now

See-Through   Survival in

Fashionables   Addiction

Fay Weldon's   Remembrance

Tale of the Unexpected   of Mary McCarthy

345

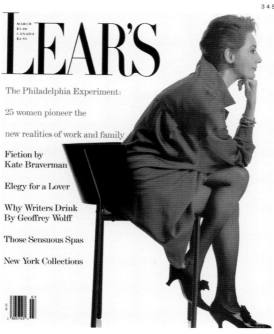

MARCH
$3.00
CANADA
$2.95

LEAR'S

The Philadelphia Experiment:

25 women pioneer the

new realities of work and family

**Fiction by
Kate Braverman**

Elegy for a Lover

**Why Writers Drink
By Geoffrey Wolff**

Those Sensuous Spas

New York Collections

346

IN QUESTE PAGINE. MINIABITO E DUE PEZ-ZI DI PIZZO MACRAMÉ COLORATO; SABOTS DI SHANTUNG; TUTTO AL-BERTA FERRETTI. FA-SHION EDITOR CARLYNE CERF DE DUDZEELE.

347

347, 348

ART DIRECTOR:

LUCA STOPPINI

PHOTOGRAPHERS:

STEVEN MEISEL (347)

ROXANNE LOWIT (348)

RONALD STOOPS (348)

BARBARA KATZ (348)

ALFA CASTALDI (348)

CLIENT:

VOGUE ITALIA

PUBLISHER:

EDIZIONE CONDÉ NAST

S.P.A.

Anni '80! Rei Kawaku-bo, Yohji Yamamoto scuotono il fashion establishment con abiti destrutturati, make-up lividi, definiti «post Hiroshima». In Inghilterra, Boy George, i New Romantics e movimenti post-punk sollecitano la «necessità» di coraggiosi look individuali. Nell'estate '89, il belga Martin Margiela presenta a Parigi la sua prima collezione. Inizia con lui un Cido di Nuovo Recupero di materiali e indumenti: gilet fatti con poster

NEW UNDERGROUND

Cappello «gabbia» realizzato da Philip Treacy per Chanel Haute Couture. Nella pagina accanto. Stivali di Martin Margiela.

D.P. di Anna Piaggi

348

■ **347, 348** SPREADS FROM TWO ISSUES OF *VOGUE ITALIA*, ONE SHOWING A MACRAMÉ MINI-DRESS AND TWO-PIECE BY ALBERTA FERRETTI, THE OTHER SHOWING UNDERGROUND FASHIONS OF THE 1980S. (ITA)

● **347, 348** DOPPELSEITEN AUS ZWEI AUSGABEN VON *VOGUE ITALIA*. VORGESTELLT WERDEN MINIMODE IN MACRAMÉ VON ALBERTA FERRETTI UND DIE UNTERGRUNDMODE DER ACHTZIGER JAHRE. (ITA)

▲ **347, 348** DOUBLES PAGES DE DEUX NUMÉROS DE *VOGUE ITALIA*. LA PREMIERE MONTRE DEUX VETEMENTS MINI EN MACRAMÉ D'ALBERTA FERRETTI, L'AUTRE LA MODE UNDERGROUND DES ANNÉES 80. (ITA)

141

349

350

349-354

Art Director:

LUCA STOPPINI

Photographers:

STEVEN MEISEL (350, 351)

GRAZIA NERI/*LIFE*

MAGAZINE (352)

ELLEN VON UNWERTH (353)

BRUNO RINALDI (354)

Still Life:

ALFA CASTALDI

Client:

VOGUE ITALIA

Publisher:

EDIZIONE CONDÉ NAST

S.P.A.

■ 349-354 A SINGLE PAGE, A COVER AND SEVERAL SPREADS FROM *VOGUE ITALIA*: NEW FASHION STYLES AND TRENDS; THE NEW SENSUAL WOMAN; AVA GARDNER AND DIZZY GILLESPIE IN 1948, FOR A FEATURE ON THE SCANDALS OF STARS; THE ACTRESS DEBBIE MAZAR; AND THE HISTORY OF ZIPPERS IN FASHION. (ITA)

● 349-354 AUFMACHERSEITE, UMSCHLAG UND DOPPELSEITEN FÜR *VOGUE ITALIA*. DIE THEMEN SIND DIE NEUEN MODETRENDS; DIE NEUE SINNLICHE FRAU; DIE SKANDALE DER STARS (GEZEIGT SIND AVA GARDNER UND DIZZY GILLESPIE 1948); DIE SCHAUSPIELERIN DEBBIE MAZAR; DIE GESCHICHTE DER REISSVERSCHLUSSMODE. (ITA)

▲ 349-354 PAGE D'INTRODUCTION, COUVERTURE ET DOUBLES PAGES DE VOGUE ITALIA: LES NOUVELLES TENDANCES DE LA MODE, LA NOUVELLE FEMME SENSUELLE, LES SCANDALES DES STARS (ICI, AVA GARDNER ET DIZZY GILLESPIE EN 1948), L'ACTRICE DEBBIE MAZAR, UNE HISTOIRE «ECLAIR» DE LA FERMETURE ECLAIR. (ITA)

con
particolari
sofisticati:
nuova
vamp

boa di marabù, bordi di
visone, polsi di
zibellino per delineare
una femminilità sensuale
e nello stesso tempo
aggressiva.

351

Tra gossip e retroscena

SCANDALI da STAR

Per ogni divo la sua biografia. O l'autobiografia. Quello di rovistare dietro le quinte delle vite famose è un imponente fenomeno editoriale e di costume. Tra i casi recenti dall'America: i Barrymore e Jean Harlow, Paul Newman e Ava Gardner. Ed è ormai impossibile sottrarsi alla curiosità di scrittori-detective. Che portano a galla virtù e vizi segreti.

352

DEBBIE BLUE

Uno sguardo intenso come quello di Lauren Bacall. Una bellezza esotica e magnetica alla Jane Russell. Dopo la sua apparizione in «Goodfellas» e nel nuovo «Jungle Fever», Debbie Mazar è ora il nome «hot» del cinema Usa.

EYES

353

storia lampo

della cerniera

D.P. di Anna Piaggi

354

home format   egoyan talks with deborah esch

355-358

ART DIRECTOR:
MARGO CHASE
DESIGNER:
MARGO CHASE
AGENCY:
MARGO CHASE DESIGN
CLIENT:
SEMIOTEXT(E)

359, 360

ART DIRECTOR:
JOHN HORNALL
DESIGNERS:
JULIA LAPINE
JOHN HORNALL
HEIDI HATLESTAD
DAVID BATES
LIAN NG
ILLUSTRATORS:
JERRY NELSON (359)
JUD GUITTEAU (360)

AGENCY:
HORNALL ANDERSON
DESIGN WORKS
CLIENT:
ROBERTS, FITZMAHAN
& ASSOC.
PUBLISHER:
COMPREHENSIVE
HEALTH EDUCATION
FOUNDATION

 355-358 TWO FOUR-PAGE ARTICLES FOR A SPECIAL "EXPERIMENTAL DESIGN" ISSUE OF SEMIOTEXT(E) MAGAZINE, FEATURING THE WORK OF SEVERAL PROMINENT GRAPHIC DESIGNERS. (USA)

■ 359, 360 COVERS FOR HERE AND NOW MAGAZINE, WHICH ADDRESSES SUCH ISSUES AS ALCOHOL, TOBACCO AND MARIJUANA DEPENDENCE, AND IS DESIGNED TO BE PART OF A DRUG-EDUCATION CURRICULUM FOR FOURTH- TO NINTH-GRADE STUDENTS. (USA)

● 355-358 ZWEI VIERSEITIGE ARTIKEL FÜR EINE SONDERAUSGABE ÜBER «EXPERIMENTELLES DESIGN» DER ZEITSCHRIFT SEMIOTEXT(E), IN DER ARBEITEN PROMINENTER DESIGNER GEZEIGT WURDEN. (USA)

● 359, 360 UMSCHLÄGE DER ZEITSCHRIFT HERE AND NOW. SIE IST TEIL DER DROGENAUFKLÄRUNG IN SCHULEN UND RICHTET SICH AN VERSCHIEDENE ALTERSSTUFEN. DIE THEMEN: ABHÄNGIGKEIT VON ALKOHOL, TABAK UND MARIHUANA. (USA)

▲ 355-358 DEUX ARTICLES POUR UN NUMÉRO SPÉCIAL CONSACRÉ AU DESIGN EXPÉRIMENTAL, PUBLIÉ DANS LE MAGAZINE SEMIOTEXT(E). ON Y PRÉSENTE DES TRAVAUX DE PLUSIEURS DESIGNERS CÉLÈBRES. (USA)

▲ 359, 360 COUVERTURES DU MAGAZINE HERE AND NOW, SUR LE THÈME DES TOXICODÉPENDANCES. CETTE PUBLICATION FAIT PARTIE D'UNE CAMPAGNE D'INFORMATION SCOLAIRE SUR LA DROGUE ET S'ADRESSE À DIVERSES CLASSES D'ÂGE. (USA)

361

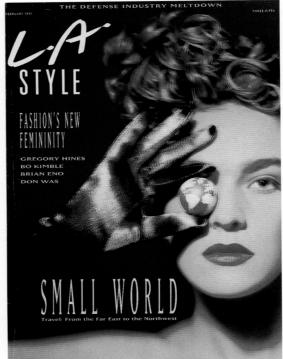

362

363

364

365

366

361-366

DESIGN DIRECTOR:

MICHAEL BROCK

ART DIRECTOR:

MICHAEL BROCK

DESIGNER:

MICHAEL BROCK

PHOTOGRAPHERS:

ANTON CORBIJN (363)

JOSÉ PICAYO (361, 365, 366)

SCOTT MORGAN (362, 364)

HAND-TINTING:

LIZ GADBOIS (361)

STYLISTS:

JODI NAKATSUKA

DENISE TERESE SOLIS (361-364)

AGENCY:

MICHAEL BROCK DESIGN

CLIENT:

L.A. STYLE

PUBLISHER:

AMERICAN EXPRESS

■ **361-366** COVERS, A CONTENTS PAGE AND SPREADS FROM *L.A. STYLE* MAGAZINE, FOCUSING ON FASHION. (USA)

● **361-366** UMSCHLÄGE, INHALTSSEITE UND DOPPELSEITEN DER ZEITSCHRIFT *L.A. STYLE* ZUM THEMA MODE. (USA)

▲ **58-63** LA MODE EST LE SUJET DE CES COUVERTURES ET DOUBLES PAGES DE *L.A. STYLE*. (USA)

367

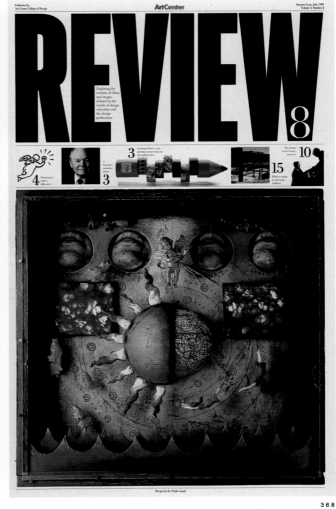

368

367

ART DIRECTOR:

ANGELO SAVAIDES

DESIGNER:

SAM CHICK

PHOTOGRAPHER:

JOSÉ PICAYO

CLIENT:

ICI FIBRES

PUBLISHER:

REDWOOD PUBLISHING

368

ART DIRECTOR:

KIT HINRICHS

DESIGNERS:

KIT HINRICHS

MARK SELFE

PIPER MURAKAMI

ILLUSTRATOR:

STEPHANIE GARCIA

EDITOR:

STUART FROLICK

AGENCY:

PENTAGRAM

CLIENT:

ART CENTER COLLEGE

OF DESIGN

369

ART DIRECTOR:

JENNIFER DOMER

ASSISTANT ART

DIRECTOR:

JACQUELINE THAW

PHOTOGRAPHERS:

LÉON OBERS

TOM WEDEL

CORINNE PFISTER

CLIENT:

INTERNATIONAL

DESIGN

PUBLISHER:

DESIGN

PUBLICATION

INC.

■ **367** COVER OF THE SPRING/SUMMER 1992 ISSUE OF *IN TOUCH*, A FASHION TRADE MAGAZINE PUBLISHED BY ICI AND ADDRESSED TO THE EUROPEAN TEXTILE INDUSTRY AND RETAIL TRADE. A SPECIAL INK AND VARNISH WERE USED. (GBR)

■ **368** THIS ISSUE OF *ART CENTER REVIEW*, A PUBLICATION OF ART CENTER COLLEGE OF DESIGN, CONTAINS A MAJOR FEATURE ARTICLE ON "DESIGNING FOR THE PUBLIC GOOD." THE COVER ILLUSTRATION ADDRESSES THAT THEME. (USA)

■ **369** IMAGES OF CHICAGO DESIGN, PAST AND PRESENT, ON THE COVER OF *INTERNATIONAL DESIGN (I.D.)* MAGAZINE. (USA)

● **367** UMSCHLAG DER FRÜHJAHR/SOMMER-AUSGABE VON *IN TOUCH*, EINE MODEFACHZEITSCHRIFT VON ICI FÜR DIE TEXTILINDUSTRIE UND DEN EINZELHANDEL. ES WURDE EINE SPEZIELLE DRUCKFARBE UND EIN MATTER FIRNIS VERWENDET. (GBR)

● **368** DIESE AUSGABE VON *ART CENTER REVIEW*, EINER PUBLIKATION DES ART CENTER COLLEGE OF DESIGN, IST STUDENTENARBEITEN ZUM WOHL DER ALLGEMEINHEIT GEWIDMET. DIE UMSCHLAGILLUSTRATION BEZIEHT SICH AUF DAS THEMA. (USA)

● **369** BILDER VON ALTEM UND NEUEM DESIGN AUS CHICAGO AUF DEM JMSCHLAG DER ZEITSCHRIFT *I.D.* (USA)

▲ **367** COUVERTURE DU NUMÉRO PRINTEMPS/ÉTÉ DE *TOUCH*, UN MAGAZINE DE MODE PUBLIÉ PAR ICI, DESTINÉ À L'INDUSTRIE TEXTILE ET AUX DÉTAILLANTS. UNE ENCRE D'IMPRIMERIE SPÉCIALE ET UN VERNIS MAT ONT ÉTÉ UTILISÉS. (GBR)

▲ **368** CE NUMÉRO DE *ART CENTER REVIEW*, UNE PUBLICATION DU ART CENTER COLLEGE OF DESIGN, EST CONSACRÉ AUX CRÉATIONS DES ÉTUDIANTS SUR LE THEME «LE BIEN DE L'HUMANITÉ», ILLUSTRÉ PAR L'IMAGE DE COUVERTURE. (USA)

▲ **369** LE DESIGN D'HIER ET D'AUJOURD'HUI À CHICAGO: COUVERTURE DU MAGAZINE *INTERNATIONAL DESIGN (I.D.)*. (USA)

JANUARY/FEBRUARY 1991 $5.00

FOCUS ON · CHICAGO DESIGN

WHAT THE
NEA DOES FOR
DESIGNERS

NEW
EXHIBITS FOR
ZOOS

CONTROVERSY
IN SOVIET
GRAPHICS

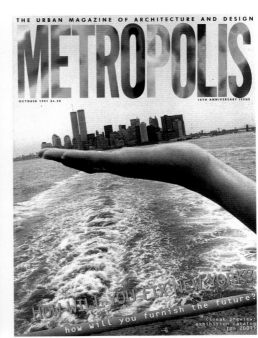

370

371

372

370-372

ART DIRECTORS:

CARL LEHMANN-HAUPT

NANCY COHEN

DESIGNERS:

CARL LEHMANN-HAUPT (371)

NANCY COHEN (371)

PHOTOGRAPHERS:

KRISTINE LARSEN (372)

DAN WINTERS (370)

MARTIN E. RICH (370)

EDITOR:

SUSAN SZENASY

CLIENT:

METROPOLIS

PUBLISHER:

HORACE HAVEMEYER III

■ 370-372 THREE COVERS OF *METROPOLIS*, "THE URBAN MAGAZINE OF ARCHITECTURE AND DESIGN." THE FIRST REFERS TO AN ARTICLE ON THE ARCHITECT LOUIS I. KAHN, THE SECOND TO AN ARTICLE ON LIGHT. THE THIRD IS A VIEW OF MANHATTAN TAKEN FROM THE STATEN ISLAND FERRY. (USA)

■ 373, 374 THE JAPANESE DESIGNER ISSEY MIYAKE AND THE AMERICAN CHOREOGRA-PHER WILLIAM FORSYTHE JOINED FORCES TO STAGE A BALLET IN FRANKFURT. *FAZ MAGA-ZIN* GAVE THE EVENT A COVER AND A NUM-BER OF INTERIOR PAGES. (GER)

■ 375, 376 THE BELGIAN ARTIST MARIE-JO LAFONTAINE AND HER VIDEO SCULPTURES ARE THE SUBJECT OF THIS COVER AND SPREAD FROM *FRANKFURTER ALLGEMEINE* MAGAZINE. (GER)

● 370-372 UMSCHLÄGE VON *METROPOLIS*, EINER ZEITSCHRIFT ÜBER ARCHITEKTUR UND DESIGN: DER UMSTRITTENE ARCHITEKT LOUIS I. KAHN; EINE ANSICHT VON STONE-HENGE IM ZUSAMMENHANG MIT DEM THEMA LICHT UND MANHATTAN, VON DER STATEN-ISLAND-FÄHRE AUS AUFGENOMMEN. (USA)

● 373, 374 DER JAPANISCHE MODESCHÖPFER ISSEY MIYAKE UND DER AMERIKANISCHE CHOREOGRAPH WILLIAM FORSYTHE MACHTEN AUF DER FRANKFURTER BALLETTBÜHNE GE-MEINSAME SACHE. DAS *FAZ MAGAZIN* BE-RICHTETE ÜBER DAS EREIGNIS. (GER)

● 375, 376 DIE BELGISCHE KÜNSTLERIN MARIE-JO LAFONTAINE UND IHRE VIDEO-SKULPTUREN SIND DAS THEMA DIESES UMSCHLAGS UND DER DOPPELSEITEN AUS DEM *FAZ MAGAZIN*. (GER)

▲ 370-372 COUVERTURES DE *METROPOLIS*, UN MAGAZINE D'ARCHITECTURE ET DE DESIGN. L'ARCHITECTE LOUIS I. KAHN, DONT LES RÉALISATIONS FONT L'OBJET DE POLÉ-MIQUES; PHOTO DE STONEHENGE POUR UN NUMÉRO SUR LA LUMIERE; MANHATTAN, VU DU FERRY-BOAT DE STATEN ISLAND. (USA)

▲ 373, 374 LE COUTURIER JAPONAIS ISSEY MIYAKE ET LE CHORÉGRAPHE AMÉRICAIN WILLIAM FORSYTHE ONT PRODUIT ENSEMBLE UN SPECTACLE DE BALLET À FRANCFORT. LE *FAZ MAGAZIN* A CONSACRÉ UNE COUVERTURE ET UN ARTICLE À CET ÉVÉNEMENT. (GER)

▲ 375, 376 L'ARTISTE BELGE MARIE-JO LAFONTAINE ET SES VIDÉOSCULPTURES SONT LE SUJET DE CETTE COUVERTURE ET DE CETTE DOUBLE PAGE DU *FRANKFURTER ALLGEMEINE MAGAZIN*. (GER)

373

374

375

376

373-376

ART DIRECTOR:

HANS-GEORG POSPISCHIL

PHOTOGRAPHERS:

SUSAN LAMER (373, 374)

SERGE COHEN (375, 376)

CLIENT:

FRANKFURTER ALLGEMEINE

MAGAZIN

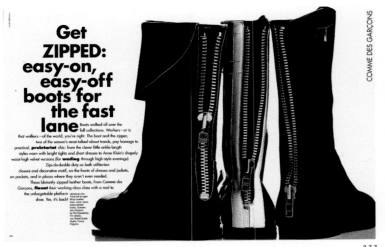

Get ZIPPED: easy-on, easy-off boots for the fast lane

Boots walked all over the fall collections. Workers—or is that walkers—of the world, you're right. The boot and the zipper, two of the season's most talked-about trends, pay homage to practical, **proletariat** chic: from the clever little ankle-length styles worn with bright tights and short dresses to Anne Klein's shapely waist-high velvet versions (for **wading** through high-style evenings). Zips do double duty as both utilitarian closure and decorative motif, on the fronts of dresses and jackets, on pockets, and in places where they aren't even needed. These blatantly zipped leather boots, from Comme des Garçons, **flaunt** their working-class class with a nod to the unforgettable platform shoe. Yes, it's back!

COMME DES GARÇONS

377

MIYAKE MAGIC

For me, a woman is always as mysterious and unfathomable as a stegosaurus, or as seductively alluring as a siren.

378

KNOCK-OUT TANK SUITS
Streamlined one-piece suits in winning colors

379

EASY does it: a modern, muted palette

380

377-380

PUBLICATION DIRECTOR:

RÉGIS PAGNIEZ

ART DIRECTOR:

OLIVIA BADRUTT-GIRON

PHOTOGRAPHERS:

GILLES BENSIMON (377)

TYEN (378, 380)

VICTORIA HESS (379)

STYLIST:

LOREN LANEY (379)

CLIENT:

ELLE

PUBLISHER:

HACHETTE MAGAZINES, INC.

■ **377-380** SPREADS FROM *ELLE* MAGAZINE SHOWING FALL 1991 BOOTS BY COMME DES GARÇONS, A LINEN JACKET BY ISSEY MIYAKE, A SELECTION OF TANK SWIMSUITS, AND THE OPENING SPREAD FROM AN ARTICLE IN THE SEPTEMBER 1991 ISSUE ON MUTED COLORS IN COSMETICS. (USA)

■ **381, 382** COVERS OF THE HUNGARIAN THEATER PUBLICATION *SZHINHAZ*. (HUN)

● **377-380** DOPPELSEITEN AUS DER ZEITSCHRIFT *ELLE*. VORGESTELLT WERDEN STIEFEL VON COMME DES GARÇONS FÜR DEN HERBST 1991; EINE LEINENJACKE VON ISSEY MIYAKE; DIE NEUEN EINTEILIGEN BADEANZÜGE UND DIE GEDÄMPFTEN FARBEN DER KOSMETIKINDUSTRIE FÜR DIE SAISON. (USA)

● **381, 382** UMSCHLÄGE EINER UNGARISCHEN ZEITSCHRIFT FÜR DAS THEATER. (HUN)

▲ **377-380** DOUBLES PAGES DU MAGAZINE *ELLE*. LES BOTTES DE LA SAISON AUTOMNE/HIVER DE COMME DES GARÇONS; UNE VESTE DE LIN D'ISSEY MIYAKE; LES NOUVEAUX MAILLOTS DE BAIN UNE PIECE ET LES COULEURS PASTEL DU MAQUILLAGE ET VERNIS À ONGLES DE L'HIVER 1991. (USA)

▲ **381, 382** COUVERTURES D'UN MAGAZINE HONGROIS SUR LE THÉATRE. (HUN)

381

382

381, 382
ART DIRECTOR:
GYÖRGY KEMÉNY
DESIGNER:
GYÖRGY KEMÉNY
PHOTOGRAPHER:
ZSUZSA KONCZ
COPYWRITER:
TAMAS KOLTAI
CLIENT:
SZINHAZ

clear was her vision, so strong her imagination, so determined her spirit that she single-handedly invented modern dance

Her life spanned nearly a century, and she wasted not a minute of it. So

MARTHA GRAHAM

383

383

ART DIRECTOR:

TOM BENTKOWSKI

DESIGNER:

NORA SHEEHAN

PHOTOGRAPHERS:

BARBARA MORGAN (LEFT)

SOICHI SUNAMI (RIGHT)

CLIENT:

LIFE

PUBLISHER:

TIME-WARNER, INC.

384-386

DESIGNERS:

KARL ULBL

DIETMAR JAKELY

EDITOR:

BOGDAN GRBIC

CLIENT:

BLIMP

■ **383** OPENING SPREAD IN *LIFE* MAGAZINE FOR AN EXCERPT FROM MARTHA GRAHAM'S AUTOBIOGRAPHY. (USA)

■ **384-386** THREE COVERS OF THE AUSTRIAN FILM-INDUSTRY MAGAZINE *BLIMP*. BECAUSE OF A LIMITED BUDGET, THE COVERS ARE DONE IN BLACK AND WHITE WITH ONE ADDITIONAL COLOR. THE RED V OF THE FALL 91 ISSUE STANDS FOR THE "VIENNALE," A VIENNA FILM FESTIVAL. ON THIS COVER A PARTIAL, HARDLY DETECTABLE VARNISH WAS ALSO USED AS AN ADDITIONAL DESIGN ELEMENT. (AUT)

● **383** AUFMACHER-DOPPELSEITE FÜR EINEN AUSZUG AUS MARTHA GRAHAMS AUTOBIOGRAPHIE IN *LIFE*. (USA)

● **384-386** UMSCHLÄGE DER ÖSTERREICHISCHEN FILMZEITSCHRIFT *BLIMP*. WEGEN DES LIMITIERTEN BUDGETS WIRD IN SCHWARZWEISS MIT EINER SCHMUCKFARBE GEARBEITET. DAS ROTE V DER AUSGABE HERBST 1991 BEZIEHT SICH AUF DIE «VIENNALE» (WIENER FILMFESTIVAL). HIER WURDE EINE PARTIELLE LACKIERUNG ALS EIGENSTÄNDIGE, FAST UNSICHTBARE BILD- UND INFORMATIONSEBENE EINGESETZT. (AUT)

▲ **383** DOUBLE PAGE INTRODUISANT UN EXTRAIT DE L'AUTOBIOGRAPHIE DE MARTHA GRAHAM, PUBLIÉ DANS *LIFE*. (USA)

▲ **384-386** TROIS COUVERTURES DE *BLIMP*, UNE REVUE AUTRICHIENNE DE CINÉMA. POUR DES RAISONS DE BUDGET, ON S'EST LIMITÉ AU NOIR ET BLANC AVEC UNE SEULE COULEUR. LE *V* ROUGE DU NUMÉRO DE L'AUTOMNE 1991 FAIT RÉFÉRENCE À LA «VIENNALE», LE FESTIVAL DU FILM DE VIENNE. LE LAQUAGE PARTIEL DE LA SURFACE, DIFFICILEMENT PERCEPTIBLE, AJOUTE UNE NOTE INFORMATIVE À L'IMAGE. (AUT)

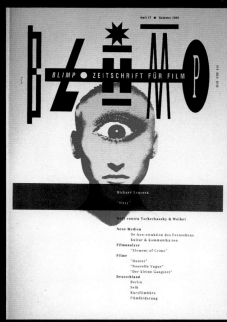

384

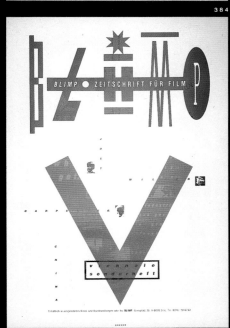

385

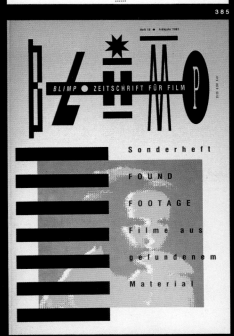

386

387

388

Primo piano sulle cinque tendenze moda più all'avan-guardia di questa primavera 1991: la mini di tulle, la gonna a palloncino di taffetà, lo scialle con nappi-

ne décor, gli shorts da paggio di faille e il piccolo abito can-can di flock, un tessuto particolare con stampa a rilievo, oggi tornato prepotentemente alla ribalta.

389

390

387-390

ART DIRECTOR:
LUCA STOPPINI

PHOTOGRAPHERS:
STEVEN MEISEL (387)
ALBERT WATSON (388-390)

CLIENT:
VOGUE ITALIA

PUBLISHER:
EDIZIONE CONDÉ NAST
S.P.A.

■ 387-390 COVER AND SPREADS FROM AN ARTICLE IN *VOGUE ITALIA* PRESENTING AVANT-GARDE SPRING 1991 FASHIONS BY FAMOUS DESIGNERS. TOP LEFT: A TOP BY GIORGIO ARMANI. TOP RIGHT: BLOOMERS BY PRADA AND A DRESS IN ORGANZA AND VOILE BY KATHARINE HAMNETT. BOTTOM LEFT: TULLE MINIS BY JEAN-PAUL GAULTIER. BOT-TOM RIGHT: AN OUTFIT BY GIANFRANCO FERRÉ, SCARF WITH POMPOMS BY CHRISTIAN DIOR. (ITA)

■ 391 COVER OF THE AUGUST 1990 ISSUE OF *EGG*, A CONSUMER MAGAZINE WITH A SQUARE FORMAT. THE ILLUSTRATION IS A PARODY OF JAPANESE MAGAZINES. UNFORTUNATELY, *EGG* IS NO LONGER BEING PUBLISHED. (USA)

● 387-390 UMSCHLAG UND DOPPELSEITEN AUS *VOGUE ITALIA*. VORGESTELLT WIRD AVANTGARDE-FRÜHJAHRSMODE DER GROS-SEN COUTURIERS. AUF DEM UMSCHLAG EIN MODELL VON GIORGIO ARMANI, AUF DEN DOPPELSEITEN V.L.N.R. UND V.O.N.U.: PUMP-HOSEN VON PRADA UND KLEID IN ORGANZA UND VOILE VON KATHARINE HAMNETT; TÜLL-MINIS VON JEAN-PAUL GAULTIER; KOMBINA-TION VON GIANFRANCO FERRÉ, TUCH MIT POMPONS VON CHRISTIAN DIOR. (ITA)

● 391 UMSCHLAG VON *EGG*, EINER ZEIT-SCHRIFT IN QUADRATISCHEM FORMAT. DIE ILLUSTRATION IST EINE PARODIE DER MACHART JAPANISCHER ZEITSCHRIFTEN. *EGG* ERSCHEINT LEIDER NICHT MEHR. (USA)

▲ 387-390 COUVERTURE ET DOUBLES PAGES DE *VOGUE ITALIA*. ON Y PRÉSENTE LES TEN-DANCES AVANT-GARDISTES DE LA MODE PRINTEMPS/ÉTÉ. EN COUVERTURE, UN MO-DÈLE DE GIORGIO ARMANI; SUR LES DOUBLES PAGES, DE G. À DR. ET DE H. EN B.: BOXER DE PRADA ET ROBE EN ORGANZA AVEC JUPON DE VOILE DE KATHARINE HAMNETT; MINI-JUPES EN TULLE DE JEAN-PAUL GAULTIER; TOP ET JUPE DE GIANFRANCO FERRÉ, CHALE À POMPONS DE CHRISTIAN DIOR. (ITA)

▲ 391 COUVERTURE DE *EGG*, UN MAGAZINE DES CONSOMMATEURS DE FORMAT CARRÉ QUI, MALHEUREUSEMENT, A CESSÉ DE PARAI-TRE. L'ILLUSTRATION PARODIE LE STYLE DES MAGAZINES JAPONAIS. (USA)

391

ART DIRECTOR:

DOUGLAS RICCARDI

DESIGNER:

LAURIE ROSENWALD

ILLUSTRATOR:

LAURIE ROSENWALD

CLIENT:

EGG

PUBLISHER:

FORBES MAGAZINES

392

ART DIRECTOR:
CHRISTIAN GUTH
DESIGNERS:
MARTIN BOCAN
WALTER PERSCHÉ
MANFRED TESCH
CLIENT:
PROFIL

393

ART DIRECTOR:
ELIANE STEPHAN
DESIGNERS:
ELIANE STEPHAN
CARLOS NADER
PHOTOGRAPHER:
EDUARDO BRANDAO
CLIENT:
CAOS
PUBLISHER:
A.N. EDITORA LTDA.

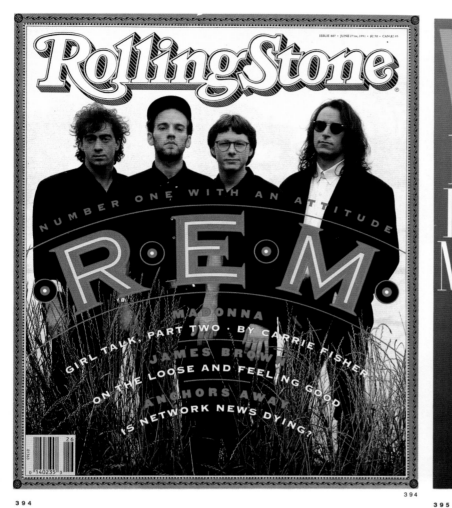

394

395

394

ART DIRECTOR:

FRED WOODWARD

PHOTOGRAPHY DIRECTOR:

LAURIE KRATOCHVIL

DESIGNER:

FRED WOODWARD

PHOTOGRAPHER:

FRANK W. OCKENFELS 3

CLIENT:

ROLLING STONE

PUBLISHER:

STRAIGHT ARROW

PUBLISHERS

395

ART DIRECTOR:

CHARLES CHURCHWARD

PHOTOGRAPHER:

ANNIE LEIBOVITZ

CLIENT:

VANITY FAIR

PUBLISHER:

CONDÉ NAST

PUBLICATIONS, INC.

■ **392** "BILLIONS IN TAX MONEY SPENT ON SADDAM"—COVER OF THE AUSTRIAN MAGAZINE *PROFIL* WITH AN ARTICLE ON TAX MONEY SPENT ON THE SUPPORT OF IRAQI FIRMS—MONEY THAT, BECAUSE OF THE GULF WAR, IS PROBABLY LOST. (AUT)

■ **393** BLUE EYES ARE THE SUBJECT OF THE COVER AND A FEATURE ARTICLE IN THE BRAZILIAN MAGAZINE *CAOS*. (BRA)

■ **394** COVER FROM *ROLLING STONE*, FEATURING THE GROUP R.E.M. (USA)

■ **395** COVER OF *VANITY FAIR*, SHOWING A PREGNANT DEMI MOORE. (USA)

● **392** DIE ÖSTERREICHISCHEN FÖRDERUNGS-GELDER (AUS STEUERMITTELN), FÜR IRAKI-SCHE FIRMEN, DIE AUFGRUND DES GOLF-KRIEGES WAHRSCHEINLICH ABGESCHRIEBEN WERDEN MÜSSEN, SIND DAS THEMA DIESES UMSCHLAGS DES MAGAZINS *PROFIL*. (AUT)

● **393** BLAUE AUGEN SIND DAS THEMA DES UMSCHLAGS UND EINES SCHÖNHEITSBEI-TRAGS IN DER ZEITSCHRIFT *CAOS*. (BRA)

● **394** DIE GRUPPE R.E.M. AUF DEM UM-SCHLAG VON *ROLLING STONE*. (USA)

● **395** UMSCHLAG VON *VANITY FAIR*: DIE SCHAUSPIELERIN DEMI MOORE. (USA)

▲ **392** CETTE COUVERTURE DU MAGAZINE *PROFIL* ÉVOQUE UN SUJET BRULANT: EN AUTRICHE, LES SOMMES DES SUBVENTIONS (PRÉLEVÉES SUR LES IMPOTS) QUI AVAIENT ÉTÉ VERSÉES À DES FIRMES IRAKIENNES, ONT PROBABLEMENT ÉTÉ PERDUES. (AUT)

▲ **393** LES YEUX BLEUS SONT LE SUJET DE LA COUVERTURE ET DES PAGES BEAUTÉ DE CE NUMÉRO DU MAGAZINE *CAOS*. (BRA)

▲ **394** LE GROUPE R.E.M. EN COUVERTURE DE *ROLLING STONE*. (USA)

▲ **395** COUVERTURE DE *VANITY FAIR*: L'AC-TRICE DEMI MOORE ENCEINTE. (USA)

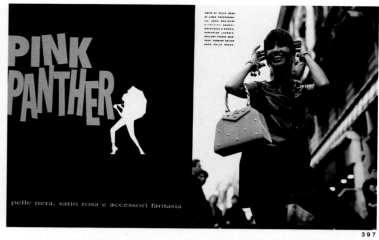

DISC-O!

396

PINK PANTHER

pelle nera, satin rosa e accessori fantasia

397

CHIC SQUAW

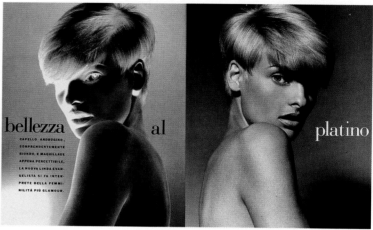

bellezza al platino

398

399

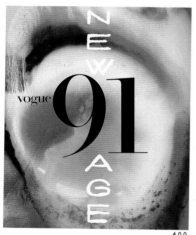

NEW AGE *vogue* 91

400

396-400

Art Director:

LUCA STOPPINI

Photographers:

IRVING PENN (396, LEFT)

DANIELLE SCOTT

(396, RIGHT)

TIZIANO MAGNI (397)

STEVEN MEISEL (398, 399)

Client:

VOGUE ITALIA

Publisher:

EDIZIONE CONDÉ

NAST S.P.A.

■ **396-400** *VOGUE ITALIA* PRESENTING FASHION TRENDS IN 1991: DISK-SHAPED JEWELRY; BLACK AND PINK COMBINATIONS; ETHNIC STYLES; PLATINUM-BLONDE HAIR (STARRING THE MODEL LINDA EVANGELISTA) AND THE COVER FOR A "NEW AGE" SECTION. (ITA)

● **396-400** DIE MODETRENDS 1991, VORGESTELLT IN *VOGUE ITALIA*: DISCO-VERRÜCKTHEITEN; KOMBINATIONEN IN SCHWARZ UND PINK; NAVAJO-STIL; LINDA EVANGELISTA IN PLATINBLOND UND DIE AUFMACHERSEITE ZUM BEITRAG «NEW AGE». (ITA)

▲ **396-400** *VOGUE ITALIA* PRÉSENTE LES NOUVEAUTÉS 1991: LES EXCEN-TRICITÉS DU STYLE DISCO, LES HARMONIES DE NOIR ET ROSE, LE STYLE NAVAJO, LINDA EVANGELISTA EN BLOND PLATINE, PAGE INTRODUISANT UN ARTICLE SUR LE «NEW AGE». (ITA)

ILLUSTRATION

ILLUSTRATIONEN

ILLUSTRATION

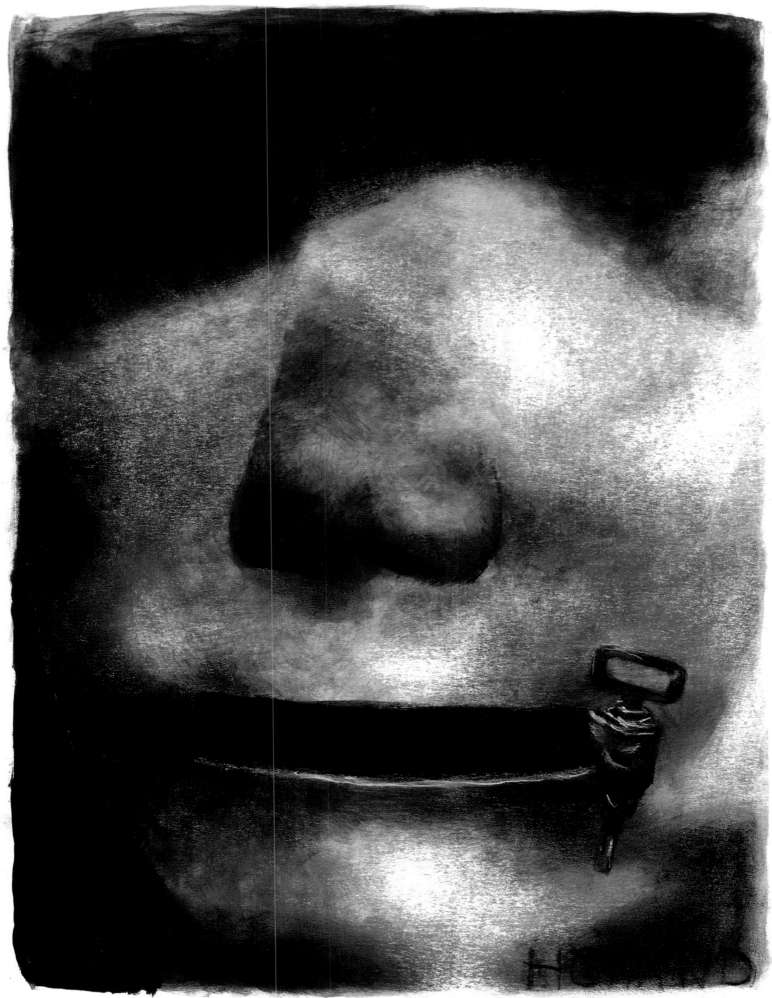

401

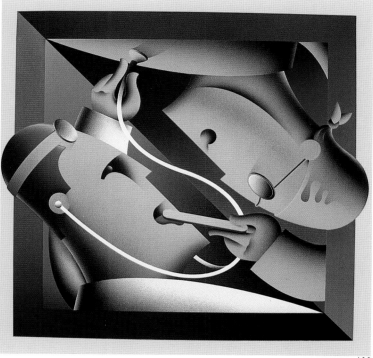

402

403

401

ART DIRECTOR:

SUSAN LIMORKELLI

ILLUSTRATOR:

BRAD HOLLAND

CLIENT:

AIGA

402, 403

ART DIRECTOR:

PAM THORNBERG (403)

ILLUSTRATOR:

JEFF KOEGEL

AGENCY:

KOEGEL DESIGN

STUDIO

CLIENT:

LOS ANGELES (403)

■ **401** ILLUSTRATION USED AS THE COVER OF AN ISSUE OF THE *AIGA JOURNAL OF GRAPHIC DESIGN* DEALING WITH FREEDOM OF EXPRESSION AND THE FIRST AMENDMENT OF THE UNITED STATES CONSTITUTION. (USA)

■ **402, 403** TWO ILLUSTRATIONS BY JEFF KOEGEL, ONE USED FOR SELF-PROMOTION, THE OTHER TO ILLUSTRATE AN ARTICLE IN *LOS ANGELES* MAGAZINE ON "THE DOCTORS DOCTORS GO TO." (USA)

● **401** UMSCHLAGILLUSTRATION FÜR DAS *AIGA JOURNAL OF GRAPHIC DESIGN*. DAS THEMA IST DIE FREIE MEINUNGSÄUSSERUNG, DIE IM ERSTEN AMENDMENT DER VERFASSUNG DER USA GARANTIERT WIRD. (USA)

● **402, 403** ZWEI ILLUSTRATIONEN VON JEFF KOEGEL. DIE EINE DIENT ALS EIGENWERBUNG, DIE ANDERE WURDE FÜR EINEN ARTIKEL MIT DEM TITEL «DIE ÄRZTE, ZU DENEN DIE ÄRZTE GEHEN» VERWENDET. (USA)

▲ **401** ILLUSTRATION POUR LA COUVERTURE DU JOURNAL DE L'AIGA. L'IMAGE ILLUSTRE LA LIBERTÉ D'EXPRESSION ET DE PAROLE, GARANTIE PAR LE PREMIER AMENDEMENT DE LA CONSTITUTION AMÉRICAINE. (USA)

▲ **402, 403** DEUX ILLUSTRATIONS DE JEFF KOEGEL: AUTOPROMOTION ET IMAGE PUBLIÉE DANS UN MAGAZINE POUR ILLUSTRER UN ARTICLE INTITULÉ: «LES MÉDECINS QUI VONT CHEZ LE MÉDECIN». (USA)

404

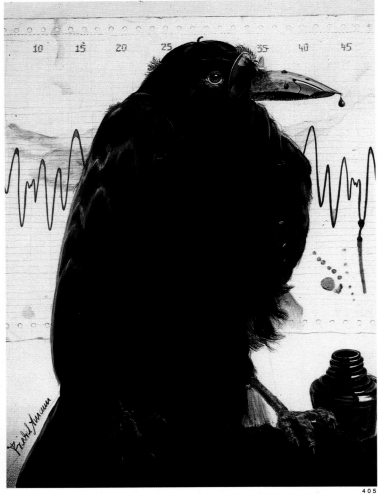

405

404

ART DIRECTOR:
GARY DANIELS
DESIGNER:
GARY DANIELS
ILLUSTRATOR:
JOE FLEMING
AGENCY:
EDS CORPORATE
COMMUNICATIONS
CLIENT:
EDS CORPORATE
COMMUNICATIONS

405

DESIGNER:
FRIEDRICH AMANN
ILLUSTRATOR:
FRIEDRICH AMANN
PUBLISHER:
DIE ZEIT

407

ART DIRECTOR:
SHUZO HIRATA
ILLUSTRATOR:
CATHLEEN TOELKE
AGENCY:
HAKUHODO INC.
CLIENT:
CÉCILENE

406

DESIGNER:
MICHAEL SCHWAB
ILLUSTRATOR:
MICHAEL SCHWAB
AGENCY:
MICHAEL SCHWAB
DESIGN
CLIENT:
PARAGRAPHICS

406

407

■ **404** ILLUSTRATION FROM THE 1990 ANNUAL REPORT OF EDS, AN INFORMATION-TECHNOLOGY SERVICES COMPANY. IT REFERS TO A MINING COMPANY THAT EDS HELPED TO RESTRUCTURE. (USA)

■ **405** ILLUSTRATION USED IN A BROCHURE PROMOTING ADVERTISING SPACE IN THE MAGAZINE SUPPLEMENT OF *DIE ZEIT*. (GER)

■ **406** THIS ILLUSTRATION OF A LEOPARD WAS PUBLISHED IN A PRINTER'S PROMOTIONAL CALENDAR. (USA)

■ **407** THIS IMAGE WAS USED ON THE SHOPPING BAG OF A JAPANESE MAIL-ORDER COMPANY TO CONVEY EUROPEAN ELEGANCE. (JPN)

● **404** ILLUSTRATION FÜR DEN JAHRESBERICHT 1990 VON EDS, INFORMATIKTECHNOLOGIE. SIE BEZIEHT SICH AUF DIE UNTERSTÜTZUNG EINES BERGBAUUNTERNEHMENS BEI DER UMSTRUKTURIERUNG. (USA)

● **405** ILLUSTRATION ALS ANZEIGEN-KUNDENWERBUNG FÜR DAS *ZEIT*-MAGAZINS. HANDKOLORIERTER SCHWARZWEISSDRUCK. (GER)

● **406** DIESER LEOPARDENKOPF, EIN FÜNFFARBENLITHO, WURDE IM KALENDER EINER DRUCKEREI VERWENDET. (USA)

● **407** FÜR EINE TRAGETASCHE EINES JAPANISCHEN VERSANDHAUSES. DAS BILD SOLLTE EUROPÄISCHE ELEGANZ AUSSTRAHLEN. (JPN)

▲ **404** ILLUSTRATION TIRÉE DU RAPPORT ANNUEL 1990 D'EDS, FIRME DE TECHNOLOGIES INFORMATIQUES. ELLE ÉVOQUE LE SOUTIEN ACCORDÉ LORS DE LA RESTRUCTURATION D'UNE SOCIÉTÉ MINIERE. (USA)

▲ **405** ILLUSTRATION POUR LE MAGAZINE DU JOURNAL *DIE ZEIT*, VISANT À GAGNER DE NOUVEAUX ANNONCEURS. (GER)

▲ **406** ILLUSTRATION SÉRIGRAPHIQUE ORNANT UNE PAGE DU CALENDRIER D'UNE IMPRIMERIE. (USA)

▲ **407** IMAGE ORNANT UN SAC DE PAPIER D'UNE GRANDE ENTREPRISE JAPONAISE DE VENTE PAR CORRESPONDANCE. (JPN)

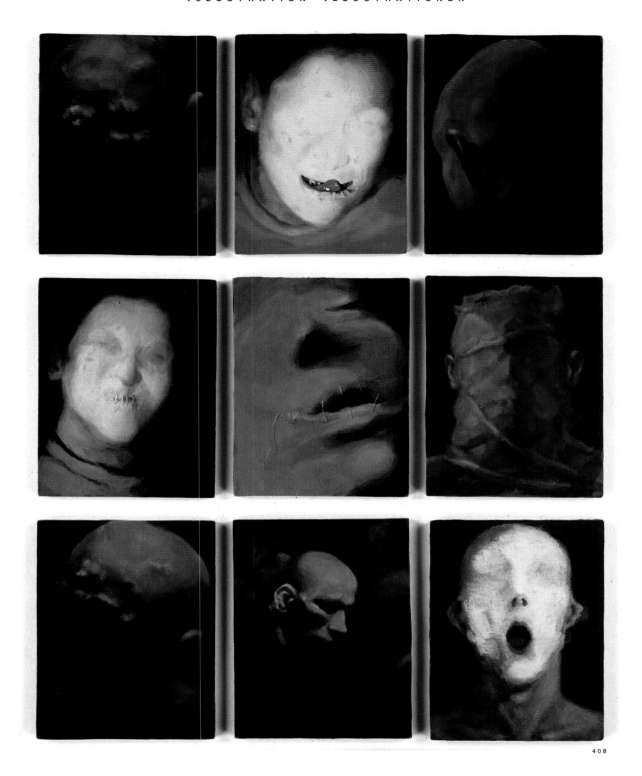

408

ILLUSTRATION · ILLUSTRATIONEN

409

409

ART DIRECTOR:

MARK ULRICKSON

ILLUSTRATOR:

JAMES STAGG

CLIENT:

SAN FRANCISCO

FOCUS

408

ART DIRECTOR:

RAFAEL OLBINSKI

ILLUSTRATOR:

JAE CHOI

CLIENT:

SCHOOL OF VISUAL

ARTS

■ **408** "POLLUTION AND THE HUMAN BEING" WAS THE THEME OF THIS ILLUSTRATION, PRODUCED FOR THE SCHOOL OF VISUAL ARTS IN NEW YORK. (USA)

■ **409** OPENING ILLUSTRATION FOR THE SECTION OF NEW RESTAURANT REVIEWS PUBLISHED EACH MONTH IN *SAN FRANCISCO FOCUS*. THE ILLUSTRATION FEATURES A CHINESE RESTAURANT, AND WAS MEANT TO CAPTURE ITS MOOD AND MOST APPEALING ASPECTS. (USA)

● **408** DER MENSCH UND DIE UMWELTVERSCHMUTZUNG IST DAS THEMA DIESER ILLUSTRATION FÜR DIE NEW YORKER SCHOOL OF VISUAL ARTS. (USA)

● **409** ILLUSTRATION ALS AUFMACHER FÜR DIE KOLUMNE ÜBER NEUE RESTAURANTS IN DER ZEITSCHRIFT *SAN FRANCISCO FOCUS*. HIER GEHT ES UM EIN NEUES CHINESISCHES RESTAURANT, DESSEN STIMMUNG UND MERKMALE MIT DIESER DARSTELLUNG EINGEFANGEN WERDEN SOLLTEN. (USA)

▲ **408** ILLUSTRATION SUR LE THEME «L'HOMME ET LA POLLUTION». ELLE A ÉTÉ RÉALISÉE POUR LA SCHOOL OF VISUAL ARTS DE NEW YORK. (USA)

▲ **409** IMAGE PUBLIÉE DANS UN MAGAZINE CULINAIRE AMÉRICAIN, LE *SAN FRANCISCO FOCUS*, POUR ILLUSTRER UN ARTICLE SUR LES NOUVEAUX RESTAURANTS. IL EST ICI QUESTION D'UN NOUVEAU RESTAURANT CHINOIS DONT L'ATMOSPHERE PARTICULIERE EST SUGGÉRÉE PAR L'ILLUSTRATION. (USA)

410

■ **410** THIS ILLUSTRATION WAS USED AS THE COVER OF *PARADISE*, A NOVEL ABOUT THREE GIRLS IN A LATIN AMERICAN CITY. (USA)

■ **411, 412** AN AIRPLANE TAIL AND A SPEEDOMETER, TWO REALISTIC RENDERINGS PUBLISHED IN LUFTHANSA'S IN-FLIGHT MAGAZINE. THE ARTICLES WERE PART OF A SERIES CALLED "CHECKLIST," COVERING MODERN FLIGHT TECHNIQUES. (GER)

● **410** ILLUSTRATION FÜR EINEN BUCHUMSCHLAG. ES GEHT UM DREI MÄDCHEN IN EINER LATEINAMERIKANISCHEN STADT. (USA)

● **411, 412** EIN TEIL DES TRAGWERKS UND FAHRTMESSER EINES FLUGZEUGS. ILLUSTRATIONEN FÜR DAS INFLIGHT-MAGAZIN DER LUFTHANSA, *BORDBUCH*. SIE ERSCHIENEN IM RAHMEN DER SERIE «CHECKLISTE» ÜBER MODERNE FLUGTECHNIK. (GER)

▲ **410** POUR LA COUVERTURE D'UN ROMAN OU IL EST QUESTION DE TROIS FILLETTES DANS UNE VILLE SUD-AMÉRICAINE. (USA)

▲ **411, 412** LA QUEUE D'UN AVION ET UN TACHYMÈTRE, DEUX ILLUSTRATIONS À L'AÉROGRAPHE. ELLES ONT ÉTÉ PUBLIÉES DANS LE MAGAZINE DE BORD DE LA LUFTHANSA, QUI INFORME DES NOUVEAUTÉS TECHNIQUES DE L'AVIATION. (GER)

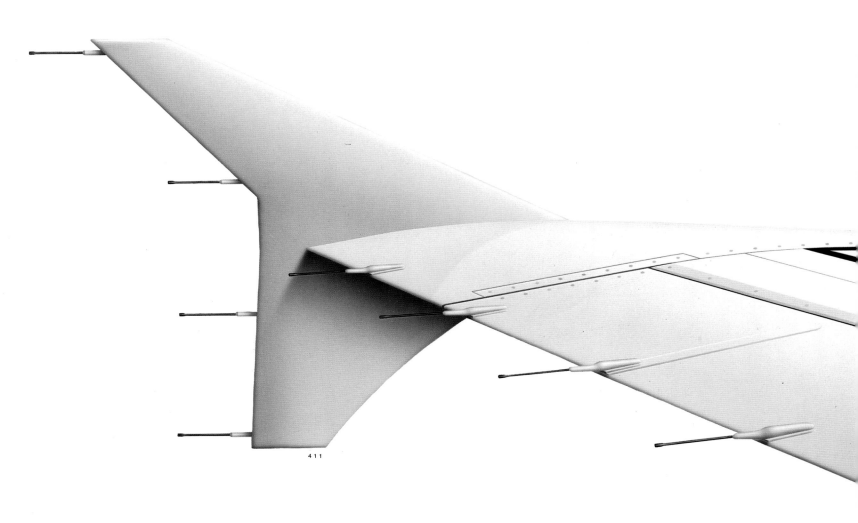

411

412

410

ART DIRECTOR:

KRYSTINA SKALSKI

DESIGNER:

KRYSTINA SKALSKI

ILLUSTRATOR:

JOHN JINKS

CLIENT:

GROVE PRESS

411, 412

ART DIRECTOR:

ULRICH VOSSNACKE

ILLUSTRATOR:

PETER KRÄMER

CLIENT:

DEUTSCHE

LUFTHANSA AG

413

414

413

ART DIRECTOR:

TOM STAEBLER

DESIGNER:

KERIG POPE

ILLUSTRATOR:

MEL ODOM

PUBLISHER:

PLAYBOY

414

ART DIRECTOR:

CARMEN DUNJKO

ILLUSTRATOR:

BRAD HOLLAND

PUBLISHER:

SATURDAY NIGHT

415

ART DIRECTOR:

LOWELL WILLIAMS

DESIGNERS:

BILL CARSON

LOWELL WILLIAMS

ILLUSTRATOR:

ANDY DEARWATER

AGENCY:

PENTAGRAM

CLIENT:

COUSINS

PROPERTIES

■ **413** "TROUBLE IN LITTLE SAIGON." ILLUSTRATION (PENCIL, DYES, GOUACHE) FOR A NONFICTION PIECE IN *PLAYBOY* ABOUT GANGS AND CRIME IN AMERICA'S LARGEST VIETNAMESE GHETTO, LOCATED IN ORANGE COUNTY, CALIFORNIA. (USA)

■ **414** "WHO IS THE FAIREST?" THIS ILLUSTRATION WAS USED FOR THE OPENING PAGE OF A STORY BY MARGARET ATWOOD IN *SATURDAY NIGHT* MAGAZINE. THE TITLE AND THE IMAGE ARE AN ALLUSION TO THE MAGIC MIRROR IN *SNOW WHITE*. (USA)

■ **415** ILLUSTRATION USED ON THE COVER OF THE LEASING BROCHURE FOR CITIZENS AND SOUTHERN PLAZA, AN ATLANTA OFFICE BUILDING. COLUMNS OF FLAME-FINISHED RED GRANITE ALTERNATE WITH ROWS OF BRONZE-TINTED WINDOWS ON THE 1,023-FOOT STRUCTURE. THE ARCHITECT WAS KEVIN ROCHE. (USA)

● **413** «ÄRGER IN KLEIN-SAIGON», ILLUSTRATION FÜR EINEN AKTUELLEN BEITRAG IM *PLAYBOY* ÜBER ORANGE COUNTY (LOS ANGELES), AMERIKAS GRÖSSTES VIETNAMESISCHES GHETTO, WO VIETNAMESISCHE STRASSENGANGS IHR UNWESEN TREIBEN. (USA)

● **414** «WER IST DIE SCHÖNSTE?» – ILLUSTRATION ALS AUFMACHER FÜR EINEN ROMAN VON MARGARET ATWOOD IN DER ZEITSCHRIFT *SATURDAY NIGHT*. TITEL UND BILD SIND EINE ANSPIELUNG AUF DEN ZAUBERSPIEGEL IN *SCHNEEWITTCHEN*. (USA)

● **415** DIESE ILLUSTRATION WURDE FÜR DEN UMSCHLAG EINER LEASING-BROSCHÜRE FÜR CITIZENS AND SOUTHERN PLAZA, EINEN NEUEN BÜROTURM IN ATLANTA, VERWENDET. SÄULEN AUS RÖTLICHEM GRANIT WECHSELN MIT KUPFERGETÖNTEN FENSTERN AB. DER ARCHITEKT DES CA. 300 METER HOHEN WOLKENKRATZERS IST KEVIN ROCHE. (USA)

▲ **413** ILLUSTRATION POUR UN ARTICLE DU MAGAZINE *PLAYBOY* SUR LES MÉFAITS DES GANGS DES RUES VIETNAMIENS DE LITTLE SAIGON, ORANGE COUNTY (LOS ANGELES), LE PLUS GRAND GHETTO VIETNAMIEN DES ETATS-UNIS. (USA)

▲ **414** «QUI ES LA PLUS BELLE?» ILLUSTRATION D'UNE NOUVELLE DE MARGARET ATWOOD, PUBLIÉE DANS LE MAGAZINE *SATURDAY NIGHT*: LE TITRE ET L'IMAGE FONT ALLUSION AU MIROIR MAGIQUE DU CONTE DE *BLANCHE-NEIGE*. (USA)

▲ **415** ILLUSTRATION PUBLIÉE EN COUVERTURE D'UNE BROCHURE PRÉSENTANT LE NOUVEAU GRATTE-CIEL D'ATLANTA, CITIZENS AND SOUTHERN PLAZA, UN IMMEUBLE COMMERCIAL DE 300 M DE HAUT AVEC FAÇADE OU ALTERNENT LES COULEURS DU GRANIT ROSE ET DES FENETRES. IL A ÉTÉ CONÇU PAR L'ARCHITECTE KEVIN ROCHE. (USA)

415

416

417

416
ART DIRECTOR:
GARY DANIELS
DESIGNER:
GARY DANIELS
ILLUSTRATOR:
BRALDT BRALDS
AGENCY:
EDS CORPORATE
COMMUNICATIONS
CLIENT:
EDS CORPORATE
COMMUNICATIONS

417
ILLUSTRATOR:
GOTTFRIED
HELNWEIN

418
ILLUSTRATOR:
GEOFFREY MOSS
AGENCY:
THE KUESTER GROUP
CLIENT:
POTLATCH PAPER
COMPANY

418

419

ART DIRECTOR:

BOB BEYN

DESIGNER:

VICKY RAND

ILLUSTRATOR:

MIKE BENNY

AGENCY:

SERAPHEIN BEYN

■ 416 CHANGING BUSINESS ENVIRONMENTS WAS THE CENTRAL THEME OF EDS INDUSTRIES' 1990 ANNUAL REPORT. THE DIFFERING STAIRCASES AND THE PEOPLE CLIMBING THEM REPRESENT CHANGING IN A POSITIVE DIRECTION. (USA)

■ 417 IN "BEAUTIFUL VICTIM," A WATERCOLOR, THE ARTIST TAKES ADVANTAGE OF THE FORCE OF A REALISTIC IMAGE AND GOES BEYOND PAINTING BY USING OTHER PROVOCATIVE ELEMENTS, SUCH AS BANDAGES. (GER)

■ 418 ILLUSTRATION PUBLISHED IN A BROCHURE BY THE POTLATCH PAPER COMPANY ON THE USES OF ITS PAPER. (USA)

■ 419 PORTRAIT (ACRYLIC, 16X16") OF JOHANNES PETER "HONUS" WAGNER (1874–1955), A FAMOUS BASEBALL PLAYER. WITH THE SLOGAN "HARD-HITTING ADVERTISING," IT WAS USED ON A PROMOTIONAL POSTER FOR AN AD AGENCY. (USA)

● 416 VERÄNDERUNGEN DES GESCHÄFTLICHEN UMFELDES WAR DAS HAUPTTHEMA DES JAHRESBERICHTES 1990 FÜR EDS INDUSTRIES. DIE VERSCHIEDENEN TREPPEN STEHEN FÜR VERÄNDERUNG, DIE MÄNNER FÜR DIE POSITIVE ENTWICKLUNG. (USA)

● 417 «BEAUTIFUL VICTIM», AQUARELL, 73X58CM. DER KÜNSTLER BENUTZT DIE WIRKSAMKEIT EINES REALISTISCHEN ABBILDES MIT PROVOZIERENDEN ELEMENTEN, UM DIE REALITÄT ZU ÜBERSCHREITEN. (GER)

● 418 ILLUSTRATION EINES POETISCHEN TEXTES ZUM THEMA SUBTILITÄT IN EINER BROSCHÜRE FÜR POTLATCH-PAPIER. (USA)

● 419 PORTRÄT (ACRYL) VON JOHANNES PETER «HONUS» WAGNER (1874–1955), EINEM BERÜHMTEN BASEBALL-SPIELER. ES WURDE VON EINER WERBEAGENTUR UNTER DEM SLOGAN «WERBUNG, DIE EINSCHLÄGT» ALS EIGENWERBUNG VERWENDET. (USA)

▲ 416 ILLUSTRATION DE BRALDT BRALDS EN COUVERTURE DU RAPPORT ANNUEL 1990 D'EDS INDUSTRIES. LES ESCALIERS SYMBOLISENT LES TRANSFORMATIONS, CEUX QUI LES GRAVISSENT LE DÉVELOPPEMENT POSITIF DE L'ENTREPRISE. (USA)

▲ 417 «BELLE VICTIME», AQUARELLE. L'ARTISTE A SU TIRER PROFIT D'UNE IMAGE RÉALISTE, Y AJOUTANT DES ÉLÉMENTS VISUELS PROVOCANTS, AFIN DE DÉPASSER LE SIMPLE NIVEAU DE LA RÉALITÉ. (GER)

▲ 418 ILLUSTRATION D'UN TEXTE POÉTIQUE SUR LE THÈME DE LA SUBTILITÉ, TIRÉ D'UNE BROCHURE DE POTLATCH PAPER. (USA)

▲ 419 PORTRAIT DE JOHANNES PETER «HONUS» WAGNER (1874-1955), UN CÉLÈBRE JOUEUR DE BASE-BALL, ILLUSTRANT L'AFFICHE AUTOPROMOTIONNELLE D'UNE AGENCE DE PUBLICITÉ, DONT LE SLOGAN ÉTAIT: «UNE PUB QUI FRAPPE». (USA)

420
ART DIRECTOR:
WAYNE ANDERSON
DESIGNER:
WAYNE ANDERSON
ILLUSTRATOR:
WAYNE ANDERSON
CLIENT:
WIZART

421
ART DIRECTOR:
PATRICK DOAB
ILLUSTRATOR:
NIGEL BUCHANAN
CLIENT:
DRAWING BOOK
STUDIOS

420

■ 420 "VIRGIN SACRIFICE," ONE OF A SERIES OF FANTASY ILLUSTRATIONS PUBLISHED AS GREETING CARDS. IT WAS CREATED WITH CRAYON AND PENCIL. (GBR)

■ 421 "MERMAID," RENDERED IN GOUACHE, AIRBRUSH AND OTHER MEDIA, WAS PUBLISHED ON THE PROMOTIONAL CALENDAR OF AN ILLUSTRATORS' AGENT. (USA)

● 420 BEISPIEL AUS EINER REIHE VON PHANTASTISCHEN ILLUSTRATIONEN FÜR EINE GRUSSKARTENSERIE: «JUNGFRAUENOPFER», KREIDE UND FARBSTIFT. (GBR)

● 421 «MEERJUNGFRAU», GOUACHE, AIRBRUSH UND ANDERE MITTEL. ILLUSTRATION FÜR DEN PROMOTIONSKALENDER EINES AGENTEN FÜR ILLUSTRATOREN. (USA)

▲ 420 EXEMPLES D'UNE SÉRIE D'ILLUS-TRATIONS FANTASTIQUES POUR DES CARTES DE VŒUX, RÉALISÉES À LA CRAIE ET AUX CRAYONS DE COULEUR. (GBR)

▲ 420 «SIRENE», GOUACHE, AÉROGRAPHE ET TECHNIQUE MIXTE. LLUSTRATION POUR LE CALENDRIER PROMOTIONNEL D'UNE AGENCE D'ILLUSTRATEURS. (USA)

421

422

422
ART DIRECTOR:
ALLEN CARROLL
ILLUSTRATOR:
RICHARD SCHLECHT
PUBLISHER:
*NATIONAL
GEOGRAPHIC*
CLIENT:
NATIONAL GEOGRAPHIC
SOCIETY

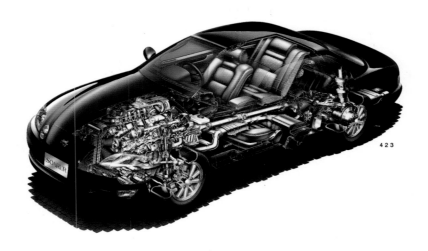

423

423
ILLUSTRATOR:
YOSHIHIRO INOMOTO
AGENCY:
NIPPON DESIGN
CENTER
CLIENT:
TOYOTA
MOTOR CORP.

424

425

424

ART DIRECTOR:

CRAIG FORSDICK

ILLUSTRATOR:

DOUGLAS FRASER

AGENCY:

JOHN HEINEY

& ASSOCIATES INC.

CLIENT:

PLM INTERNATIONAL

INC.

425

ART DIRECTOR:

PATRICIA BRADBURY

DESIGNER:

PETER COMITINI

ILLUSTRATOR:

DANIEL ADEL

PUBLISHER:

NEWSWEEK, INC.

■ **422** THIS ILLUSTRATION WAS USED ON THE FOLD-OUT PAGE OF AN ARTICLE IN *NATIONAL GEOGRAPHIC* ABOUT NORTH AMERICAN WHALING. IT SHOWS PEOPLE OF THE MAKAH TRIBE IN 36-FOOT CEDAR CANOES. ONE OF THE INDIANS IS SEWING THE MOUTH OF THE HARPOONED WHALE SHUT IN ORDER TO KEEP THE CARCASS FROM SINKING AS THE CANOES TOW IT TO SHORE. (USA)

■ **423** TECHNICAL RENDERING OF A TOYOTA SOARER. (JPN)

■ **424** ILLUSTRATION USED IN THE ANNUAL REPORT OF PLM INTERNATIONAL TO SHOW THE AIR GROUP OF THE COMPANY. (CAN)

■ **425** THE COVER LINE FOR THIS ISSUE OF *NEWSWEEK* MAGAZINE READ "THE VICTIMS OF RAPE: SHOULD THEIR NAMES BE KEPT SECRET?" (USA)

● **422** DIESE ILLUSTRATION WURDE ÜBER DREI SEITEN EINES ARTIKELS IN *NATIONAL GEOGRAPHIC* ÜBER DEN WALFANG IN NORDAMERIKA GEZEIGT. MAN SIEHT ANGEHÖRIGE DES MAKAH-STAMMES IN CA. ZEHN METER LANGEN KANUS AUS ZEDERNHOLZ, WOBEI EINER DAS MAUL DES WALS ZUNÄHT, UM ZU VERHINDERN, DASS WASSER EINDRINGT UND DER WAL DADURCH SINKT. (USA)

● **423** TECHNISCHE DARSTELLUNG EINES TOYOTA-SOARER. (JPN)

● **424** AUF DIE FLUGZEUGDIVISION VON PLM BEZOGENE ILLUSTRATION (ACRYL) FÜR EINEN JAHRESBERICHT DER FIRMA. (CAN)

● **425** ILLUSTRATION FÜR EINEN *NEWSWEEK*-UMSCHLAG. DIE SCHLAGZEILE: «OPFER VON VERGEWALTIGUNGEN – SOLLTE MAN IHRE NAMEN GEHEIMHALTEN?». (USA)

▲ **422** DOUBLE PAGE AVEC RABAT ILLUSTRANT LA PECHE À LA BALEINE AU NORD DE L'AMÉRIQUE, POUR UN ARTICLE PARU DANS LE *NATIONAL GEOGRAPHIC*. LES INDIENS MAKAH, APRES AVOIR HARPONNÉ L'ANIMAL, LE MAINTENAIENT À LA SURFACE DE L'EAU À L'AIDE DE BOUÉES ET COUSAIENT SA GUEULE POUR EMPECHER L'EAU DE PÉNÉTRER ET LE CORPS DE COULER. (USA)

▲ **423** ILLUSTRATION TECHNIQUE REPRÉSENTANT LE COUPÉ TOYOTA-SOARER. (JPN)

▲ **424** IMAGE ILLUSTRANT LE RAPPORT ANNUEL DE PLM. ELLE SE RAPPORTE À LA DIVISION AÉRONAUTIQUE DE PLM. (CAN)

▲ **425** ILLUSTRATION PUBLIÉE EN COUVERTURE D'UN NUMÉRO DU MAGAZINE *NEWSWEEK* CONSACRÉ AUX VICTIMES DU RAPT: «LEURS NOMS DOIT-IL RESTER SECRET?» (USA)

426-428
ART DIRECTOR:
FRAN BLACK
ARTIST:
JOSÉ ORTEGA
STYLIST:
EDNA GARCES
COPYWRITER:
LONA BENNEY
AGENCY:
ARTS COUNSEL
CLIENT:
ARTS COUNSEL

■ **426-428** HALLOWEEN MASKS, ILLUSTRATED BY JOSÉ ORTEGA. (USA)

● **426-428** HALLOWEEN-MASKEN ILLUSTRIERT VON JOSÉ ORTEGA. (USA)

▲ **426-428** DES MASQUES POUR HALLOWEEN ILLUSTRÉS PAR JOSÉ ORTEGA. (USA)

CORPORATE IDENTITY

FIRMENERSCHEINUNGSBILDER

IDENTITÉ CORPORATE

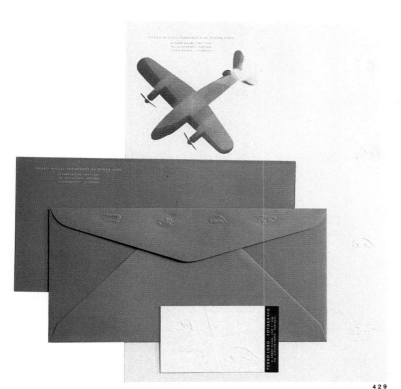

429

430

429

DESIGNERS:

ANA MENEZES

NE SANTELMO

AGENCY:

PAN DESIGN

CLIENT:

PEDRO LOBO

430

ART DIRECTOR:

PAUL VICKERS

DESIGNER:

ANDREW HEATH

ILLUSTRATOR:

PAUL ROBINSON

AGENCY:

TOTAL DESIGN

SOLUTION

CLIENT:

GILBERT MULLER

■ **429** STATIONERY FOR PEDRO LOBO, A PHOTOGRAPHER. (POR)

■ **430** LOGO AND STATIONERY FOR A PRODUCER OF FOIE GRAS AND OTHER GASTRONOMIC SPECIALTIES FROM THE SOUTHWEST OF FRANCE. (FRA)

■ **431** PROMOTIONAL POSTCARD AND BUSINESS CARD FOR A COMPANY RENTING RESTORED CHECKER TAXICABS FOR FILMS AND OTHER USES. THE DESIGN AND TYPOGRAPHY HAD TO EVOKE THE CLASSIC AND DISTINCT STYLE OF CHECKER CABS, AND THE INTENT WAS ALSO TO CREATE AN EYE-CATCHING PIECE THAT WOULD WORK IN DIFFERENT SIZES. (USA)

● **429** BRIEFPAPIER FÜR DEN PHOTOGRAPHEN PEDRO LOBO. (POR)

● **430** LOGO UND BRIEFPAPIER FÜR EINEN HERSTELLER VON LEBERPASTETE UND ANDEREN SPEZIALITÄTEN AUS DEM SÜDWESTEN FRANKREICHS. (FRA)

● **431** WERBEPOSTKARTE UND VISITENKARTE FÜR EINE FIRMA, DIE RESTAURIERTE ALTE TAXIS FÜR FILME UND WERBUNG VERMIETET. DESIGN UND TYPOGRAPHIE SOLLTEN AN DIE ZEIT UND DEN SPEZIELLEN STIL DIESER TAXIS MIT DEM TYPISCHEN SCHACHBRETT-MUSTER ERINNERN. ZUDEM SOLLTE DAS DESIGN ANSPRECHEND UND FÜR VERSCHIEDENE FORMATE GEEIGNET SEIN. (USA)

▲ **429** PAPIER À LETTRES DU PHOTOGRAPHE PEDRO LOBO. (POR)

▲ **430** LOGO ET PAPIER À LETTRES D'UN PRODUCTEUR DE FOIE GRAS ET DE SPÉCIALITÉS GASTRONOMIQUES DU SUD-OUEST DE LA FRANCE. (FRA)

▲ **431** CARTE POSTALE PUBLICITAIRE ET CARTE DE VISITE POUR UNE COMPAGNIE QUI LOUE DE VIEUX TAXIS REMIS À NEUF POUR DES FILMS, ÉMISSIONS DE TV OU OPÉRATIONS PROMOTIONNELLES. LE MOTIF DE DAMIERS ÉTAIT UN ÉLÉMENT DE DÉCOR CARACTÉRISTIQUE DE CES VÉHICULES. LE DESIGN, CONÇU POUR DIFFÉRENTS FORMATS, ÉVOQUE LES ANNÉES CINQUANTE. (USA)

431
ART DIRECTOR:
ROBERT PADOVANO
DESIGNER:
ROBERT PADOVANO
ILLUSTRATOR:
ROBERT PADOVANO
AGENCY:
ROBERT PADOVANO
DESIGN
CLIENT:
PETER YANELLO/
CHECKER CAB

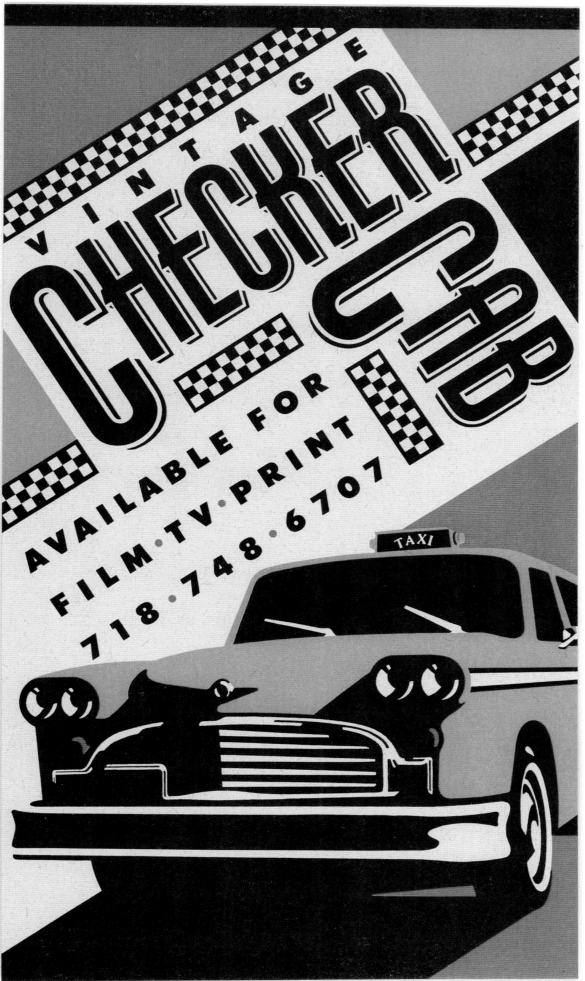

432

ART DIRECTOR:

CHAN MAYER

DESIGNER:

CHAN MAYER

CLIENT:

BEAUTYMED (BEAUTY
PRODUCTS/KOSMETIK
PRODUKTE/PRODUITS
DE BEAUTÉ)

(HKG)

432

433

ART DIRECTOR:

SCOTT GRIFFITHS

DESIGNER:

JAY VIGON

AGENCY:

GRIFFITHS + ASSOCI-
ATES

CLIENT:

VARITRANS (HAIR-
DRESSER/COIFFEUR-
SALON/SALON DE
COIFFURE)

(USA)

433

434

ART DIRECTOR:

JOSE SERRANO

DESIGNER:

JOSE SERRANO

ILLUSTRATOR:

DAN THONER

AGENCY:

MIRES DESIGN, INC.

CLIENT:

SAN DIEGO
HIKING CLUB
(ASSOCIATION/
WANDERCLUB/
CLUB DE RANDON-
NEURS)

(USA)

434

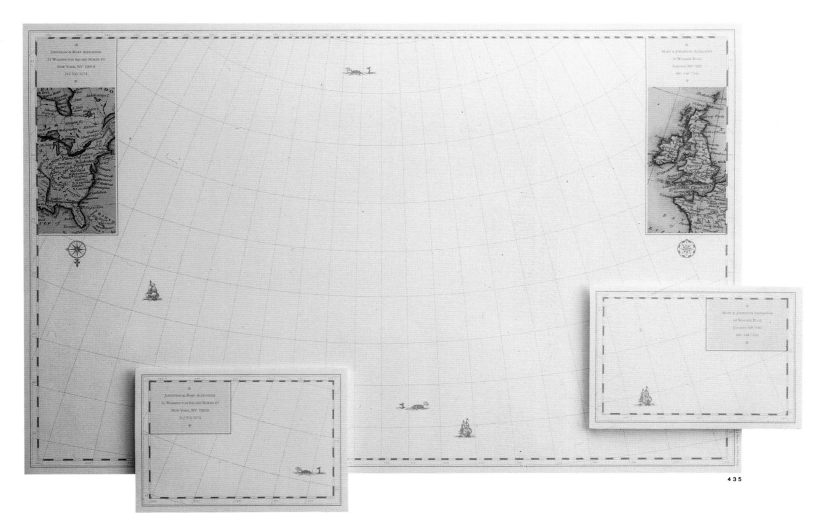

435

435

ART DIRECTOR:
WOODY PIRTLE
DESIGNERS:
JENNIFER LONG,
LESLIE PIRTLE
AGENCY:
PENTAGRAM DESIGN
CLIENT:
MARY & JONATHAN
ALEXANDER
(INDIVIDUALS/PRIVAT/
PRIVÉ)
(USA)

436

ART DIRECTOR:
ROBERT PADOVANO
DESIGNER:
ROBERT PADOVANO
AGENCY:
ROBERT PADOVANO
DESIGN
CLIENT:
MUSIC EMPORIUM
(RECORD STORE/
SCHALL-
PLATTENLADEN/
MAGASIN DE
DISQUES)
(USA)

436

438
ART DIRECTOR:
STEFAN WASSAK
AGENCY:
WASSAK & FRIK
CLIENT:
ULRIKE ECKER
(FASHIONS FOR
OVERWEIGHT PEOPLE/
MODE FÜR GROSSE
GRÖSSEN/
MODE GRANDES
TAILLES)
(AUT)

439
ART DIRECTOR:
SUPON PHORNIRUNLIT
DESIGNER:
SUPON PHORNIRUNLIT
AGENCY:
SUPON DESIGN GROUP
CLIENT:
ULMAN PAPER BAG
COMPANY (BAG MANU-
FACTURER/FABRIKANT VON
PAPIERTÜTEN/
FABRICANT DE SACS
EN PAPIER)
(USA)

440
ART DIRECTOR:
DOO KIM
DESIGNER:
DOO KIM
AGENCY:
DOO KIM DESIGN
CLIENT:
ID&A (DESIGN STUDIO/
STUDIO DE
DESIGN)
(KOR)

441
ART DIRECTORS:
MARY CAWEIN,
WALTER MCCORD
ILLUSTRATORS:
MARY CAWEIN,
WALTER MCCORD
CLIENT:
BOB HOWER
(PHOTOGRAPHER/
PHOTOGRAPH/
PHOTOGRAPHE)
(USA)

442
ART DIRECTOR:
RÜDIGER GÖTZ
DESIGNER:
RÜDIGER GÖTZ
ILLUSTRATOR:
RÜDIGER GÖTZ
AGENCY:
STUBENRAUCH & SIMON
CLIENT:
PROF. DR. WEISSMAN
(MARKETING CON-
SULTANCY/MARKETING-
BERATUNGSFIRMA/
FIRME DE CONSEIL EN
MARKETING)
(GER)

443
ART DIRECTORS:
ART GARCIA
RON SULLIVAN ·
DESIGNER:
ART GARCIA
ILLUSTRATOR:
ART GARCIA
AGENCY:
SULLIVAN PERKINS
CLIENT:
NORTHERN TELECOM
(CELLULAR PHONE
COMPANY. THIS LOGO IS
FOR A MEETING IN THE
BAHAMAS/KONGRESS AUF
DEN BAHAMAS ÜBER
ZELLULARTELEPHONE/
CONGRES SUR LES
TÉLÉPHONES
CELLULAIRES)
(USA)

444
ART DIRECTOR:
FREEMAN LAU SIU HONG
DESIGNER:
FREEMAN LAU SIU HONG
AGENCY:
KAN TAI-KEUNG DESIGN &
ASSOCIATES LTD
CLIENT:
MARDEN FOUNDATION INC.
(CHARITY FOUNDATION/
KARIKATIVE STIFTUNG/
ASSOCIATION
CARITATIVE)
(USA)

445
ART DIRECTOR:
ANDREY LOGVIN
DESIGNER:
ANDREY LOGVIN
CLIENT:
IMA-PRESS
(PUBLISHING HOUSE/
VERLAG/
MAISON D'ÉDITIONS)
(RUS)

446
ART DIRECTORS:
CHARLES S. ANDERSON
HALEY JOHNSON
DESIGNER:
HALEY JOHNSON
AGENCY:
C.S. ANDERSON
DESIGN CO.
CLIENT:
OVERSEAS PROD. INT'L.
(WATCHMAKER/
UHRENFIRMA/
HORLOGERIE)
(USA)

ULRIKE ECKER

438

439

ID&A
International Design & Advertising

440

MOTORHEAD

441

442

443

444

ИМА
ПРЕСС

445

446

447

448

449

450

451

452

453

454

■ **447** DESIGNER: MICHAEL MABRY AGENCY: MICHAEL MABRY DESIGN CLIENT: LUNAR DESIGN (USA) ■ **448** ART DIRECTOR: LAUREN SMITH DESIGNER: LAUREN SMITH CLIENT: BELISSIMA (MATERNITY CLOTHING RETAILER/GESCHÄFT FÜR SCHWANGERSCHAFTSMODE/MAGASIN DE VETEMENTS DE GROSSESSE) (USA) ■ **449** ART DIRECTORS: JOHN NORMAN, JEFF WEITHMAN DESIGNER: JOHN NORMAN ARTIST: JOHN NORMAN AGENCY: NIKE DESIGN CLIENT: NIKE, INC. (USA) ■ **450** ART DIRECTOR: EARL GEE DESIGNERS: FANI CHUNG, EARL GEE ARTIST: EARL GEE AGENCY: EARL GEE DESIGN CLIENT: SAN FRANCISCO ARTS COMMISSION (CULTURAL AGENCY/KULTURELLE VERANSTALTUNGEN/MANIFESTATIONS PUBLIQUES) (USA) ■ **451** ART DIRECTOR/ DESIGNER: RÜDIGER GÖTZ ILLUSTRATOR: RÜDIGER GÖTZ AGENCY: STUBENRAUCH & SIMON CLIENT: MERCATOR AUTOLEASING GMBH (GER) ■ **452** DESIGNER: STEVE SANDSTROM ILLUSTRATOR: GEORGE CHENEY AGENCY: SANDSTROM DESIGN CLIENT: MARK WEXLER (PHOTOGRAPHER/PHOTOGRAPH/PHOTOGRAPHE) (USA) ■ **453** ART DIRECTORS/DESIGNERS: CHARLES S. ANDERSON, DANIEL OLSON AGENCY: C.S . ANDERSON DESIGN CO. CLIENT: PARAMOUNT PICTURES (PRODUCT LINE/PRODUKTELINIE/LIGNE DE PRODUITS) (USA) ■ **454** ART DIRECTORS: COLIN FORBES, MICHAEL GERICKE DESIGNER: MICHAEL GERICKE ILLUSTRATOR: MIRKO ILIC AGENCY: PENTAGRAM DESIGN CLIENT: ATHENEUM HOTEL (USA) ■

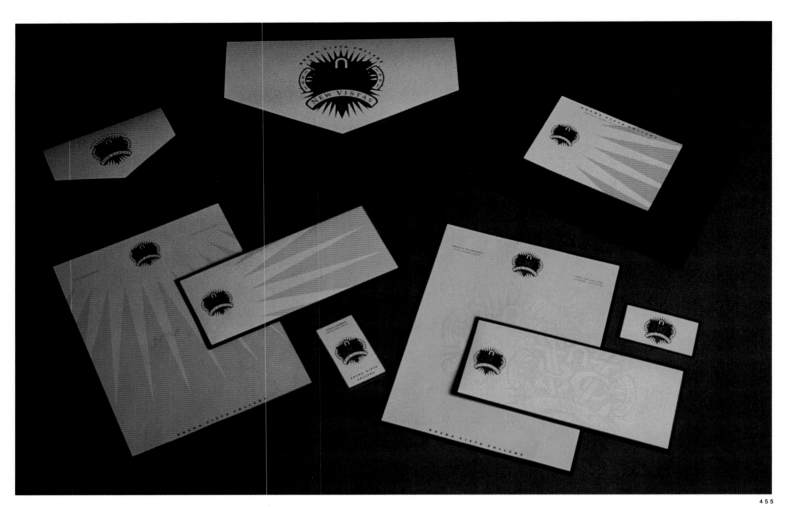

455

455

ART DIRECTOR:

JOHN SAYLES

DESIGNER:

JOHN SAYLES

AGENCY:

SAYLES GRAPHIC DESIGN

CLIENT:

BUENA VISTA COLLEGE

456

ART DIRECTOR:

ROBERT SCHALLENBERG

DESIGNER:

ROBERT SCHALLENBERG

AGENCY:

HÜTTER UND

SCHALLENBERG

CLIENT:

FOTOSTUDIO A. MEYER

456

457

457

ART DIRECTOR:

KAN TAI-KEUNG

DESIGNER:

KAN TAI-KEUNG

AGENCY:

KAN TAI-KEUNG DESIGN

& ASSOCIATES LTD

CLIENT:

FAMOUS DECORATION CO.

■ 455 A STATIONARY SYSTEM FOR BUENA VISTA COLLEGE. (USA)

● 455 BRIEFBOGEN FÜR DAS BUENA VISTA COLLEGE. (USA)

▲ 455 PAPIER À LETTRES DU BUENA VISTA COLLEGE. (USA)

■ 456 STATIONERY FOR A PHOTOGRAPHER'S STUDIO. (GER)

● 456 BRIEFPAPIER FÜR EIN PHOTOSTUDIO IN KÖLN. (GER)

▲ 456 PAPIER À LETTRES POUR UN STUDIO DE PHOTOGRAPHIE. (GER)

■ 457 STATIONERY AND PRINTED MATERIALS FOR THE FAMOUS DECORATION CO., AN INTERIOR-DESIGN FIRM. (HKG)

● 457 AUSWAHL DES GESCHÄFTSPAPIERS FÜR EINE INNENARCHITEKTEN-FIRMA IN HONGKONG. (HKG)

▲ 457 LIGNE DE PAPIER À LETTRES CONÇUE POUR UN ARCHITECTE D'INTÉRIEUR. (HKG)

458

458

CREATIVE DIRECTOR:
KAN TAI-KEUNG
DESIGNERS:
KAN TAI-KEUNG
EDDY YU CHI KONG
AGENCY:
KAN TAI-KEUNG
DESIGN &
ASSOCIATES LTD
CLIENT:
LUTEX CO LTD
(SOAP MANUFAC-
TURER/SEIFE/
SAVON)
(HKG)

460

460

ART DIRECTOR:
JOSE SERRANO
DESIGNER:
JOSE SERRANO
ILLUSTRATOR:
DAN THONER
AGENCY:
MIRES DESIGN, INC.
CLIENT:
ADVENTURE 16
(TRAVEL OUTFITTERS/
FREIZEITBE-KLEIDUNG/
VETEMENTS
DE LOISIRS)
(USA)

459

459

ART DIRECTOR:
MICHAEL CRONAN
DESIGNER:
MICHAEL CRONAN
AGENCY:
CRONAN DESIGN, INC.
CLIENT:
CRONAN ARTEFACT
(CLOTHING
MANUFACTURER/
TEXTILIEN/
FABRICANT DE
VETEMENTS)
(USA)

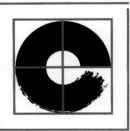

461

461

ART DIRECTOR:
KAN TAI-KEUNG
DESIGNER:
KAN TAI-KEUNG
AGENCY:
KAN TAI-KEUNG
DESIGN & ASSOCI-
ATES LTD
CLIENT:
CITY GALLERY
(ART GALLERY/
KUNSTGALERIE/
GALERIE D'ART)
(HKG)

PACKAGING

PACKUNGEN

PACKAGING

462

462
DESIGNER:
MICHAEL MABRY
COPYWRITER:
LYNNE GALLER
AGENCY:
MICHAEL MABRY
DESIGN
CLIENT:
MON JARDINET,
LTD.

463
ART DIRECTOR:
BARRIE TUCKER
DESIGNERS:
BARRIE TUCKER
JODY TUCKER
ILLUSTRATOR:
JODY TUCKER
CLIENT:
MORRIS WINES
PTY LTD

■ 462 PACKAGING FOR A SERIES OF MON JARDINET PERFUMED SOAPS, EACH WITH A DIFFERENT TYPOGRAPHIC SOLUTION. (USA)

● 462 VERPACKUNG FÜR MON-JARDINET-SEIFEN; JEDE MIT EINER ANDEREN TYPOGRAPHISCHEN LÖSUNG. (USA)

▲ 462 EMBALLAGES POUR DES SAVONS PARFUMÉS; CHACUN PRÉSENTE UNE SOLUTION TYPOGRAPHIQUE DIFFÉRENTE. (USA)

■ 463 A BOTTLE OF MORRIS OF RUTHERGLEN LIQUEUR MUSCAT WITH ITS GIFT CARTON. IT IS PART OF A SERIES OF PACKAGES FOR THE MORRIS COMPANY, EMPHASIZING THE COMPANY'S LONG TRADITION. (AUS)

● 463 GESTALTUNG EINER FLASCHE MIT GESCHENKKARTON FÜR EINEN MUSKAT-LIKÖR. SIE SIND TEIL EINER VERPACKUNGS-LINIE, DIE DIE TRADITION DES HAUSES MORRIS WIDERSPIEGELN SOLL. (AUS)

▲ 463 LA BOUTEILLE D'UNE LIQUEUR MUSCAT ET SON EMBALLAGE CADEAU. D'UNE SÉRIE DE CONDITIONNEMENTS POUR LES APÉRITIFS ET DIGESTIFS PRODUITS PAR UNE MAISON DE GRANDE TRADITION. (AUS)

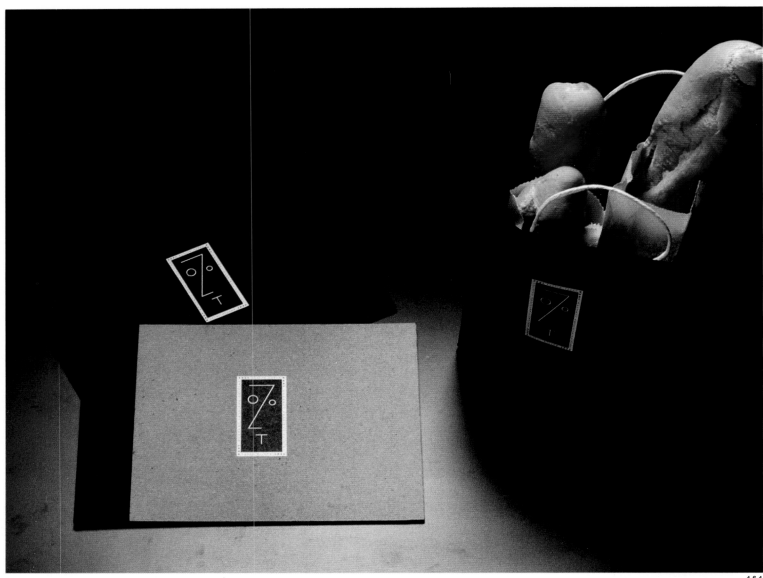

464

464

Art Director:
LANA RIGSBY
Designer:
LANA RIGSBY
Illustrator:
LANA RIGSBY
Agency:
RIGSBY DESIGN
Client:
ZOOT RESTAURANT

465

Art Director:
GEOFF SMITH
Designer:
GEOFF SMITH
Illustrator:
DOUG MARTIN
Agency:
SMITH + COMPANY
Client:
BRIDGEHEAD TRADING

465

466

467

466

ART DIRECTOR:

JACK ANDERSON

DESIGNERS:

JACK ANDERSON

MARY HERMES

ILLUSTRATOR:

LARRY JOST

AGENCY:

HORNALL ANDERSON

DESIGN WORKS

CLIENT:

BROADMOOR BAKER

467

ART DIRECTOR:

PIERO VENTURA

DESIGNER:

ROSSELLA RABUFFI

ILLUSTRATOR:

ROSSELLA RABUFFI

AGENCY:

IMMAGINE DESIGN

CLIENT:

CRIPPA & BERGER

■ **464** PACKAGING AS PART OF A CORPO-RATE-IDENTITY DESIGN FOR AN UPSCALE RESTAURANT IN AUSTIN, TEXAS. (USA)

■ **465** PACKAGE DESIGN FOR A SPECIALTY TEA IMPORTED FROM SMALL COOPERATIVES AND SOLD MAINLY BY CATALOG. (USA)

■ **466** PACKAGING FOR AN ITALIAN BREAD BAKED AND SOLD IN THE UNITED STATES. THE PACKAGE HIGHLIGHTS THE BREAD-BAK-ING HERITAGE OF THE ITALIAN REGION OF COMO AND THE SPECIAL TASTE OF THIS RUS-TIC BREAD. (USA)

■ **467** SEALED BAG FOR A DECAFFEINATED COFFEE CALLED "DAY AND NIGHT." (ITA)

● **464** VERPACKUNGEN ALS TEIL DES VISU-ELLEN ERSCHEINUNGSBILDES EINES ERST-KLASSRESTAURANTS IN AUSTIN. (USA)

● **465** PACKUNG FÜR QUALITÄTS-TEE, DER VON KLEINEN KOOPERATIVEN PRODUZIERT UND PER KATALOG VERKAUFT WIRD. (USA)

● **466** VERPACKUNG FÜR IN DEN USA VER-KAUFTES ITALIENISCHES BROT. ES GEHT UM DIE BETONUNG DER HANDWERKLICHEN TRA-DITION DES BACKENS AUS DER REGION VON COMO UND DEN SPEZIELLEN GESCHMACK DIESES RUSTIKALEN BROTES. (USA)

● **467** VERSIEGELTE TÜTE FÜR DEN KOFFEIN-FREIEN KAFFEE «TAG UND NACHT». (ITA)

▲ **464** LE PACKAGING A ÉTÉ CONÇU DANS LE CADRE DU PROGRAMME D'IDENTITÉ VISUELLE D'UN GRAND RESTAURANT D'AUSTIN. (USA)

▲ **465** BOITE POUR UNE MARQUE DE THÉ PRODUIT PAR DE PETITES COOPÉRATIVES ET VENDU PAR CORRESPONDANCE. (USA)

▲ **466** SACHETS SPÉCIALEMENT CRÉÉS POUR DU PAIN ITALIEN VENDU AUX USA. LE DESIGN SOULIGNE LE COTÉ ARTISANAL DE LA FABRI-CATION DE CE PAIN AU GOUT RUSTIQUE, CUIT DANS LA TRADITION DES BOULANGERS DE LA RÉGION DE COME. (USA)

▲ **467** SACHET POUR UN CAFÉ DÉCAFÉINÉ ITALIEN: «NUIT ET JOUR». (ITA)

468

468

ART DIRECTION:

ALPERN, HASLER, SCHNELL

DESIGN:

ALPERN, HASLER, SCHNELL

ILLUSTRATION:

ALPERN, HASLER, SCHNELL

AGENCY:

HAS DESIGN AG

CLIENT:

COOP SCHWEIZ

469

469

Art Directors:

HARALD SCHWEERS

HOLGER SINN

Designer:

HOLGER SINN

Illustrator:

ULF NAWROT

Copywriter:

MICHAEL LEWE

Agency:

ATELIER HAASE & KNELS

Client:

STANWELL VERTRIEBS

GMBH

■ **468** UPDATED LABEL DESIGNS FOR A LINE OF JAMS, THE HOUSE BRAND OF THE COOP CHAIN IN SWITZERLAND. (SWI)

■ **469** EXAMPLES OF A PACKAGING DESIGN FOR A TOBACCO BLEND INCORPORATING THE AROMA OF CALIFORNIAN CHARDONNAY. CARTONS WITH PLASTIC FOIL ON THE INSIDE WERE CHOSEN INSTEAD OF THE USUAL TIN BOXES. (GER)

● **468** NEUGESTALTUNG DER ETIKETTS FÜR VERSCHIEDENE SORTEN MARMELADE, HAUSMARKE DER LADENKETTE COOP. (SWI)

● **469** ANWENDUNGEN EINES PACKUNGS-DESIGNS FÜR EINE TABAKMISCHUNG, DIE MIT KALIFORNISCHEM CHARDONNAY AROMATISIERT WURDE. STATT BLECHDOSEN WURDE EIN INNEN MIT KUNSTSTOFF-FOLIE BESCHICHTETER KARTON GEWÄHLT. (GER)

▲ **468** CONDITIONNEMENT D'UN ASSORTIMENT DE CONFITURES VENDUES DANS LES MAGASINS COOP EN SUISSE. (SWI)

▲ **469** DIVERSES APPLICATIONS DU DESIGN CONÇU POUR UN TABAC AROMATISÉ AU CHARDONNAY CALIFORNIEN. AU LIEU DES TRADITIONNELLES DOSES EN FER BLANC, ON A CHOISI ICI UN CARTON DOUBLÉ DE PLASTIQUE À L'INTÉRIEUR. (GER)

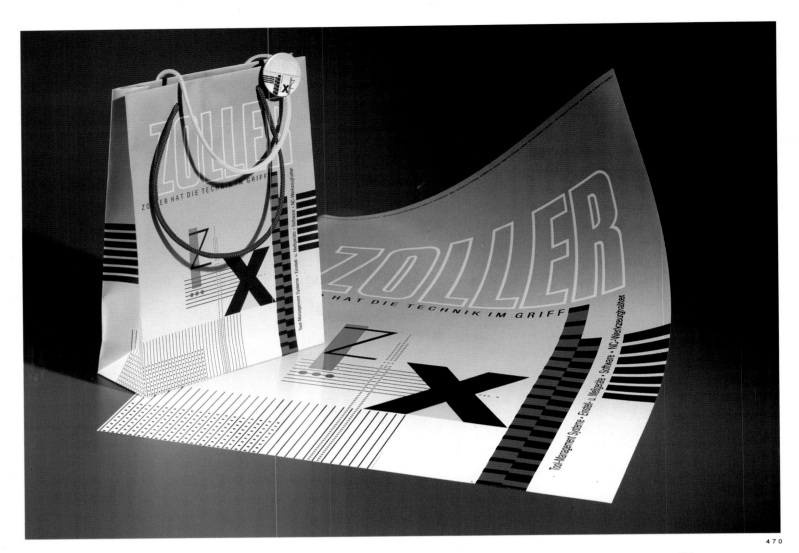

470

470
DESIGNER:
METZGER & METZGER
AGENCY:
METZGER & METZGER
CLIENT:
E. ZOLLER GMBH
& CO KG

471
ART DIRECTORS:
PEP CARRIO
PACO DIAZ
DESIGNER:
COMUNICARTE
AGENCY:
COMUNICARTE
CLIENT:
UNIMOL

472
ART DIRECTOR:
JOHN SWIETER
DESIGNERS:
JOHN SWIETER
JIM VOGEL
ILLUSTRATOR:
PAUL MUNSTERMAN
AGENCY:
SWIETER DESIGN
CLIENT:
NATIONAL OATS CO.

471

472

473

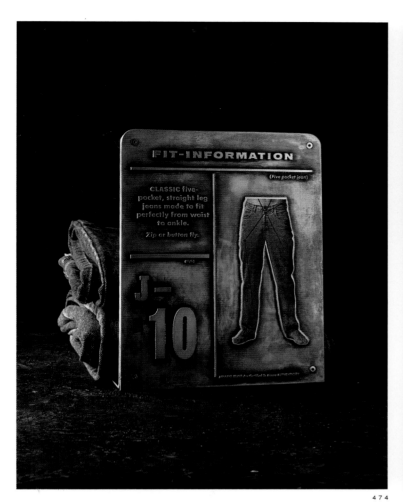

474

475

473-475

ART DIRECTORS:

JOE DUFFY (473, 475)

SHARON WERNER (474)

TODD WATERBURY

DESIGNERS:

SHARON WERNER (474)

TODD WATERBURY

COPYWRITER:

CHUCK CARLSON

AGENCY:

THE DUFFY DESIGN

GROUP

CLIENT:

SIMINT USA, INC.

■ 473-475 EXAMPLES FROM A SERIES OF PACKAGES FOR ARMANI PRODUCTS. A UTILITARIAN LOOK WAS CHOSEN FOR THE BAGS AND BOXES IN VARIOUS SIZES. INDIVIDUAL METAL BOOKENDS, INSPIRED BY THE NO-NONSENSE MILITARY LOOK, DISPLAY THE FEATURES OF THE DIFFERENT STYLES OF JEANS AVAILABLE. (USA)

● 473-475 VERPACKUNG UND PRÄSENTATION VON ARMANI-PRODUKTEN. BEI DEN TÜTEN UND SCHACHTELN STANDEN VERPACKUNGEN AUS EISENWARENLÄDEN PATE; WÄHREND EINZELNE BUCHSTÜTZEN AUS METALL MIT INFORMATIONEN ÜBER DIE JEANS VON DEN NÜCHTERNEN INFORMATIONSTAFELN DER ARMEE INSPIRIERT WURDEN. (USA)

▲ 473-475 EXEMPLES DE LA GAMME DE PACKAGING CONÇUE POUR LES PRODUITS ARMANI. POUR LES SACS ET LES BOITES, L'ASPECT UTILITAIRE A ÉTÉ DÉTERMINANT; LE SERRE-LIVRES, INSPIRÉ DU SYSTEME DE CLASSIFICATION UTILISÉ PAR L'ARMÉE, PERMET D'IDENTIFIER LES DIFFÉRENTS STYLES DE JEANS. (USA)

476

477

478

476

Art Directors:

CHARLES ANDERSON

DANIEL OLSON

Designers:

CHARLES ANDERSON

DANIEL OLSON

Agency:

C.S. ANDERSON

DESIGN CO.

Client:

DISTILLERIE DES

ARAVIS

477

Art Directors:

CHARLES ANDERSON

HALEY JOHNSON

DANIEL OLSON

Designers:

HALEY JOHNSON

DANIEL OLSON

Illustrators:

RANDALL DAHLK

HALEY JOHNSON

DANIEL OLSON

Agency:

C.S. ANDERSON DESIGN CO.

Client:

OVERSEAS PROD. INT'L., INC.

478

Art Directors:

CHARLES ANDERSON

DANIEL OLSON

Designers:

CHARLES ANDERSON

DANIEL OLSON

Illustrator:

CHARLES ANDERSON

Agency:

C.S. ANDERSON

DESIGN CO.

Client:

REGIS CORP.

■ **476** A CORDIAL LABEL BASED ON ANTIQUE POSTAGE STAMPS. THE LABEL WAS DESIGNED TO REFLECT THE HERITAGE OF THIS 200-YEAR-OLD FRENCH DISTILLERY. SUBTLE COLORS, UNCOATED PAPER AND A DISCREET, CLASSIC TYPOGRAPHY SUPPORT THE APPROACH. (USA)

■ **477** A SERIES OF SILKSCREENED TIN BOXES DESIGNED FOR THE FOSSIL WATCH CO., DEMONSTRATING VARIOUS TYPOGRAPHIC AND DESIGN APPROACHES. THE COVER DESIGNS WILL CHANGE CONSTANTLY WITH MORE THAN 20 VARIATIONS PER YEAR. (USA)

■ **478** PROPOSED PACKAGING AND IDENTITY FOR THE REGIS HAIR SALONS' HOUSE BRAND OF HAIR AND SKIN PRODUCTS. (USA)

● **476** ETIKETT FÜR DEN FRUCHTLIKÖR EINER 200 JAHRE ALTEN BRENNEREI IN FRANKREICH. ALTE BRIEFMARKEN; SANFTE FARBEN, UNGESTRICHENES PAPIER UND EINE DISKRETE, KLASSISCHE TYPOGRAPHIE VERSTÄRKEN DEN GEWÜNSCHTEN EINDRUCK VON HANDARBEIT UND SORGFALT. (USA)

● **477** WEISSBLECHDOSEN MIT SIEBDRUCK-ILLUSTRATIONEN FÜR DIE FOSSIL WATCH CO. IN VERSCHIEDENEN GRAPHISCHEN AUSFÜHRUNGEN. ES IST VORGESEHEN, PRO JAHR 20 VARIANTEN DER DOSENDESIGNS AUF DEN MARKT ZU BRINGEN. (USA)

● **478** VERPACKUNGSPROJEKT FÜR DIE KOSMETIK- UND HAARPFLEGEPRODUKTE EINER COIFFEUR-KETTE. (USA)

▲ **476** ÉTIQUETTE POUR DES BOUTEILLES DE LIQUEURS PRODUITES PAR UNE DISTILLERIE FONDÉE VOICI DEUX SIECLES. ELLES SONT DÉCORÉES D'ANCIENNES GRAVURES DE TIMBRES-POSTE QUI RAPPELLENT L'HÉRITAGE CULTUREL FRANÇAIS DE CETTE MAISON ET SONT FAITES ARTISANALEMENT. (USA)

▲ **477** EXEMPLES D'UNE SÉRIE DE 16 BOITES EN FER BLANC, ORNÉES D'IMAGES SÉRIGRAPHIÉES, POUR LES MONTRES DE LA MARQUE FOSSIL WATCH: IL EST PRÉVU DE CRÉER PLUS DE 20 VARIATIONS DE CES DÉCORS CHAQUE ANNÉE. (USA)

▲ **478** PACKAGING CRÉÉ POUR DES COSMÉTIQUES ET PRODUITS CAPILLAIRES D'UNE CHAINE DE SALONS DE COIFFURE. (USA)

479

479

Art Directors:

FREEMAN LAU SIU HONG

KAN TAI-KEUNG

Designers:

BENSON KWUN TIN YAU

FREEMAN LAU SIU HONG

KAN TAI-KEUNG

Agency:

KAN TAI-KEUNG DESIGN

& ASSOCIATES LTD

Client:

THE HOUSE OF KWONG

SANG HONG LTD

■ **479** A SERIES OF SHOPPING BAGS PROMOTING A HONG KONG STORE. (HKG)

■ **480** PACKAGE DESIGN USED FOR THE INTRODUCTION OF A NEW TYPE OF FONT CARTRIDGE FOR HEWLETT-PACKARD LASER PRINTERS. (USA)

■ **481** THIS PACKAGE DESIGN HAD TO BE ADAPTABLE TO THE VARIOUS PRODUCTS OF A COSTA RICAN PLANTATION: BLACK PEPPERCORNS, VANILLA BEANS, COCONUTS AND HEARTS OF PALM. (USA)

● **479** TRAGTASCHEN ALS WERBUNG FÜR EINEN LADEN IN HONGKONG. (HKG)

● **480** PACKUNGSGESTALTUNG FÜR DIE EINFÜHRUNG EINER NEUEN SCHRIFTKASSETTE FÜR LASERPRINTER DER FIRMA HEWLETT-PACKARD. (USA)

● **481** DIESE FLASCHENGESTALTUNG MUSSTE SICH FÜR VERSCHIEDENE PRODUKTE (PFEFFER, VANILLESCHOTEN, KOKOSFLOCKEN UND ARTISCHOKENHERZEN) EINER PLANTAGE IN COSTA RICA EIGNEN. (USA)

▲ **479** UNE SÉRIE DE SACS POUR LA PUBLICITÉ D'UN MAGASIN. (HKG)

▲ **480** EMBALLAGE CRÉÉ POUR LE LANCEMENT D'UNE NOUVELLE POLICE DE CARACTERES POUR IMPRIMANTES LASER DE LA FIRME HEWLETT-PACKARD. (USA)

▲ **481** PETITES BOUTEILLES D'ÉPICES ET AROMES NATURELS (POIVRE, GOUSSES DE VANILLE, NOIX DE COCO PILÉE ET CŒURS DE PALMIER) PRODUITS PAR UNE PLANTATION DU COSTA RICA. (USA)

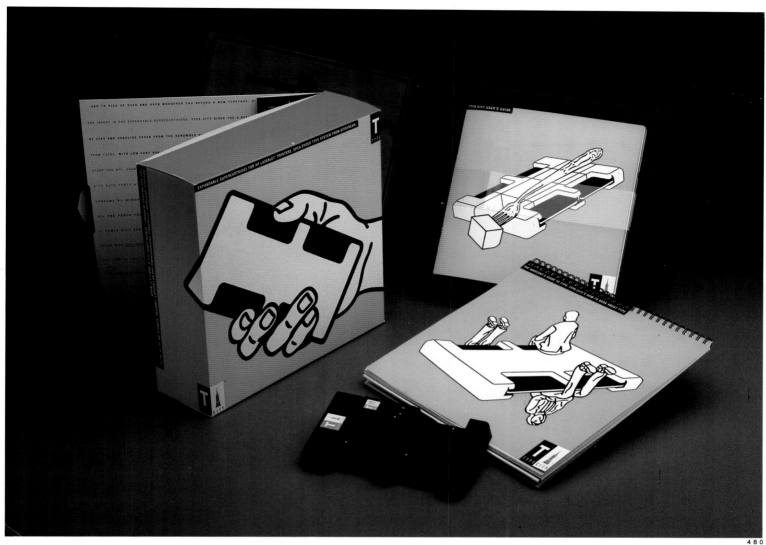

480

481

482

483

482
ART DIRECTORS:
CHARLES ANDERSON
DANIEL OLSON
DESIGNERS:
CHARLES ANDERSON
DANIEL OLSON
ILLUSTRATOR:
RANDALL DAHLK
AGENCY:
C.S. ANDERSON DESIGN CO.
CLIENT:
THE EL PASO CHILE CO.

483
ART DIRECTOR:
MICHAEL DUNLAVEY
DESIGNER:
MICHAEL DUNLAVEY
ILLUSTRATOR:
DAVE STEVENSON
AGENCY:
THE DUNLAVEY STUDIO
CLIENT:
WORLD OF GOOD TASTES

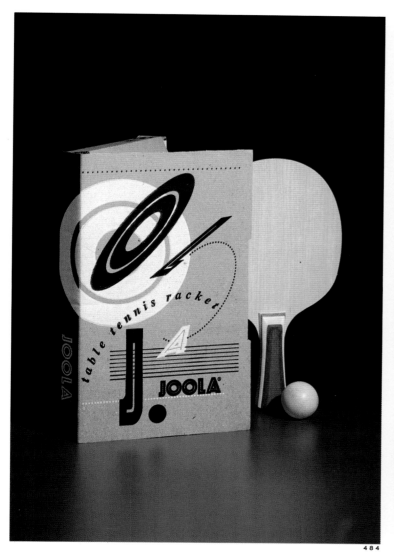

484

485

484

DESIGNER:
METZGER & METZGER
AGENCY:
METZGER & METZGER
CLIENT:
E. ZOLLER GMBH &
CO KG

485

ART DIRECTOR:
JACK ANDERSON
DESIGNERS:
JACK ANDERSON
JULIA LAPINE
ILLUSTRATOR:
JULIA LAPINE
AGENCY:
HORNALL ANDERSON
DESIGN WORKS
CLIENT:
ITALIA

■ **482** PACKAGING CREATED FOR DESERT PEPPER'S NEW LINE OF SALSAS. THE LABELS FEATURE MEXICAN WOODCUTS. (USA)

■ **483** BOX DESIGN FOR UNBLEACHED COFFEE FILTERS. THE BOXES, CORRUGATED CARDBOARD WITH A SCRATCHBOARD ILLUSTRATION, PRINTED ON RECYCLED STOCK, SUPPORT THE NATURAL LOOK DESIRED. (USA)

■ **484** THIS PACKAGE IS MADE OUT OF SIMPLE BROWN CARDBOARD, IN CONSIDERATION OF THE GERMAN ENVIRONMENTAL LAW ORDERING RETAILERS TO TAKE BACK THE PACKAGES THEIR GOODS ARE SOLD IN. (GER)

■ **485** THIS LABEL IS PART OF THE CORPORATE-IDENTITY DESIGN FOR AN ITALIAN RESTAURANT. (USA)

● **482** VERPACKUNG FÜR NEUE SAUCEN VON DESERT PEPPER. MEXIKANISCHE HOLZSCHNITTE DIENEN ALS ILLUSTRATION. (USA)

● **483** SCHACHTEL FÜR UNGEBLEICHTES KAFFEEFILTERPAPIER. WELLKARTON UND DIE SCHABILLUSTRATION (THERMODRUCK AUF RECYCLINGPAPIER) UNTERSTÜTZEN DEN ERWÜNSCHTEN NATUR-LOOK. (USA)

● **484** DIESE PACKUNG AUS GROBEM BRAUNEN KARTON WURDE IM HINBLICK AUF DAS DEUTSCHE UMWELTSCHUTZGESETZ GESTALTET, DAS ANBIETER VERPFLICHTET, PACKUNGEN ZURÜCKZUNEHMEN. (GER)

● **485** ETIKETT ALS TEIL DES CORPORATE IDENTITY DESIGNS FÜR EIN ITALIENISCHES RESTAURANT. (USA)

▲ **482** EMBALLAGES D'UN ASSORTISSEMENT DE SALSAS. LES ÉTIQUETTES SONT ORNÉES DE GRAVURES SUR BOIS MEXICAINES. (USA)

▲ **483** BOITES CONÇUES POUR DES FILTRES À CAFÉ EN PAPIER NON BLANCHI. L'EMPLOI DE CARTON ONDULÉ ET L'ILLUSTRATION ESQUISSÉE RENFORCENT LE COTÉ NATUREL DU DESIGN. (USA)

▲ **484** CET EMBALLAGE EN CARTON D'UN JEU DE TENNIS DE TABLE A ÉTÉ CONÇU EN FONCTION DE LA NOUVELLE RÉGLEMENTATION SUR L'ENVIRONNEMENT QUI OBLIGE LES MAGASINS À REPRENDRE LES EMBALLAGES. (GER)

▲ **485** ÉTIQUETTES DE BOUTEILLES FAISANT PARTIE DU PROGRAMME D'IDENTITÉ VISUELLE D'UN RESTAURANT ITALIEN. (USA)

486

■ **486** WINE BOTTLE AND CARTON SENT BY A PRINTER TO CLIENTS AT CHRISTMAS. LABEL AND CARTON DEMONSTRATE THE CRAFTSMANSHIP OF THE PRINTER, DRAWING A COMPARISON TO THAT OF A VINTNER. (CAN)

■ **487** LABEL AND CARTON DESIGN FOR A 14-YEAR-OLD MALT WHISKY. THE DESIGN EMPHASIZES AUTHENTICITY, HERITAGE, QUALITY AND DISTINCTION. (GBR)

■ **488** BOTTLE AND CARTON FOR A JAPANESE WHISKY. (JPN)

■ **489** EMBOSSED TIN FOR HAND-PACKED PIPE TOBACCO. (GER)

● **486** WEINFLASCHE MIT KARTON, VON EINEM DRUCKER ALS WEIHNACHTSGESCHENK AN SEINE KUNDEN VERSANDT. ETIKETT UND VERPACKUNG DEMONSTRIEREN DIE SORGFÄLTIGE ARBEIT DES DRUCKERS. (CAN)

● **487** ETIKETT UND KARTONGESTALTUNG FÜR EINEN 14 JAHRE ALTEN MALT WHISKY. DAS DESIGN SOLLTE ECHTHEIT, TRADITION UND QUALITÄT HERVORHEBEN. (GBR)

● **488** FLASCHENAUSSTATTUNG UND KARTON FÜR EINEN JAPANISCHEN WHISKY. (JPN)

● **489** WEISSBLECHDOSE MIT PRÄGUNG FÜR HOCHWERTIGEN PFEIFENTABAK. (GER)

▲ **486** BOUTEILLE ENVOYÉE PAR UNE IMPRIMERIE À SES CLIENTS POUR NOEL: L'ÉTIQUETTE ET L'EMBALLAGE METTENT EN VALEUR LE TRAVAIL SOIGNEUX DE CETTE ENTREPRISE. (CAN)

▲ **487** EMBALLAGE CADEAU D'UNE BOUTEILLE DE WHISKY DE 14 ANS D'AGE. L'AUTHEN-TIC-ITÉ ET LA QUALITÉ DU PRODUIT SONT SOULIGNÉES PAR LE DESIGN. (GBR)

▲ **488** UN WHISKY VENDU AU JAPON ET SON EMBALLAGE CADEAU. (JPN)

▲ **489** BOITE EN FER BLANC ESTAMPÉE POUR UN TABAC DE QUALITÉ SUPÉRIEURE. (GER)

487

488

486

ART DIRECTOR:
PAUL HASLIP
DESIGNER:
PAUL HASLIP
ILLUSTRATOR:
GERARD GAUCI
COPYWRITER:
JAMES HYNES
AGENCY:
HM + E INCORPORATED
CLIENT:
GRENVILLE PRINTING

487

ART DIRECTOR:
MARY LEWIS
DESIGNER:
MARY LEWIS
ILLUSTRATOR:
BILL SANDERSON
COPYWRITER:
MARY LEWIS
AGENCY:
LEWIS MOBERLY
CLIENT:
UNITED DISTILLERS

488

ART DIRECTOR:
KEN-YA HARA
DESIGNER:
KEN-YA HARA
AGENCY:
NIPPON DESIGN CENTER,
INC.
CLIENT:
THE NIKKA WHISKY DIS-
TILLING CO., LTD.

489

ART DIRECTORS:
FRITZ HAASE
HARALD SCHWEERS
DESIGNER:
ANDREAS WILHELM
AGENCY:
ATELIER HAASE & KNELS
CLIENT:
STANWELL VERTRIEB
GMBH

489

490

490

ART DIRECTOR:

JOSE SERRANO

DESIGNER:

JOSE SERRANO

ILLUSTRATOR:

TRACY SABIN

COPYWRITER:

KELLY SMOTHERMON

AGENCY:

MIRES DESIGN, INC.

CLIENT:

DELEO CLAY TILE

491

ART DIRECTORS:

AUBYN GWINN

MICHAEL MABRY

DESIGNER:

MICHAEL MABRY

PHOTOGRAPHER:

ALBERT WATSON

STYLISTS:

BUTLER REGHANTI

JESSE RODRIGUEZ

AGENCY:

FOOTE CONE &

BELDING

CLIENT:

LEVI STRAUSS & CO.

491

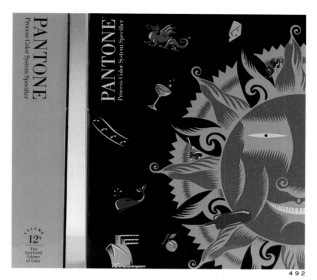

492

493

492-494

ART DIRECTOR:

WOODY PIRTLE

DESIGNERS:

MATT HECK

WOODY PIRTLE

ILLUSTRATORS:

TIM LEWIS (492)

WOODY PIRTLE (493)

ERIN VAN SLYCK (493)

ANTHONY RUSSO (494)

AGENCY:

PENTAGRAM DESIGN

CLIENT:

PANTONE, INC.

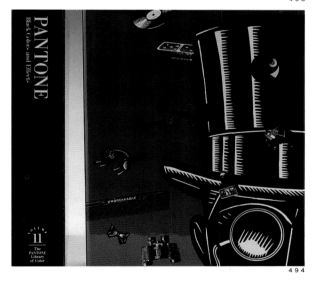

494

■ **490** THIS PACKAGE DESIGN FOR DELEO ROOFING TILES HAD TO CONVEY THE NATURAL QUALITY OF THE PRODUCT. (USA)

■ **491** LABEL DESIGNS FOR DIFFERENT STYLES OF LEVI STRAUSS JEANS. (USA)

■ **492-494** SERIES OF BOOKS CONTAINING PANTONE COLOR-MATCHING SYSTEMS, AIMED AT THE GRAPHICS INDUSTRY. (USA)

● **490** DIESE VERPACKUNG FÜR DELEO-DACH-ZIEGEL SOLLTE DIE NATÜRLICHKEIT DES PRODUKTES UNTERSTREICHEN. (USA)

● **491** VERSCHIEDENE ETIKETT-DESIGNS FÜR LEVI-STRAUSS-JEANS. (USA)

● **492-494** EINE FÜR DIE GRAPHISCHE INDUSTRIE BESTIMMTE REIHE VON PANTONE-FARBMUSTERBÜCHERN. (USA)

▲ **490** BOITES DE PRÉSENTATION DES ÉCHANTILLONS DE TUILES DELEO SOULIGNANT LE COTÉ NATUREL DU PRODUIT. (USA)

▲ **491** ETIQUETTES POUR LES JEANS LEVI-STRAUSS. (USA)

▲ **492-494** UNE SÉRIE DE LIVRES RENFERMANT LES NUANCIERS PANTONE, CONÇUS POUR L'INDUSTRIE GRAPHIQUE. (USA)

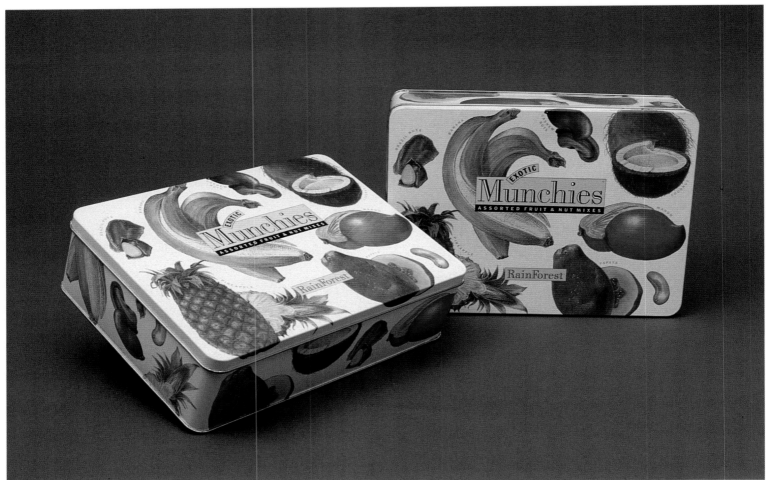

495

495

ART DIRECTOR:

PAULA SCHER

DESIGNER:

PAULA SCHER

ILLUSTRATOR:

DUGALD STERMER

AGENCY:

PENTAGRAM DESIGN

CLIENT:

FROM THE RAINFOREST, INC.

496

ART DIRECTOR:

BARRIE TUCKER

DESIGNERS:

DAVID LANCASHIRE

BARRIE TUCKER

ILLUSTRATOR:

ROBERT MARSHALL

CLIENT:

SOUTH AUSTRALIAN BREWING

COMPANY

496

497

ART DIRECTOR:

ARNO SCHMID

DESIGNER:

ARNO SCHMID

ILLUSTRATOR:

ARNO SCHMID

AGENCY:

SCHMID GRAFIK-

WERBUNG-DESIGN

CLIENT:

BRAUEREI SONNEN-

BRÄU AG

497

498

ART DIRECTOR:

SUZANNE LYKIARD

DESIGNER:

COLIN LEIGH

ILLUSTRATOR:

STEFAN CHABLUK

AGENCY:

NUCLEUS DESIGN

LIMITED

CLIENT:

G.E. THORN

■ 495 PACKAGE FOR SNACK FOOD. DRAWINGS WHICH WERE REMINISCENT OF 19TH-CENTURY BOTANICAL ILLUSTRATIONS WERE CHOSEN, AND VEGETABLE INKS AND REUSABLE TINS WERE USED. (USA)

■ 496 BOTTLE FOR A LOW-ALCOHOL BEER MADE BY AN AUSTRALIAN BREWERY. (AUS)

■ 497 BEER BOTTLE WITH GLASS RELIEF AND LID, CREATED FOR THE CENTENNIAL CELEBRATION OF A GERMAN BREWERY. (GER)

■ 498 PRODUCT ILLUSTRATIONS WITH VIBRANT BACKGROUND COLORS PRODUCE BOLD GEOMETRIC REPEAT PATTERNS ON THESE PACKAGES FOR MAZDA HOUSEHOLD LIGHT BULBS. (GBR)

● 495 VERPACKUNG FÜR SNACKS AUS DER REGENWALDREGION. DIE ILLUSTRATIONEN ERINNERN AN ALTE BOTANISCHE DARSTELLUNGEN. ES WURDEN DRUCKFARBEN AUF PFLANZLICHER BASIS VERWENDET. (USA)

● 496 FLASCHE FÜR EIN AUSTRALISCHES BIER MIT NIEDRIGEM ALKOHOLGEHALT. (AUS)

● 497 BIERFLASCHE MIT GLASRELIEF UND BÜGELVERSCHLUSS ZUM HUNDERTJÄHRIGEN BESTEHEN EINER BRAUEREI. (GER)

● 498 DIE PRODUKTDARSTELLUNG UND DIE LEUCHTENDEN HINTERGRUNDFARBEN ERGEBEN EIN STARKES GEOMETRISCHES FORTSETZUNGSMUSTER AUF DIESEN VERPACKUNGEN FÜR HAUSHALTGLÜHBIRNEN. (GBR)

▲ 495 CONDITIONNEMENTS POUR FRUITS SECS DE LA FORET TROPICALE. LES ILLUSTRATIONS RAPPELLENT LES VIEILLES PLANCHES DE BOTANIQUE. ON A UTILISÉ DES ENCRES VÉGÉTALES. (USA)

▲ 496 ETIQUETTE POUR UNE BIERE AUSTRALIENNE PEU ALCOOLISÉE. (AUS)

▲ 497 BOUTEILLE ET CHOPE DE BIERE CRÉÉES À L'OCCASION DU 100E ANNIVERSAIRE DE LA BRASSERIE SONNENBRÄU. (GER)

▲ 498 LA FORME SE PROFILANT SUR DES FONDS DE COULEURS LUMINEUSES PERMET D'ASSEMBLER LES BOITES AFIN DE RECRÉER L'IMAGE DU PRODUIT, DES AMPOULES ÉLECTRIQUES POUR LA MAISON. (GBR)

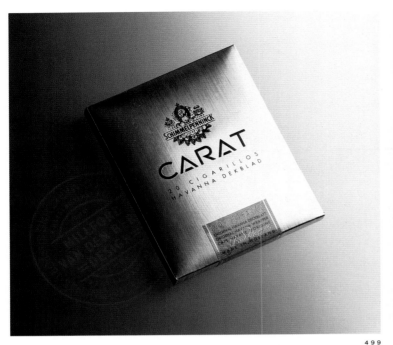

499

500

499

ART DIRECTOR:

JOS VAN DER ZWAAL

DESIGNER:

JOS VAN DER ZWAAL

AGENCY:

MILLFORD-VAN DEN

BERG DESIGN B.V.

CLIENT:

ROTHMANS

INTERNATIONAL

500

ART DIRECTOR:

ROB VAN DEN BERG

DESIGNER:

ROB VAN DEN BERG

AGENCY:

MILLFORD-VAN DEN

BERG DESIGN B.V.

CLIENT:

VAN NELLE ROTTERDAM

■ **499** THE INTERNATIONAL PACKAGE DESIGN FOR SCHIMMELPENNINCK, A DUTCH BRAND OF CIGARILLOS. (NLD)

■ **500** PACKAGE DESIGN FOR A VACUUM-SEALED GROUND COFFEE. IT IS PART OF A COLOR-CODED SERIES OF PACKAGES FOR VARIOUS TYPES OF COFFEE SOLD AS THE HOUSE BRAND OF THE DUTCH HEMA SUPER-MARKET CHAIN. (NLD)

● **499** FÜR DEN INTERNATIONALEN MARKT BESTIMMTE VERPACKUNG FÜR SCHIMMEL-PENNINCK-ZIGARILLOS. (NLD)

● **500** VAKUUMPACKUNG FÜR GEMAHLENEN KAFFEE. SIE GEHÖRT ZU EINER FARBKODIER-TEN SERIE FÜR VERSCHIEDENE KAFFEE-SORTEN, DIE ALS HAUSMARKE DER HOLLÄN-DISCHEN SUPERMARKT-KETTE HEMA ANGE-BOTEN WERDEN. (NLD)

▲ **499** BOITE DE CIGARILLOS PUR HAVANE DE TRES GRANDE QUALITÉ DESTINÉS AU MARCHÉ INTERNATIONAL. (NLD)

▲ **500** EMBALLAGE SOUS VIDE DE CAFÉ MOULU. IL FAIT PARTIE D'UNE SÉRIE DE PACKAGING AVEC CODES COULEURS POUR DIVERSES SORTES DE CAFÉ VENDUES COMME MARQUE MAISON DE LA CHAINE DE SUPER-MARCHÉS HOLLANDAIS HEMA. (NLD)

RECORD COVERS, BOOKS, CALENDARS

SCHALLPLATTEN, BÜCHER, KALENDER

DISQUES, LIVRES, CALENDRIERS

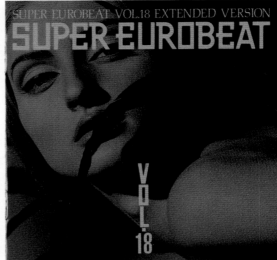

501

502

503

504

■ **501** THE DETAILED ILLUSTRATION ON THE COVER OF MICHAEL JACKSON'S ALBUM *DANGEROUS* INCLUDES HIS PET CHIMP. (USA)

■ **502** COVER DESIGN FOR THE SMALL BOOKLET THAT COMES WITH THE CD *SUPER EUROBEAT*, AS MARKETED IN JAPAN. (JPN)

■ **503** A MELANCHOLY PHOTOGRAPH ON THE COVER OF OZZY OSBOURNE'S ALBUM *NO MORE TEARS*. (USA)

■ **504** COVER FOR A COMPILATION CD OF EUROPEAN MUSIC, MARKETED IN JAPAN. (JPN)

■ **505** THESE CD' AND ALBUM COVERS FOR THE SONGWRITING TEAM OF TUCK AND PATTY WERE INSPIRED BY THE RECORD'S TITLE, *DREAM*. THE PALE BLUE ROSE SERVES AS A SYMBOL OF A DREAM. (USA)

● **501** EINE GEISTERBAHN AUF DER HÜLLE EINER LP VON MICHAEL JACKSON MIT DEM TITEL *DANGEROUS*. (USA)

● **502** UMSCHLAG EINER BROSCHÜRE, DIE ZU EINER CD MIT EUROPÄISCHEM BEAT FÜR DEN JAPANISCHEN MARKT GEHÖRT. (JPN)

● **503** DER MELANCHOLISCHE GRUNDTON DES PLATTENTITELS «KEINE TRÄNEN MEHR» WIRD AUF DIESER HÜLLE WIEDERGEGEBEN. (USA)

● **504** FÜR EINE IN JAPAN VERKAUFTE CD MIT EINEM MIX EUROPÄISCHER MUSIK. (JPN)

● **505** DAS THEMA TRAUM INSPIRIERTE DAS KONZEPT FÜR DIESES BÜCHLEIN UND DIE PLATTENVERPACKUNG MIT MUSIK DES PAARES TUCK UND PATTY. DIE BLAUE ROSE DIENT ALS TRAUMSYMBOL. (USA)

▲ **501** UN TRAIN-FANTOME SUR LA COUVERTURE DE L'ALBUM *DANGEROUS* DE MICHAEL JACKSON. (USA)

▲ **502** PLAQUETTE ACCOMPAGNANT UN DISQUE COMPACT QUI RASSEMBLE UNE SÉLECTION DE MUSIQUE EUROPÉENNE. (JPN)

▲ **503** ATMOSPHERE MÉLANCOLIQUE POUR LA POCHETTE D'UN DISQUE INTITULÉ «PLUS DE LARMES». (USA)

▲ **504** COUVERTURE D'UN DISQUE COMPACT DE MUSIC EUROPÉENNE. (JPN)

▲ **505** LE DÉCOR DE L'ÉTUI ET LA COUVERTURE DE L'ALBUM D'UN COUPLE D'AUTEURS INTERPRETES, TUCK ET PATTI, ONT POUR SUJET LE REVE. LES PAROLES DES CHANSONS ONDULENT SUR LE FOND. (USA)

505

501

ART DIRECTORS:
NANCY DONALD
MARK RYDEN
ILLUSTRATOR:
MARK RYDEN
CLIENT:
SONY MUSIC

502, 504

ART DIRECTOR:
MASUMI OHASHI
DESIGNER:
NAONOBU NAKAMURA
PHOTOGRAPHER:
YUTAKA SAKANO (502)
AGENCY:
ROUND TABLE
ASSOCIATES INC.
CLIENT:
AVEX DD CO., LTD.

503

ART DIRECTORS:
NANCY DONALD
DAVID COLEMAN
PHOTOGRAPHER:
MATT MAHURIN
CLIENT:
SONY MUSIC

505

ART DIRECTOR:
JENNIFER MORLA
DESIGNERS:
JEANETTE ARAMBURU
JENNIFER MORLA
PHOTOGRAPHER:
BYBEE STUDIOS
AGENCY:
MORLA DESIGN
CLIENT:
WINDHAM HILL

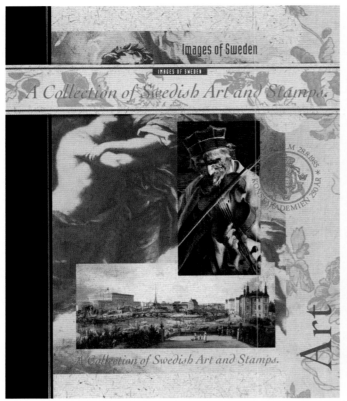

506

507

506

ART DIRECTORS:
RANDY BRAATEN
LEIF ABJÖRNSSON
DESIGNERS:
RANDY BRAATEN
LEIF ABJÖRNSSON
ARTISTS:
D.K. EHRENSTRAHL
J.F. MARTIN
C. SLANIA
J. MAGNUSSON
PUBLISHER:
SWEDEN POST
STAMPS

507

ART DIRECTOR:
KYM ABRAMS
DESIGNER:
MIKE STEES
AGENCY:
KYM ABRAMS DESIGN
CLIENT:
ILLINOIS FILM
OFFICE

■ 506 COVER OF A BOOK SHOWING THE CUL-TURAL HISTORY OF SWEDEN THROUGH ART AND STAMPS. (SWE)

■ 507 COVER OF A GUIDE TO LOCATIONS IN ILLINOIS, SENT TO FILM DIRECTORS AND PRODUCERS IN ORDER TO PROMOTE FILM-MAKING IN THE STATE. (USA)

■ 508-513 THE COVER AND SEVERAL INSIDE SPREADS FROM A CATALOG OF THE GEN TARUMI COLLECTION OF 1960'S NEON CLOCKS. THE CATALOG WAS PUBLISHED TO RAISE MONEY FOR CHARITY. (USA)

● 506 DIE KULTURGESCHICHTE SCHWEDENS, DARGESTELLT ANHAND VON GEMÄLDEN UND BRIEFMARKEN. (SWE)

● 507 UMSCHLAG EINES AN FILM-PROFIS GERICHTETEN KATALOGS MIT LANDSCHAFTEN ILLINOIS', DER DIE FILMPRODUKTION IN DIESEM STAAT FÖRDERN SOLL. (USA)

● 508-513 UMSCHLAG UND DOPPELSEITEN AUS EINEM KATALOG DER GRÖSSTEN PRIVA-TEN SAMMLUNG VON LEUCHTUHREN AUS DEN SECHZIGER JAHREN, DIE GEN TARUMI GE-HÖRT. (USA)

▲ 506 COUVERTURE D'UN LIVRE RETRAÇANT L'HISTOIRE DE LA CULTURE EN SUEDE, VUE AU TRAVERS DE SES TIMBRES-POSTE. (SWE)

▲ 507 COUVERTURE D'UN CATALOGUE DES-TINÉ AUX PRODUCTEURS ET RÉALISATEURS DE FILMS: LES SITES INTÉRESSANTS DE L'ILLINOIS Y SONT RÉPERTORIÉS. (USA)

▲ 508-513 COUVERTURE ET PAGES INTÉ-RIEURES D'UN CATALOGUE PRÉSENTANT LA PLUS GRANDE COLLECTION PRIVÉE D'HOR-LOGES LUMINEUSES DES ANNÉES SOIXANTE, RASSEMBLÉE PAR GEN TARUMI. (USA)

NEON CLOCK

A Neon Clock Collection by Gen Tarumi Photography by Roberto Carra

HOLLYWOOD RANCH MARKET

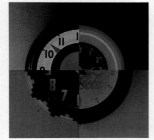

508

509

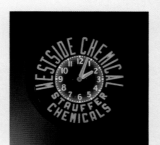

510

511

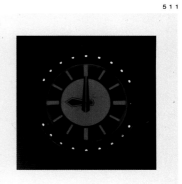

512

513

508-513

ART DIRECTOR:

TAMOTSU YAGI

DESIGNER:

TAMOTSU YAGI

PHOTOGRAPHER:

ROBERTO CARRA

AGENCY:

TAMOTSU YAGI

DESIGN

CLIENT:

HOLLYWOOD

RANCH MARKET

THE LEGEND OF SLEEPY HOLLOW

WASHINGTON IRVING   GARY KELLEY

514

515

516

517

518

514-518

ART DIRECTOR:

RITA MARSHALL

DESIGNER:

RITA MARSHALL

ILLUSTRATOR:

GARY KELLEY

PUBLISHER:

STEWART, TABORI

+ CHANG, INC.

■ **514-518**. COVER AND EXAMPLES OF THE ILLUSTRATED PAGES FROM A NEW EDITION OF WASHINGTON IRVING'S STORY *THE LEGEND OF SLEEPY HOLLOW*, IN WHICH HE PRESENTS THE LIVES AND SUPERSTITIONS OF THE EARLY DUTCH SETTLERS WHO FARMED THE HUDSON RIVER VALLEY. THE METICULOUSLY RESEARCHED, FULL-COLOR CHALK DRAWINGS RE-CREATE THE TIME AND PLACE, WHILE BLACK-AND-WHITE IMAGES OF GRAVESTONE RUBBINGS EVOKE THE EERINESS OF THIS GHOST STORY. (USA)

● **514-518** UMSCHLAG UND ILLUSTRIERTE SEITEN EINER AUSGABE VON WASHINGTON IRVINGS KLASSIKER ÜBER DAS LEBEN UND DEN ABERGLAUBEN DER ERSTEN HOLLÄNDISCHEN SIEDLER IM TAL DES HUDSONFLUSSES. DIE SORGFÄLTIG RECHERCHIERTEN, MEHRFARBIGEN KREIDEZEICHNUNGEN VERMITTELN EIN AUTHENTISCHES BILD VON ZEIT UND ORT DER HANDLUNG; DIE KLEINEN, AN GRABSTEINE ERINNERNDEN SCHWARZWEISSBILDER ENTSPRECHEN DEM CHARAKTER DER GEISTERGESCHICHTE. (USA)

▲ **514-518** COUVERTURE ET PAGES INTÉRIEURES D'UN LIVRE DE L'ÉCRIVAIN AMÉRICAIN WASHINGTON IRVING (1783-1859). IL S'AGIT D'UNE LÉGENDE QUI ÉVOQUE LA VIE ET LES SUPERSTITIONS DES PREMIERS IMMIGRANTS HOLLANDAIS ÉTABLIS DANS LA VALLÉE DE L'HUDSON. LES ILLUSTRATIONS EN COULEURS, RÉALISÉES À LA CRAIE COLORÉE, RECRÉENT L'ATMOSPHÈRE DE L'ÉPOQUE. LES IMAGES EN NOIR ET BLANC SOULIGNENT LE CÔTÉ MACABRE DE CETTE HISTOIRE DE FANTOMES. (USA)

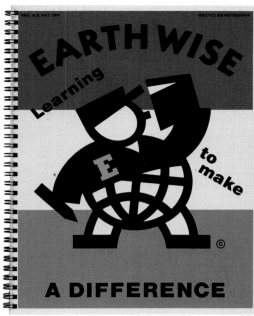

519

520

521

519

ART DIRECTOR:
ALEXANDER
BELOSLUDCEV
DESIGNER:
ANDREY LOGVIN
ILLUSTRATOR:
ANDREY LOGVIN
PUBLISHER:
OTECNESTVO
PUBLISHING HOUSE

520

ART DIRECTORS:
CHARLES S.
ANDERSON
DANIEL OLSON
DESIGNERS:
CHARLES S.
ANDERSON
DANIEL OLSON
AGENCY:
C.S. ANDERSON
DESIGN CO.
CLIENT:
BON MARCHÉ
DEPARTMENT STORES

521

ART DIRECTOR:
STEVEN BROWER
DESIGNER:
STEVEN BROWER
PUBLISHER:
CAROL PUBLISHING
GROUP

522

ART DIRECTOR:
VICTOR WEAVER
DESIGNER:
MICHAEL SCHWAB
ILLUSTRATOR:
MICHAEL SCHWAB
STUDIO:
MICHAEL SCHWAB
DESIGN
CLIENT:
WALT DISNEY ADULT
PUBLICATIONS

■ **519** COVER FOR A BOOK ON THE RUSSIAN REVOLUTION. (RUS)

■ **520** ONE COVER FROM A SERIES OF SPI-RAL-BOUND NOTEBOOKS PRODUCED FOR A BACK-TO-SCHOOL CAMPAIGN BY BON MARCHÉ DEPARTMENT STORES. IT IS SILK-SCREENED IN FOUR COLORS ON RECYCLED, CORRUGAT-ED CARDBOARD, AND THE BOOKS ARE PRINT-ED ON RECYCLED STOCK. (USA)

■ **521** COVER FOR A BOOK ON THE FILMS OF CHARLES CHAPLIN. (USA)

■ **522** COVER FOR A NOVEL BY SUSAN STRAIGHT, PUBLISHED BY WALT DISNEY ADULT PUBLICATIONS. (USA)

● **519** UMSCHLAG EINES BUCHES ÜBER DIE RUSSISCHE REVOLUTION. (RUS)

● **520** BEISPIEL AUS EINER REIHE VON SPIRALGEBUNDENEN SCHULHEFTEN AUS RECYCLINGPAPIER FÜR EINE KAMPAGNE DER BON-MARCHÉ-KAUFHÄUSER. DIE ILLUSTRA-TION AUF DEM UMSCHLAG AUS WIEDERVER-WERTETEM WELLKARTON IST EIN VIER-FARBENSIEBDRUCK. (USA)

● **521** UMSCHLAG EINES BUCHES ÜBER DAS FILMWERK CHARLIE CHAPLINS. (USA)

● **522** «ICH WAR IN KUMMERS KÜCHE UND HABE ALLE TÖPFE AUSGELECKT.» BUCHUM-SCHLAG. (USA)

▲ **519** COUVERTURE D'UN LIVRE SUR LA RÉVOLUTION RUSSE. (RUS)

▲ **520** EXEMPLE D'UNE SÉRIE DE CAHIERS EN PAPIER RECYCLÉ À RELIURE SPIRALE ET COUVERTURE DE CARTON ONDULÉ ORNÉE D'UNE ILLUSTRATION RÉALISÉE EN SÉ-RIGRAPHIE. POUR UNE CAMPAGNE DE BON MARCHÉ, UNE CHAINE DE MAGASINS DE SEATTLE. (USA)

▲ **521** COUVERTURE D'UN LIVRE SUR L'ŒUVRE DE CHARLIE CHAPLIN. (USA)

▲ **522** POUR UN LIVRE DE SUSAN STRAIGHT: «J'ÉTAIS DANS LA CUISINE DES CHAGRINS ET J'AI LÉCHÉ TOUS LES PLATS.» (USA)

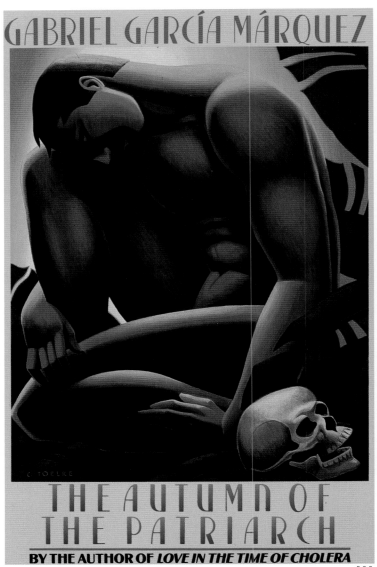

523

524

523

ART DIRECTOR:

JOSEPH MONTEBELLO

DESIGNER:

SUZANNE NOLI

ILLUSTRATOR:

CATHLEEN TOELKE

PUBLISHER:

HARPER COLLINS

PUBLISHERS

524

DESIGNER:

HENRIK BARENDS

PUBLISHER:

IN DE KNIPSCHEER

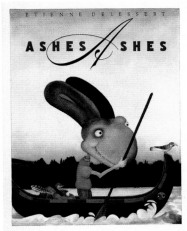

525

526

527

528

525-528

Art Director:

RITA MARSHALL

Designer:

RITA MARSHALL

Illustrator:

ETIENNE DELESSERT

Publisher:

STEWART, TABORI

+ CHANG, INC.

■ **523** COVER ART FOR AN EDITION OF *THE AUTUMN OF THE PATRIARCH*, BY GABRIEL GARCIA MARQUEZ. (USA)

■ **524** COVER ART FROM ONE BOOK IN A SERIES CONTAINING POEMS BY YOUNG AUTHORS. (NLD)

■ **525-528** A CHILDREN'S BOOK ILLUSTRATED BY ETIENNE DELESSERT. IT TELLS THE STORY OF A DISSATISFIED YOUNGSTER WHO LEAVES A WORLD WITH "MOUNTAINS OF RUSTED WASTE" TO EMBARK ON A SEARCH FOR PURITY AND TRUTH. SHOWN ARE THE COVER AND SOME INTERIOR SPREADS. (USA)

● **523** UMSCHLAG FÜR «DER HERBST DES PATRIARCHEN» VON GABRIEL GARCIA MARQUEZ. (USA)

● **524** «MAXIMAAL» – UMSCHLAG FÜR EINEN POESIEBAND MIT GEDICHTEN JUNGER AUTOREN. (NLD)

● **525-528** EIN VON ETIENNE DELESSERT ILLUSTRIERTES KINDERBUCH. ES ERZÄHLT DIE GESCHICHTE EINES UNZUFRIEDENEN KINDES, DAS SICH AUF DIE SUCHE NACH REINHEIT UND WAHRHEIT BEGIBT. GEZEIGT SIND DER UMSCHLAG UND EINIGE SEITEN AUS DEM INHALT. (USA)

▲ **523** COUVERTURE DU LIVRE INTITULÉ «L'AUTOMNE DU PATRIARCHE» DE GABRIEL GARCIA MARQUEZ. (USA)

▲ **524** «MAXIMAAL». L'UNE DES COUVERTURES D'UNE SÉRIE DE RECUEILS DE POÉSIE DE JEUNES ÉCRIVAINS. (NLD)

▲ **525-528** COUVERTURE ET EXEMPLES DE PAGES D'UN LIVRE POUR ENFANTS ILLUSTRÉ PAR ETIENNE DELESSERT. IL RACONTE L'HISTOIRE D'UN JEUNE ENFANT QUI, INSATISFAIT, S'ÉVADE DANS UN AUTRE MONDE, À LA RECHERCHE DE LA PURETÉ ET DE LA VÉRITÉ. (USA)

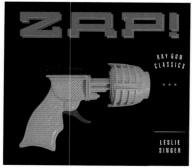

529

530

531

532

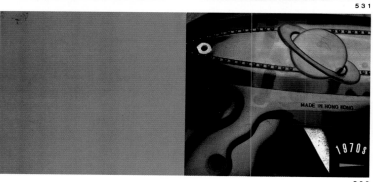

533

534

529-534

ART DIRECTOR:

KAREN PIKE

DESIGNER:

KAREN SMIDTH

PHOTOGRAPHER:

DIXIE KNIGHT

PUBLISHER:

CHRONICLE BOOKS

535

ART DIRECTOR:

OSWALDO MIRANDA

DESIGNER:

OSWALDO MIRANDA

AGENCY:

CASA DE IDEIAS

PUBLISHER:

BIBLIOTECA

PUBLICA P.R.

■ 529-534 COVER AND SPREADS FROM A BOOK BY LESLIE SINGER, ADVERTISING CREATIVE DIRECTOR AND COLLECTOR OF TOY RAY GUNS. THESE TOY GUNS ORIGINATED WITH THE ART DECO RAY GUNS OF THE 1930S. (USA)

■ 535 THIS COVER FOR A BOOK ON THE POSTER ARTIST AND DESIGNER CASSANDRE WAS INSPIRED BY HIS WORK. (BRA)

● 529-534 UMSCHLAG UND SEITEN AUS EINEM BUCH VON LESLIE SINGER, KREATIVDIREKTOR EINER WERBEAGENTUR UND SAMMLER VON SPIELZEUGPISTOLEN, DIE SEIT DEN DREISSIGER JAHREN AUF DEM AMERIKANISCHEN MARKT SIND. (USA)

● 535 DIESER UMSCHLAG EINES BUCHES ÜBER DEN PLAKATKÜNSTLER CASSANDRE WURDE VON DESSEN STIL INSPIRIERT. (BRA)

▲ 529-534 COUVERTURE ET PAGES D'UN LIVRE DE LESLIE SINGER, DIRECTEUR DE LA CRÉATION DANS UNE AGENCE DE PUBLICITÉ ET LUI-MEME COLLECTIONNEUR, SUR LES PISTOLETS CRÉÉS PAR LES FABRICANTS DE JOUETS DEPUIS LES ANNÉES TRENTE. (USA)

▲ 535 COUVERTURE D'UN LIVRE SUR L'AFFICHISTE CASSANDRE, DIRECTEMENT INSPIRÉE DE SON ŒUVRE. (BRA)

LAST CALL CASSANDRE POSTERS

CASSANDRE

535

536

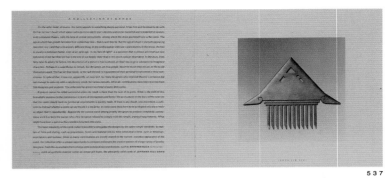

537

538

539

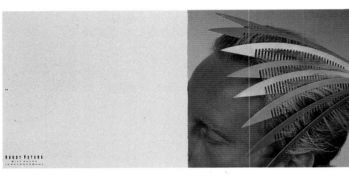

540

541

542

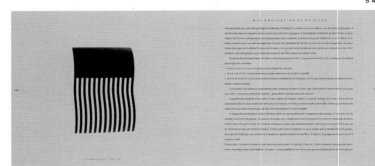

543

536-543

DESIGNER:

HENRIK BARENDS

PHOTOGRAPHER:

MICHEL S.
KRZYZANOWSKI

COPYWRITERS:

MARIJKE HILHORST

MARJAN UNGER

PUBLISHER:

MARZEE/KAMMEN

544

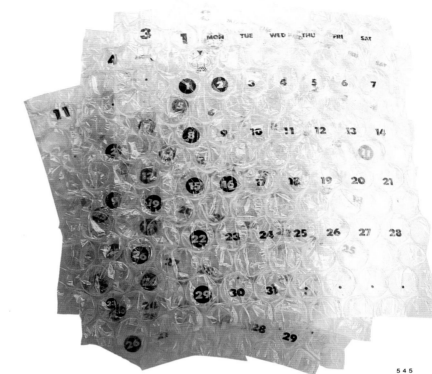

545

544-545

ART DIRECTOR:
AKIO OKUMURA
DESIGNERS:
AKIO OKUMURA
KATSUJI MINAMI
AGENCY:
PACKAGING
CREATE INC.
CLIENT:
PACKAGING
CREATE INC.

■ 536-543 COVER AND SOME INSIDE SPREADS FROM A CATALOG SHOWING COMBS FROM JEWELRY DESIGNERS AROUND THE WORLD, AT THE INVITATION OF THE DUTCH GALLERY MARZEE IN NIJMEGEN. (NLD)

● 536-543 VERSCHIEDENE KÄMME WURDEN AUF EINLADUNG DER GALERIE MARZEE IN NIJMEGEN VON SCHMUCKDESIGNERN ENTWORFEN. GEZEIGT SIND DER UMSCHLAG UND SEITEN AUS DEM KATALOG. (NLD)

▲ 536-543 COUVERTURE ET PAGES D'UN CATALOGUE PRÉSENTANT LES DIFFÉRENTS MODÈLES DE PEIGNE CONÇUS PAR DES CRÉATEURS DE BIJOUX À L'INVITATION DE LA GALERIE MARZEE À NIMÈGUE. (NLD)

■ 544, 545 TWO SHEETS FROM A THREE-DIMENSIONAL CALENDAR MADE OF BUBBLE-PACK MATERIAL, DESIGNED FOR A MANUFACTURER OF PACKAGING PRODUCTS. (JPN)

● 544, 545 ZWEI BLÄTTER VON EINEM DREI-DIMENSIONALEN KALENDER AUS BLASENVER-PACKUNGSMATERIAL, FÜR EINEN HERSTELLER VON VERPACKUNGSMATERIAL. (JPN)

▲ 544, 545 DEUX PAGES D'UN CALENDRIER TRIDIMENSIONNEL EN MATÉRIEL D'EMBALLAGE «BUBBLE», CRÉÉ POUR UN FABRICANT D'EMBALLAGES. (JPN)

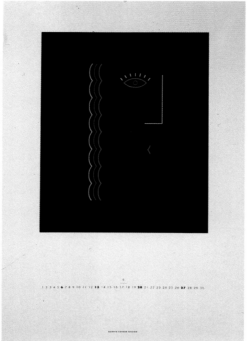

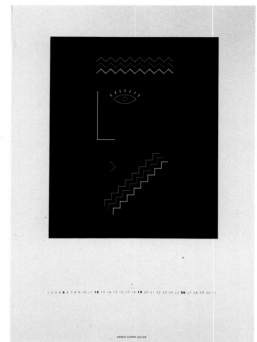

546

547

548

546-548

ART DIRECTOR:

BARRIE TUCKER

DESIGNER:

BARRIE TUCKER

COMPUTER GRAPHICS:

CLAIRE ROSE

CLIENT:

BARRIE TUCKER

DESIGN

549 550 551

549-551

ART DIRECTOR:

GEORGE TSCHERNY

DESIGNER:

GEORGE TSCHERNY

TYPOGRAPHY &

LETTERING:

ELIZABETH LAUB

MICHELLE NOVAK

GEORGE TSCHERNY

AGENCY:

GEORGE

TSCHERNY, INC.

CLIENT:

SEI CORPORATION

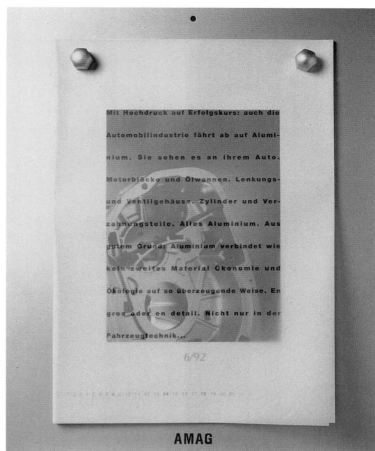

552

553

552, 553

ART DIRECTOR:

PETRA RADEL

DESIGNER:

PETRA RADEL

PHOTOGRAPHER:

RALF HÄSELICH

COPYWRITER:

KARIN WALDHER

CLIENT:

AMAG (AUSTRIA

METALL AG)

■ 546-548 THE CONCEPT BEHIND THIS SILK-SCREENED CALENDAR IS THAT OF COMMUNICATION AMONG PEOPLE GIVING RISE TO IDEAS, FANTASIES AND SPIRITUAL UNDERSTANDING. IT WAS PUBLISHED IN A LIMITED EDITION OF 50 COPIES DISTRIBUTED WORLDWIDE. (AUS)

■ 549-551 SHEETS FROM A SPIRAL-BOUND WALL CALENDAR, APPROXIMATELY THREE FEET HIGH, WHICH WAS DESIGNED AS A CORPORATE GIFT. (USA)

■ 552, 553 THIS CALENDAR FOR AUSTRIA METALL AG IS HELD BY A SOLID ALUMINUM SHEET AND HUGE SCREWS. THE COPY (ON TRANSPARENT PAPER) AND THE IMAGES DISCUSS AND SHOW THE PROPERTIES AND USES OF ALUMINUM. (AUT)

● 546-548 DAS KONZEPT FÜR DIESEN SIEB-DRUCK-KALENDER BASIERT AUF DEM POSITIVEN ZUSAMMENSPIEL UND DER KOMMUNIKATION ZWISCHEN MENSCHEN. DAS THEMA IST DURCH DAS SPIEL DER GRAPHISCHEN FORMEN ILLUSTRIERT. ES WURDE EINE AUFLAGE VON NUR 50 EXEMPLAREN GEDRUCKT. (AUS)

● 549-551 BLÄTTER EINES SPIRALGEBUNDENEN WANDKALENDERS IN EINER HÖHE VON CA. EIN METER. ER IST ALS FIRMENGESCHENK GEDACHT. (USA)

● 552, 553 FÜR DIE INDUSTRIELLE ANMUTUNG DIESES KALENDERS FÜR AUSTRIA METALL AG SORGEN DIE ALUMINIUMPLATTE UND DIE SCHRAUBEN. DER WERKSTOFF ALUMINIUM WIRD IN WORT (AUF TRANSPARENT-PAPIER) UND BILD BESCHRIEBEN. (AUT)

▲ 546-548 DEUX PAGES D'UN CALENDRIER ORNÉ DE SÉRIGRAPHIES PUBLIÉ À 50 EXEMPLAIRES. LE CONCEPT REPOSE SUR L'INTERACTION ET LA COMMUNICATION, PRIVILÉGIANT L'INVENTION ET LA FANTAISIE, ILLUSTRÉES PAR LES JEUX GRAPHIQUES DES FORMES. (AUS)

▲ 549-551 PAGES D'UN CALENDRIER MURAL À RELIURE SPIRALE DE PRES D'UN METRE DE HAUT, IMPRIMÉ RECTO-VERSO, OFFERT PAR UNE ENTREPRISE À SES CLIENTS. (USA)

▲ 552, 553 CALENDRIER MURAL DONT LES PAGES SONT FIXÉES À UNE PLAQUE D'ALUMINIUM PAR DEUX BOULONS. LE TEXTE, SUR DES FEUILLES DE PAPIER TRANSPARENT, DÉCRIT LES PROPRIÉTÉS ET USAGES DU MATÉRIAU, ILLUSTRÉS PAR DES IMAGES. (AUT)

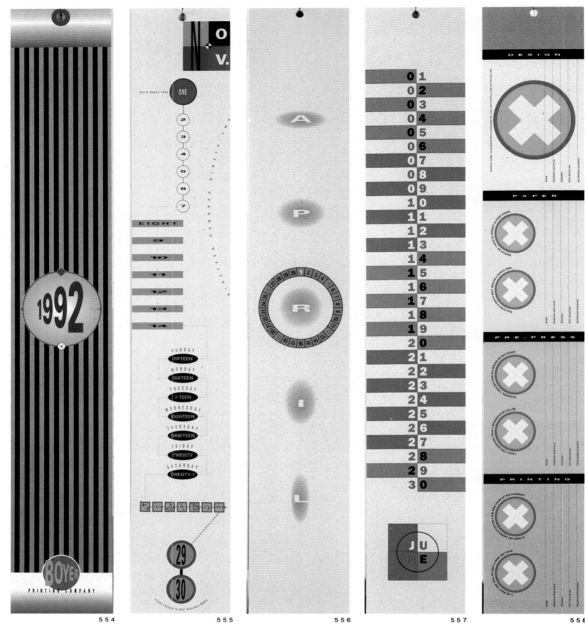

554

555

556

557

558

554-558

ART DIRECTOR:
JERRY KING MUSSER
DESIGNER:
JERRY KING MUSSER
AGENCY:
JERRY KING MUSSER
CLIENT:
BOYER PRINTING

■ 554-558 CALENDAR IN A LONG, NARROW FORMAT TO DEMONSTRATE THE ABILITIES OF THE DESIGNER AND THE PRINTER. THE FOUR-COLOR PIECE WAS PRODUCED WITH A MACINTOSH COMPUTER USING ONLY TYPO-GRAPHIC ELEMENTS, AND IT REQUIRED NO SEPARATELY PRODUCED INK TRAPS. (USA)

● 554-558 KALENDER IN LANGEM, SCHMALEN FORMAT, VOLLKOMMEN MIT HILFE EINES MACINTOSH COMPUTERS PRODUZIERT, WOBEI NUR TYPOGRAPHISCHE ELEMENTE VERWEN-DET WURDEN. DER DESIGNER UND DRUCKER DEMONSTRIEREN IHR KÖNNEN IM UMGANG MIT ANSPRUCHSVOLLER TECHNIK. (USA)

▲ 554-558 CALENDRIER DE FORMAT OBLONG CRÉÉ SUR ORDINATEUR MACINTOSH ET UTI-LISANT EXCLUSIVEMENT DES ÉLÉMENTS TY-POGRAPHIQUES. IL S'AGISSAIT DE DÉMON-TRER LA COMPÉTENCE D'UNE IMPRIMERIE QUI APPLIQUE LES PROCÉDÉS TECHNIQUES LES PLUS MODERNES. (USA)

INDEX

VERZEICHNIS

INDEX

CALL FOR ENTRIES

EINLADUNGEN

APPEL D'ENVOIS

CALL FOR ENTRIES

GRAPHIS DESIGN 94

ENTRY DEADLINE: NOVEMBER 30, 1992

ADVERTISING: Newspaper and magazine. **DESIGN:** Promotion brochures, catalogs, invitations, record covers, announcements, logos, corporate campaigns, calendars, books, book covers, packaging (single or series, labels or complete packages). **EDITORIAL:** Company magazines, newspapers, consumer magazines, house organs, annual reports. **ILLUSTRATION:** All categories, black-and-white or color. **ELIGIBILITY:** All work produced between December 1, 1991 and November 30, 1992, including unpublished work by professionals or students.

GRAPHIS PHOTO 94

ENTRY DEADLINE: AUGUST 31, 1993

ADVERTISING PHOTOGRAPHY: Ads, catalogs, invitations, announcements, record covers and calendars on any subject. **EDITORIAL PHOTOGRAPHY:** Photos subject for journals, books and corporate publications. **FINE ART PHOTOGRAPHY:** Personal studies on any subject. **UNPUBLISHED PHOTOGRAPHS:** Experimental or student work on any subject. **ELIGIBILITY:** All work produced between Sept. 1, 1992 and Aug. 31, 1993.

GRAPHIS POSTER 94

ENTRY DEADLINE: APRIL 30, 1993

CULTURAL POSTERS: Exhibitions, film, music and theater. **ADVERTISING POSTERS:** Consumer goods and self-promotion. **SOCIAL POSTERS:** Education, conferences, political issues. **ELIGIBILITY:** All work produced between May 1, 1992 and April 30, 1993.

GRAPHIS ANNUAL REPORTS 4

ENTRY DEADLINE: APRIL 30, 1993

All annual reports, brochures, and other corporate collateral material. **ELIGIBILITY:** Work published between May 1, 1991 and April 30, 1993.

RULES

By submitting work, the sender grants permission for it to be published in any Graphis book, any article in Graphis magazine, or any advertisement, brochure or other printed matter produced specifically for the purpose of promoting the sale of these publications.

■ **ELIGIBILITY:** All work produced in the 12-month period previous to the submission deadline, including unpublished work by professionals or students, is eligible.

■ **WHAT TO SEND:** Please send the printed pieces or duplicate transparencies (please mark the dupes with your name) accompanied by a completed entry label. ALL 35MM SLIDES MUST BE CARDBOARD-MOUNTED, NO GLASS! *We regret that entries cannot be returned.*

■ **HOW AND WHERE TO SEND:** Please tape (do not glue) the completed entry form (or a copy) to the back of each piece. Entries can be sent by air mail, air parcel post or surface mail. Please do not send anything by air freight. Write "No Commercial Value" on the package, and label it "Art for Contest." The number of photographs and transparencies enclosed should also be marked on the parcel. (If sending by air courier—Federal Express or DHL, for instance—label the package "Documents, Commercial Value $00.00".) For entries from countries with exchange controls, please contact us.

■ **SINGLE ENTRIES:** North America, U.S. $15; Germany, DM 15, All other countries, SFr 15.

■ **FOR AN ENTRY OF THREE OR MORE PIECES IN A SINGLE CONTEST:** North America, U.S. $35, Germany DM 40, All other countries SFr 40.

■ **STUDENTS' ENTRIES:** Free with copy of student identification.

Please make checks payable to **GRAPHIS PRESS CORP., ZÜRICH,** and include in parcel. A confirmation of receipt will be sent to each entrant, and all entrants will be notified whether their work has been accepted for publication. By submitting work, you qualify for a 25 percent discount on the purchase of the published book. Please send entries to:

GRAPHIS PRESS CORP., 107 DUFOURSTRASSE CH-8008 ZÜRICH, SWITZERLAND

ENTRY LABEL

SENDER:

FIRM, ADDRESS, TELEPHONE/TELEFAX

ART DIRECTOR:

ADDRESS, TELEPHONE/TELEFAX

DESIGNER:

ADDRESS, TELEPHONE/TELEFAX

ILLUSTRATOR, PHOTOGRAPHER, STYLIST:

ADDRESS, TELEPHONE/TELEFAX

COPYWRITER:

ADDRESS, TELEPHONE/TELEFAX

AGENCY, STUDIO:

ADDRESS, TELEPHONE/TELEFAX

CLIENT, PUBLISHER:

ADDRESS, TELEPHONE/TELEFAX

DESCRIPTION OF ASSIGNMENT AND YOUR SOLUTION:

SIGNATURE:

I HEREBY GRANT **GRAPHIS PRESS** NON-EXCLUSIVE PERMISSION FOR USE OF THE SUBMITTED MATERIAL, FOR WHICH I HAVE FULL REPRO-DUCTION RIGHTS (COPY, PHOTOGRAPHY, ILLUSTRATION, AND DESIGN).

ETIKETT/FICHE

ABSENDER/ENVOYÉ PAR:

FIRMA(E), ADRESSE, TELEPHON(E), TELEFAX

ART DIRECTOR/DIRECTEUR ARTISTIQUE:

ADRESSE, TELEPHON(E), TELEFAX

GESTALTER/DESIGNER:

ADRESSE, TELEPHON(E), TELEFAX

KÜNSTLER/ARTISTE, PHOTOGRAPH(E), STYLIST(E):

ADRESSE, TELEPHON(E), TELEFAX

TEXTER/RÉDACTEUR:

ADRESSE, TELEPHON(E), TELEFAX

AGENTUR/AGENCE:

ADRESSE, TELEPHON(E), TELEFAX

KUNDE/CLIENT:

ADRESSE, TELEPHON(E), TELEFAX

BESCHREIBUNG DES AUFTRAGS UND DER AUSFÜHRUNG:
DESCRIPTION DE LA COMMANDE ET DE SA REALISATION:

UNTERSCHRIFT/SIGNATURE:

ICH ERTEILE HIERMIT DEM **GRAPHIS VERLAG** DIE NICHT-EXKLUSIVE ERLAUBNIS ZUR VERÖFFENTLICHUNG DER EINGEREICHTEN ARBEITEN, FÜR DIE ICH DIE REPRODUKTIONSRECHTE BESITZE (TEXT, PHOTOGRAPHIE, ILLUSTRATION UND DESIGN).

J'ACCORDE PAR LA PRÉSENTE AUX **EDITIONS GRAPHIS** L'AUTORISATION NON EXCLUSIVE D'UTILISER LE MATÉRIEL SOUMIS Á LEUR APPRÉCIA-TION, POUR LEQUEL JE DÉTIENS LES DROITS DE REPRODUCTION (TEXTE, PHOTOGRAPHIE, ILLUSTRATION ET DESIGN).

GRAPHIS PRESS CORP., 107 DUFOURSTRASSE CH-8008 ZÜRICH, SWITZERLAND

EINLADUNG

GRAPHIS DESIGN 94

EINSENDESCHLUSS: 30. NOVEMBER 1992

WERBUNG: In Zeitungen und Zeitschriften. **DESIGN**: Werbeprospekte, Kataloge, Einladungen, Schallplattenhüllen, Anzeigen, Signete, Image-Kampagnen, Kalender, Bücher, Buchumschläge, Packungen. **REDAKTIONELLES DESIGN**: Firmenpublikationen, Zeitungen, Zeitschriften, Jahresberichte. **ILLUSTRATIONEN**: Alle Kategorien, schwarzweiss oder farbig. **IN FRAGE KOMMEN**: Alle Arbeiten von Fachleuten und Studenten – auch nicht publizierte Arbeiten –, die zwischen Dezember 1991 und November 1992 entstanden sind.

GRAPHIS PHOTO 94

EINSENDESCHLUSS: 31. AUGUST 1993

WERBEPHOTOGRAPHIE: Anzeigen, Kataloge, Einladungen, Plattenhüllen, Kalender. **REDAKTIONELLE PHOTOGRAPHIE**: Pressephotos, Firmenpublikationen usw. **KÜNSTLERISCHE PHOTOGRAPHIE**: Persönliche Studien. **UNVERÖFFENTLICHTE PHOTOS**: Experimentelle Photographie und Arbeiten von Studenten. **IN FRAGE KOMMEN**: Arbeiten, die zwischen September 1992 und August 1993 entstanden sind.

GRAPHIS POSTER 94

EINSENDESCHLUSS: 30. APRIL 1993

KULTUR: Plakate für Ausstellungen, Film-, Theater-, Ballettaufführungen etc. **WERBUNG**: Plakate für Konsumgüter, Eigenwerbung **GESELLSCHAFT**: Ausbildung, Politik, Umwelt **IN FRAGE KOMMEN**: Arbeiten, die zwischen Mai 1992 und April 1993 entstanden sind.

GRAPHIS ANNUAL REPORTS 4

EINSENDESCHLUSS: 30. APRIL 1993

IN FRAGE KOMMEN: Jahresberichte einer Firma oder Organisation, die zwischen Mai 1991 und April 1993 publiziert wurden.

TEILNAHMEBEDINGUNGEN

Durch Ihre Einsendung erteilen Sie dem Graphis Verlag die Erlaubnis zur Veröffentlichung der Arbeiten in den Graphis-Büchern und in der Zeitschrift *Graphis* oder für die Wiedergabe im Zusammenhang mit Besprechungen und Werbematerial für Graphis-Publikationen.

■ **IN FRAGE KOMMEN**: Alle Arbeiten von Fachleuten und Studenten – auch nicht publizierte Arbeiten –, die in der angegebenen Periode vor Einsendeschluss entstanden sind.

■ **WAS EINSENDEN**: Senden Sie uns das gedruckte Beispiel oder Duplikatdias (bitte Dias mit Ihrem Namen versehen) zusammen mit dem ausgefüllten Etikett. KLEINBILDDIAS BITTE IM KARTONRAHMEN, KEIN GLAS! *Bitte beachten Sie, dass Einsendungen nicht zurückgeschickt werden können.*

■ **WIE SCHICKEN**: Befestigen Sie das ausgefüllte Etikett (oder eine Kopie) mit Klebstreifen (nicht mit Klebstoff) auf der Rückseite jeder Arbeit. Bitte per Luftpost oder auf normalem Postweg einsenden.

Keine Luftfrachtsendungen. Deklarieren Sie «ohne jeden Handelswert» und «Arbeitsproben». Die Anzahl der Dias und Photos sollte auf dem Paket angegeben werden. Bei Luftkurier-Sendungen vermerken Sie «Dokumente, ohne jeden Handelswert».

■ **GEBÜHREN**: SFr. 15.–/DM 15,– für einzelne Arbeiten; SFr. 40.–/DM 40,– pro Kampagne oder Serie von mehr als drei Stück.

■ **STUDENTEN**: Diese Gebühren gelten nicht für Studenten. Senden Sie uns bitte eine Kopie des Studentenausweises.

Bitte senden Sie uns einen Scheck (SFr.-Schecks bitte auf eine Schweizer Bank ziehen) oder überweisen Sie den Betrag auf PC Zürich 80-23071-9 oder PSchK Frankfurt 3000 57-602. Jeder Einsender erhält eine Empfangsbestätigung und wird über Erscheinen oder Nichterscheinen seiner Arbeit informiert. Durch Ihre Einsendung erhalten Sie 25% Rabatt auf das betreffende Buch. Bitte senden Sie Ihre Arbeit an folgende Adresse:

GRAPHIS VERLAG, DUFOURSTRASSE 107, CH-8008 ZURICH, SCHWEIZ

APPEL D'ENVOIS

GRAPHIS DESIGN 94

DATE LIMITE D'ENVOI: 30 NOVEMBRE 1992

PUBLICITÉ: journaux, magazines. **DESIGN:** brochures, catalogues, invitations, pochettes de disque, annonces, logos, campagnes d'identité visuelle, calendriers, livres, jaquettes, packaging (spécimen ou série, étiquettes ou emballages complets). **DESIGN ÉDITORIAL:** magazines de sociétés, journaux, revues, publications d'entreprise, rapports annuels. **ILLUSTRATION:** toutes catégories noir et blanc ou couleurs. **ADMISSION:** tous travaux réalisés entre le 1er décembre 1991 et le 30 novembre 1992, y compris les inédits de professionnels ou d'étudiants.

GRAPHIS PHOTO 94

DATE LIMITE D'ENVOI: 31 AOUT 1993

PHOTO PUBLICITAIRE: publicités, catalogues, invitations, annonces, pochettes de disque et calendriers sur tous sujets. **PHOTO RÉDACTIONNELLE:** reportages pour périodiques, livres et publications d'entreprise. **PHOTO D'ART:** études personnelles. **PHOTOS INÉDITES:** travaux expérimentaux ou projets d'étudiants. **ADMISSION:** tous travaux réalisés entre le 1er septembre 1992 et le 31 août 1993.

GRAPHIS POSTER 94

DATE LIMITE D'ENVOI: 30 AVRIL 1993

AFFICHES CULTURELLES: expositions, films, musique, théâtre etc. **AFFICHES PUBLICITAIRES:** produits de consommation, autopromotion. **AFFICHES SOCIALES:** formation, conférences, politique. **ADMISSION:** tous travaux réalisés entre le 1er mai 1992 et le 30 avril 1993.

GRAPHIS ANNUAL REPORTS 4

DATE LIMITE D'ENVOI: 30 AVRIL 1993

Rapports annuels, brochures et tout matériel d'identité corporate. **ADMISSION:** travaux publiés entre le 1er mai 1991 et le 30 avril 1993.

REGLEMENT

Par votre envoi, vous donnez aux Editions Graphis l'autorisation de publier les travaux reçus dans nos livres Graphis, dans tout article du magazine Graphis ou toute publicité, brochure ou autre matériel publicitaire destiné à promouvoir la vente de ces publications.

■ **ADMISSION:** sont acceptés tous les travaux de professionnels et d'étudiants – même inédits – réalisés pendant les douze mois précédant le délai limite d'envoi.

■ **QUE NOUS ENVOYER:** un exemplaire imprimé ou un duplicata de la diapositive (n'oubliez pas d'inscrire votre nom dessus) avec l'étiquette ci-jointe, dûment remplie. NE PAS ENVOYER DE DIAPOSITIVES SOUS VERRE! *Les travaux ne peuvent pas être retournés.*

■ **COMMENT ET OÙ ENVOYER:** veuillez scotcher (ne pas coller) au dos de chaque spécimen les étiquettes (ou photocopies) dûment remplies. Envoyez les travaux par avion ou par voie de surface. Ne nous envoyez rien en fret aérien. Indiquez «Sans aucune valeur commerciale» et «Echantillons pour concours». Inscrire le nombre de diapositives et photos sur le paquet. (Pour les envois par courrier, indiquer «Documents, sans aucune valeur commerciale). Pour les envois en provenance de pays soumis au contrôle des changes, veuillez nous contacter.

■ **ENVOI D'UN SEUL TRAVAIL:** droits d'admission, SFr 15.–/US$ 15.00

■ **ENVOI D'UNE SÉRIE DE TROIS TRAVAUX OU PLUS POUR UN SEUL CONCOURS:** SFr 40.–/US 35.00

■ **ÉTUDIANTS:** les étudiants sont exemptés de la taxe d'admission. Prière de joindre une photocopie de la carte d'étudiant.

Veuillez joindre à votre envoi un chèque tiré sur une banque suisse ou verser ce montant au compte chèque postal Zurich, 80.23071.9. Nous vous ferons parvenir un accusé de réception. Tous les candidats seront informés de la parution ou non-parution de leurs travaux. Votre envoi vous vaudra une réduction de 25% sur l'annuel en question. Veuillez envoyer vos travaux à l'adresse suivante:

EDITIONS GRAPHIS, DUFOURSTRASSE 107, CH-8008 ZURICH, SUISSE

MAGAZINE	USA	CANADA

☐ NEW   ☐ RENEW
☐ GRAPHIS (TWO YEARS/12 ISSUES)   US $149.00   US $166.00
☐ GRAPHIS (ONE YEAR/6 ISSUES)   US $79.00   US $88.00
IMPORTANT! CHECK THE LANGUAGE VERSION DESIRED:
☐ ENGLISH   ☐ GERMAN   ☐ FRENCH
☐ CHECK ENCLOSED
☐ PLEASE BILL ME
☐ 25% DISCOUNT FOR STUDENTS WITH COPY OF VALID,
   DATED STUDENT ID AND PAYMENT WITH ORDER
FOR CREDIT CARD PAYMENT:
☐ VISA   ☐ MASTERCARD

ACCT. NO   EXP. DATE

SIGNATURE

PLEASE PRINT

NAME   DATE

TITLE

COMPANY

ADDRESS

CITY   POSTAL CODE

COUNTRY

SEND ORDER FORM AND MAKE CHECK PAYABLE TO:
GRAPHIS US, INC.,
141 LEXINGTON AVENUE
NEW YORK, NY 10016-8191
SERVICE WILL BEGIN WITH ISSUE THAT IS CURRENT
WHEN ORDER IS PROCESSED.   (DESIGN 93)

REQUEST FOR CALL FOR ENTRIES
PLEASE PUT ME ON THE "CALL FOR ENTRIES" LIST FOR THE
FOLLOWING TITLES:

☐ GRAPHIS DESIGN   ☐ GRAPHIS ANNUAL REPORTS
☐ GRAPHIS DIAGRAM   ☐ GRAPHIS CORPORATE IDENTITY
☐ GRAPHIS POSTER   ☐ GRAPHIS PACKAGING
☐ GRAPHIS PHOTO   ☐ GRAPHIS LETTERHEAD
☐ GRAPHIS LOGO   ☐ GRAPHIS TYPOGRAPHY

SUBMITTING MATERIAL TO ANY OF THE ABOVE TITLES QUALIFIES
SENDER FOR A 25% DISCOUNT TOWARD PURCHASE OF THAT TITLE.

MAGAZINE	GERMANY	U.K.	WORLD

☐ NEW   ☐ RENEW
☐ GRAPHIS (TWO YEARS/12 ISSUES)   DM 326,–   £ 106.00   SFR 280.–
☐ GRAPHIS (ONE YEAR/6 ISSUES)   DM 181,–   £ 63.00   SFR 156.–
IMPORTANT! CHECK THE LANGUAGE VERSION DESIRED:
☐ ENGLISH   ☐ GERMAN   ☐ FRENCH
☐ SUBSCRIPTION FEES INCLUDE POSTAGE TO ANY
   PART OF THE WORLD
☐ AIRMAIL SURCHARGES (PER YEAR)   DM 75,–   £ 26.00   SFR 65.–
☐ REGISTERED MAIL (PER YEAR)   DM 20,–   £ 7.00   SFR 20.–
☐ CHECK ENCLOSED (PLEASE MAKE SFR.–CHECK PAYABLE
   TO A SWISS BANK.
☐ STUDENTS MAY REQUEST A 25% DISCOUNT BY SENDING STUDENT ID
FOR CREDIT CARD PAYMENT (ALL CARDS DEBITED IN SWISS FRANCS):
☐ AMERICAN EXPRESS   ☐ DINER'S CLUB
☐ EURO/MASTERCARD   ☐ VISA/BARCLAY/CARTE BLEUE

ACCT. NO   EXP. DATE

SIGNATURE

PLEASE PRINT

NAME   DATE

TITLE

COMPANY

ADDRESS

CITY   POSTAL CODE

COUNTRY

SEND ORDER FORM AND MAKE CHECK PAYABLE TO:
GRAPHIS PRESS CORP.,
DUFOURSTRASSE 107
CH-8008 ZÜRICH, SWITZERLAND
SERVICE WILL BEGIN WITH ISSUE THAT IS CURRENT
WHEN ORDER IS PROCESSED.   (DESIGN 93)

REQUEST FOR CALL FOR ENTRIES
PLEASE PUT ME ON THE "CALL FOR ENTRIES" LIST FOR THE
FOLLOWING TITLES:

☐ GRAPHIS DESIGN   ☐ GRAPHIS ANNUAL REPORTS
☐ GRAPHIS DIAGRAM   ☐ GRAPHIS CORPORATE IDENTITY
☐ GRAPHIS POSTER   ☐ GRAPHIS PACKAGING
☐ GRAPHIS PHOTO   ☐ GRAPHIS LETTERHEAD
☐ GRAPHIS LOGO   ☐ GRAPHIS TYPOGRAPHY

SUBMITTING MATERIAL TO ANY OF THE ABOVE TITLES QUALIFIES
SENDER FOR A 25% DISCOUNT TOWARD PURCHASE OF THAT TITLE.

BOOK ORDER FORM: USA AND CANADA		
BOOKS	**USA**	**CANADA**
☐ GRAPHIS DESIGN 93	US $69.00	US $94.00
☐ GRAPHIS DESIGN 92	US $69.00	US $94.00
☐ GRAPHIS POSTER 92	US $69.00	US $94.00
☐ GRAPHIS POSTER 91	US $69.00	US $94.00
☐ GRAPHIS PHOTO 92	US $69.00	US $94.00
☐ GRAPHIS ANNUAL REPORTS 3	US $75.00	US$100.00
☐ GRAPHIS LETTERHEAD 1	US $69.00	US $94.00
☐ GRAPHIS LOGO 1	US $50.00	US $70.00
☐ THE GRAPHIC DESIGNER'S GREENBOOK	US $25.00	US $41.00
☐ GRAPHIS PUBLICATION 1/MAGAZINDESIGN 1 ☐ ENGLISH ☐ GERMAN	US $75.00	US$100.00
☐ ART FOR SURVIVAL: THE ILLUSTRATOR AND THE ENVIRONMENT	US $40.00	US $60.00
☐ GRAPHIS NUDES	US $75.00	US$100.00
☐ GRAPHIS PACKAGING 5	US $75.00	US$100.00
☐ GRAPHIS DIAGRAM 1	US $69.00	US $94.00

☐ CHECK ENCLOSED (GRAPHIS AGREES TO PAY MAILING COSTS)

☐ PLEASE BILL ME (MAILING COSTS IN ADDITION TO ABOVE BOOK PRICES WILL BE CHARGED. BOOK(S) WILL BE SENT WHEN PAYMENT IS RECEIVED)

PLEASE PRINT

NAME   DATE

TITLE

COMPANY

ADDRESS

CITY   POSTAL CODE

COUNTRY

DATE   SIGNATURE

SEND ORDER FORM AND MAKE CHECK PAYABLE TO:
GRAPHIS US, INC.
141 LEXINGTON AVENUE,
NEW YORK, NY 10016, USA

REQUEST FOR CALL FOR ENTRIES
PLEASE PUT ME ON YOUR "CALL FOR ENTRIES" LIST FOR THE FOLLOWING TITLES:

☐ GRAPHIS DESIGN   ☐ GRAPHIS ANNUAL REPORTS
☐ GRAPHIS DIAGRAM   ☐ GRAPHIS CORPORATE IDENTITY
☐ GRAPHIS POSTER   ☐ GRAPHIS PACKAGING
☐ GRAPHIS PHOTO   ☐ GRAPHIS LETTERHEAD
☐ GRAPHIS LOGO   ☐ GRAPHIS TYPOGRAPHY

SUBMITTING MATERIAL TO ANY OF THE ABOVE TITLES QUALIFIES SENDER FOR A 25% DISCOUNT TOWARD PURCHASE OF THAT TITLE.

BOOK ORDER FORM: EUROPE AND WORLD			
BOOKS	**GERMANY**	**U.K.**	**WORLD**
☐ GRAPHIS DESIGN 93	DM 149,–	£ 49.00	SFR. 123.–
☐ GRAPHIS DESIGN 92	DM 149,–	£ 49.00	SFR. 123.–
☐ GRAPHIS POSTER 92	DM 149,–	£ 49.00	SFR. 123.–
☐ GRAPHIS POSTER 91	DM 149,–	£ 49.00	SFR. 123.–
☐ GRAPHIS PHOTO 92	DM 149,–	£ 49.00	SFR. 123.–
☐ GRAPHIS ANNUAL REPORTS 3	DM 162,–	£ 52.00	SFR. 137.–
☐ GRAPHIS LETTERHEAD 1	DM 149,–	£ 49.00	SFR. 123.–
☐ GRAPHIS LOGO 1	DM 108,–	£ 36.00	SFR. 92.–
☐ THE GRAPHIC DESIGNER'S GREENBOOK	DM 54,–	£ 18.00	SFR. 46.–
☐ GRAPHIS PUBLICATION 1/MAGAZINDESIGN 1 ☐ ENGLISH ☐ GERMAN	DM 162,–	£ 52.00	SFR. 137.–
☐ ART FOR SURVIVAL: THE ILLUSTRATOR AND THE ENVIRONMENT	DM 89,–	£ 33.00	SFR. 79.–
☐ GRAPHIS NUDES	DM 162,–	£ 48.00	SFR. 137.–
☐ GRAPHIS PACKAGING 5	DM 160,–	£ 48.00	SFR. 132.–
☐ GRAPHIS DIAGRAM 1	DM 138,–	£ 49.00	SFR. 112.–

☐ CHECK ENCLOSED (PLEASE MAKE CHECK PAYABLE TO EUROPEAN BOOK SERVICE, DE MEERN)

☐ PLEASE BILL ME (MAILING COSTS WILL BE CHARGED)

FOR CREDIT CARD PAYMENT (ALL CARDS DEBITED IN SWISS FRANCS):
☐ AMERICAN EXPRESS   ☐ DINER'S CLUB
☐ EURO/MASTERCARD   ☐ VISA/BARCLAY/CARTE BLEUE

ACCOUNT NO.   EXPIRATION DATE

SIGNATURE   DATE

PLEASE PRINT

NAME   DATE

TITLE

COMPANY

ADDRESS

CITY   POSTAL CODE

COUNTRY

DATE   SIGNATURE

PLEASE SEND ORDER FORM TO:
GRAPHIS PRESS CORP.,
DUFOURSTRASSE 107,
CH–8008 ZÜRICH, SWITZERLAND

REQUEST FOR CALL FOR ENTRIES
PLEASE PUT ME ON YOUR "CALL FOR ENTRIES" LIST FOR THE FOLLOWING TITLES:

☐ GRAPHIS DESIGN   ☐ GRAPHIS ANNUAL REPORTS
☐ GRAPHIS DIAGRAM   ☐ GRAPHIS CORPORATE IDENTITY
☐ GRAPHIS POSTER   ☐ GRAPHIS PACKAGING
☐ GRAPHIS PHOTO   ☐ GRAPHIS LETTERHEAD
☐ GRAPHIS LOGO   ☐ GRAPHIS TYPOGRAPHY

SUBMITTING MATERIAL TO ANY OF THE ABOVE TITLES QUALIFIES SENDER FOR A 25% DISCOUNT TOWARD PURCHASE OF THAT TITLE.